Machine Learning for Multimedia Content Analysis

T0138051

Softcover reprint of the hardcover 1st edition 2006

MULTIMEDIA SYSTEMS AND APPLICATIONS SERIES

Consulting Editor

Borko Furht
Florida Atlantic University

Recently Published Titles:

Visit the series on our website: www.springer.com

Machine Learning for Multimedia Content Analysis

by

Yihong Gong
and
Wei Xu
NEC Laboratories America, Inc.
USA

 Springer

Yihong Gong
NEC
Laboratories of America, Inc.
10080 N. Wolfe Road SW3-350
Cupertino CA 95014
ygong@sv.nec-labs.com

Wei Xu
NEC
Laboratories of America, Inc.
10080 N. Wolfe Road SW3-350
Cupertino CA 95014
xw@sv.nec-labs.com

Machine Learning for Multimedia Content Analysis by Yihong Gong and Wei Xu

ISBN 978-1-4419-4353-8   e-ISBN 978-0-387- 69942-4

Printed on acid-free paper.

9 8 7 6 5 4 3 2 1

springer.com

Preface

Nowadays, huge amount of multimedia data are being constantly generated in various forms from various places around the world. With ever increasing complexity and variability of multimedia data, traditional rule-based approaches where humans have to discover the domain knowledge and encode it into a set of programming rules are too costly and incompetent for analyzing the contents, and gaining the intelligence of this glut of multimedia data.

The challenges in data complexity and variability have led to revolutions in machine learning techniques. In the past decade, we have seen many new developments in machine learning theories and algorithms, such as boosting, regressions, Support Vector Machines, graphical models, etc. These developments have achieved great successes in a variety of applications in terms of the improvement of data classification accuracies, and the modeling of complex, structured data sets. Such notable successes in a wide range of areas have aroused people's enthusiasms in machine learning, and have led to a spate of new machine learning text books. Noteworthily, among the ever growing list of machine learning books, many of them attempt to encompass most parts of the entire spectrum of machine learning techniques, resulting in a shallow, incomplete coverage of many important topics, whereas many others choose to dig deeply into a specific branch of machine learning in all aspects, resulting in excessive theoretical analysis and mathematical rigor at the expense of loosing the overall picture and the usability of the books. Furthermore, despite a large number of machine learning books, there is yet a text book dedicated to the audience of the multimedia community to address unique problems and interesting applications of machine learning techniques in this area.

The objectives we set for this book are two-fold: (1) bring together those important machine learning techniques that are particularly powerful and effective for modeling multimedia data; and (2) showcase their applications to common tasks of multimedia content analysis. Multimedia data, such as digital images, audio streams, motion video programs, etc, exhibit much richer structures than simple, isolated data items. For example, a digital image is composed of a number of pixels that collectively convey certain visual content to viewers. A TV video program consists of both audio and image streams that complementally unfold the underlying story and information. To recognize the visual content of a digital image, or to understand the underlying story of a video program, we may need to label sets of pixels or groups of image and audio frames jointly because the label of each element is strongly correlated with the labels of the neighboring elements. In machine learning field, there are certain techniques that are able to explicitly exploit the spatial, temporal structures, and to model the correlations among different elements of the target problems. In this book, we strive to provide a systematic coverage on this class of machine learning techniques in an intuitive fashion, and demonstrate their applications through various case studies.

There are different ways to categorize machine learning techniques. Chapter 1 presents an overview of machine learning methods through four different categorizations: (1) Unsupervised versus supervised; (2) Generative versus discriminative; (3) Models for i.i.d. data versus models for structured data; and (4) Model-based versus modeless. Each of the above four categorizations represents a specific branch of machine learning methodologies that stem from different assumptions/philosophies and aim at different problems. These categorizations are not mutually exclusive, and many machine learning techniques can be labeled with multiple categories simultaneously. In describing these categorizations, we strive to incorporate some of the latest developments in machine learning philosophies and paradigms.

The main body of this book is composed of three parts: I. unsupervised learning, II. Generative models, and III. Discriminative models. In Part I, we present two important branches of unsupervised learning techniques: dimension reduction and data clustering, which are generic enabling tools for many multimedia content analysis tasks. Dimension reduction techniques are commonly used for exploratory data analysis, visualization, pattern recognition, etc. Such techniques are particularly useful for multimedia content analysis because multimedia data are usually represented by feature vectors of extremely high dimensions. The curse of dimensionality usually results in deteriorated performances for content analysis and classification tasks. Dimension reduction techniques are able to transform the high dimensional raw feature space into a new space with much lower dimensions where noise and irrelevant information are diminished. In Chapter 2, we describe three representative techniques: Singular Value Decomposition (SVD), Independent Component Analysis (ICA), and Dimension Reduction by Locally Linear Embedding (LLE). We also apply the three techniques to a subset of handwritten digits, and reveal their characteristics by comparing the subspaces generated by these techniques.

Data clustering can be considered as unsupervised data classification that is able to partition a given data set into a predefined number of clusters based on the intrinsic distribution of the data set. There exist a variety of data clustering techniques in the literature. In Chapter 3, instead of providing a comprehensive coverage on all kinds of data clustering methods, we focus on two state-of-the-art methodologies in this field: spectral clustering, and clustering based on non-negative matrix factorization (NMF). Spectral clustering evolves from the spectral graph partitioning theory that aims to find the best cuts of the graph that optimize certain predefined objective functions. The solution is usually obtained by computing the eigenvectors of a graph affinity matrix defined on the given problem, which possess many interesting and preferable algebraic properties. On the other hand, NMF-based data clustering strives to generate semantically meaningful data partitions by exploring the desirable properties of the non-negative matrix factorization. Theoretically speaking, because the non-negative matrix factorization does not require the derived factor-space to be orthogonal, it is more likely to generate the set of factor vectors that capture the main distributions of the given data set.

In the first half of Chapter 3, we provide a systematic coverage on four representative spectral clustering techniques from the aspects of problem formulation, objective functions, and solution computations. We also reveal the characteristics of these spectral clustering techniques through analytical examinations of their objective functions. In the second half of Chapter 3, we describe two NMF-based data clustering techniques, which stem from our original works in recent years. At the end of this chapter, we provide a case study where the spectral and NMF clustering techniques are applied to the text clustering task, and their performance comparisons are conducted through experimental evaluations.

In Part II and III, we focus on various graphical models that are aimed to explicitly model the spatial, temporal structures of the given data set, and therefore are particularly effective for modeling multimedia data. Graphical models can be further categorized as either generative or discriminative. In Part II, we provide a comprehensive coverage on generative graphical models. We start by introducing basic concepts, frameworks, and terminologies of graphical models in Chapter 4, followed by in-depth coverages of the most basic graphical models: Markov Chains and Markov Random Fields in Chapter 5 and 6, respectively. In these two chapters, we also describe two important applications of Markov Chains and Markov Random Fields, namely Markov Chain Monte Carlo Simulation (MCMC) and Gibbs Sampling. MCMC and Gibbs Sampling are the two powerful data sampling techniques that enable us to conduct inferences for complex problems for which one can not obtain closed-form descriptions of their probability distributions. In Chapter 7, we present the Hidden Markov Model (HMM), one of the most commonly used graphical models in speech and video content analysis, with detailed descriptions of the forward-backward and the Viterbi algorithms for training and finding solutions of the HMM. In Chapter 8, we introduce more general graphical models and the popular algorithms such as sum-production, max-product, etc. that can effectively carry out inference and training on graphical models.

In recent years, there have been research works that strive to overcome the drawbacks of generative graphical models by extending the models into discriminative ones. In Part III, we begin with the introduction of the Conditional Random Field (CRF) in Chapter 9, a pioneer work in this field. In the last chapter of this book, we present an innovative work, Max-Margin Markov Networks (M^3-nets), which strives to combine the advantages of both the graphical models and the Support Vector Machines (SVMs). SVMs are known for their abilities to use high-dimensional feature spaces, and for their strong theoretical generalization guarantees, while graphical models have the advantages of effectively exploiting problem structures and modeling correlations among inter-dependent variables. By implanting the kernels, and introducing a margin-based objective function, which are the core ingredients of SVMs, M^3-nets successfully inherit the advantages of the two frameworks. In Chapter 10, we first describe the concepts and algorithms of SVMs and Kernel methods, and then provide an in-depth coverage of the M^3-nets. At the end of the chapter, we also provide our insights into why discriminative graphical models generally outperform generative models, and M^3-nets are generally better than discriminative models.

This book is devoted to students and researchers who want to apply machine learning techniques to multimedia content analysis. We assume that the reader has basic knowledge in statistics, linear algebra, and calculus. We do not attempt to write a comprehensive catalog covering the entire spectrum of machine learning techniques, but rather to focus on the learning methods that are powerful and effective for modeling multimedia data. We strive to write this book in an intuitive fashion, emphasizing concepts and algorithms rather than mathematical completeness. We also provide comments and discussions on characteristics of various methods described in this book to help the reader to get insights and essences of the methods. To further increase the usability of this book, we include case studies in many chapters to demonstrate example applications of respective techniques to real multimedia problems, and to illustrate factors to be considered in real implementations.

California, U.S.A.   *Yihong Gong*
May 2007   *Wei Xu*

Contents

Part II Generative Graphical Models

1

Introduction

The term *machine learning* covers a broad range of computer programs. In general, any computer program that can improve its performance at some task through experience (or training) can be called a learning program [1]. There are two general types of learning: *inductive*, and *deductive*. Inductive learning aims to obtain or discover general rules/facts from particular training examples, while deductive learning attempts to use a set of known rules/facts to derive hypotheses that fit the observed training data. Because of its commercial values and variety of applications, inductive machine learning has been the focus of considerable researches for decades, and most machine learning techniques in the literature fall into the inductive learning category. In this book, unless otherwise notified, the term machine learning will be used to denote inductive learning.

During the early days of machine learning research, computer scientists developed learning algorithms based on heuristics and insights into human reasoning mechanisms. Many early works modeled the learning problem as a hypothesis search problem where the hypothesis space is searched through to find the hypothesis that best fits the training examples. Representative works include concept learning, decision trees, etc. On the other hand, neuroscientists attempted to devise learning methods by imitating the structure of human brains. Various types of neural networks are the most famous achievement from such endeavors.

Along the course of machine learning research, there are several major developments that have brought significant impacts on, and accelerated evolutions of the machine learning field. The first such development is the merging of research activities between statisticians and computer scientists. This has resulted in mathematical formulations of machine learning techniques using statistical and probabilistic theories. A second development is the significant progress in linear and nonlinear programming algorithms which have dramatically enhanced our abilities to optimize complex and large-scale problems. A third development, less relevant but still important, is the dramatic increase in computing power which has made many complex, heavy weight training/optimaization algorithms computationally possible and feasible. Compared to early stages of machine learning techniques, recent methods are more theoretic instead of heuristic, reply more on modern numerical optimization algorithms instead of ad hoc search, and consequently, produce more accurate and powerful inference results.

As most modern machine learning methods are either formulated using, or can be explained by statistical/probabilisic theories, in this book, our main focus will be devoted to statistical learning techniques and relevant theories. This chapter provides an overview of machine learning techniques and shows the strong relevance between typical multimedia content analysis and machine learning tasks. The overview of machine learning techniques is presented through four different categorizations, each of which characterizes the machine learning techniques from a different point of view.

1.1 Basic Statistical Learning Problems

Statistical learning techniques generally deal with random variables and their probabilities. In this book, we will use uppercase letters such as X, Y, or Z to denote random variables, and use lowercase letters to denote observed values of random variables. For example, the i'th observed value of the variable X is denoted as x_i. If X is a vector, we will use the bold lowercase letter $\mathbf{x}$ to denote its values. Bold uppercase letters (i.e., $\mathbf{A}$, $\mathbf{B}$, $\mathbf{C}$) are used to represent matrices.

In real applications, most learning tasks can be formulated as one of the following two problems.

Regression: Assume that X is an input (or independent) variable, and that Y is an output (or dependent) variable. Infer a function $f(X)$ so that given a value x of the input variable X, $\hat{y} = f(x)$ is a good prediction of the true value y of the output variable Y.

Classification: Assume that a random variable X can belong to one of a finite set of classes $C = \{1, 2, \ldots, K\}$. Given the value x of variable X, infer its class label $l = g(x)$, where $l \in C$. It is also of great interest to estimate the probability $P(k|x)$ that X belongs to class k, $k \in C$.

In fact both the regression and classification problems in the above list can be formulated using the same framework. For example, in the classification problem, if we treat the random variable X as an independent variable, use a variable L (a dependent variable) to represent X's class label, $L \in C$, and think of the function $g(X)$ as a regression function, then it becomes equivalent to the regression problem. The only difference is that in regression Y takes continuous, real values, while in classification L takes discrete, categorical values.

Despite the above equivalence, quite different loss functions and learning algorithms, however, have been employed/devised to tackle each of the two problems. Therefore, in this book, to make the descriptions less confused, we choose to clearly distinguish the two problems, and treat the learning algorithms for the two problems separately.

In real applications, regression techniques can be applied to a variety of problems such as:

- Predict a person's age given one or more face images of the person.
- Predict a company's stock price in one month from now, given both the company's performances measures and the macro economic data.
- Estimate tomorrow's high and low temperatures of a particular city, given various meteorological sensor data of the city.

On the other hand, classification techniques are useful for solving the following problems:

- Detect human faces from a given image.
- Predict the category of the object contained in a given image.
- Detect all the home run events from a given baseball video program.
- Predict the category of a given video shot (news, sport, talk show, etc).
- Predict whether a cancer patient will die or survive based on demographic, living habit, and clinical measurements of that patient.

Besides the above two typical learning problems, other problems, such as confidence interval computing and hypothesis testing, have been also among the main topics in the statistical learning literature. However, as we will not cover these topics in this book, we omit their descriptions here, and recommend interested readers to additional reading materials in [1, 2].

1.2 Categorizations of Machine Learning Techniques

In this section, we present an overview of machine learning techniques through four different categorizations. Each categorization represents a specific branch of machine learning methodologies that stem from different assumptions/philosophies and aim at different problems. These categorizations are not mutually exclusive, and many machine learning techniques can be labeled with multiple categories simultaneously.

1.2.1 Unsupervised vs. Supervised

In Sect. 1.1, we described two basic learning problems: regression and classification. Regression aims to infer a function $\hat{y} = f(x)$ that is a good prediction of the true value y of the output variable Y given a value x of the input variable X, while classification attempts to infer a function $l = g(x)$ that predicts the class label l of the variable X given its value x. For inferring the functions $f(x)$ and $g(x)$, if pairs of training data (x_i, y_i) or (x_i, l_i), $i = 1, \ldots, N$ are available, where y_i is the observed value of the output variable Y given the value x_i of the input variable X, l_i is the true class label of the variable X given its value x_i, then the inference process is called a *supervised learning* process; otherwise, it is called a *unsupervised learning* process.

Most regression methods are supervised learning methods. Conversely, there are many supervised as well as unsupervised classification methods in the literature. Unsupervised classification methods strive to automatically partition a given data set into the predefined number of clusters based on the analysis of the intrinsic data distribution of the data set. Normally no training data are required by such methods to conduct the data partitioning task, and some methods are even able to automatically guess the optimal number of clusters into which the given data set should be partitioned. In the machine learning field, we use a special name *clustering* to refer to unsupervised classification methods. In Chap. 3, we will present two types of data clustering techniques that are the state of the art in this field.

1.2.2 Generative Models vs. Discriminative Models

This categorization is more related to statistical classification techniques that involve various probability computations.

Given a finite set of classes $C = \{1, 2, \ldots, K\}$ and an input data x, probabilistic classification methods typically compute the probabilities $P(k|x)$ that

x belongs to class k, where $k \in C$, and then classify x into the class l that has the highest conditional probability $l = \arg\max_k P(k|x)$. In general, there are two ways of learning $P(k|x)$: *generative* and *discriminative*. Discriminative models strive to learn $P(k|x)$ directly from the training set without the attempt to modeling the observation x. Generative models, on the other hand, compute $P(k|x)$ by first modeling the class-conditional probabilities $P(x|k)$ as well as the class probabilities $P(k)$, and then applying the Bayes' rule as follows:

$$P(k|x) \propto P(x|k)P(k) . \tag{1.1}$$

Because $P(x|k)$ can be interpreted as the probability of generating the observation x by class k, classifiers exploring $P(x|k)$ can be viewed as modeling how the observation x is generated, which explains the name "generative model".

Popular generative models include Naive Bayes, Bayesian Networks, Gaussian Mixture Models (GMM), Hidden Markov Models (HMM), etc, while representative discriminative models include Neural Networks, Support Vector Machines (SVM), Maximum Entropy Models (MEM), Conditional Random Fields (CRF), etc. Generative models have been traditionally popular for data classification tasks because modeling $P(x|k)$ is often easier than modeling $P(k|x)$, and there exist well-established, easy-to-implement algorithms such as the EM algorithm [3] and the Baum-Welch algorithm [4] to efficiently estimate the model through a learning process. The ease of use, and the theoretical beauty of generative models, however, do come with a cost. Many complex data entities, such as a beach scene, a home run event, etc, need to be represented by a vector **x** of many features that depend on each other. To make the model estimation process tractable, generative models commonly assume conditional independence among all the features comprising the feature vector **x**. Because this assumption is for the sake of mathematical convenience rather than the reflection of a reality, generative models often have limited performance accuracies for classifying complex data sets. Discriminative models, on the other hand, typically make very few assumptions about the data and the features, and in a sense, let the data speak for themselves. Recent research studies have shown that discriminative models outperform generative models in many applications such as natural language processing, webpage classifications, baseball highlight detections, etc.

In this book, Part II and III will be devoted to covering representative generative and discriminative models that are particularly powerful and effective for modeling multimedia data, respectively.

1.2.3 Models for Simple Data vs. Models for Complex Data

Many data entities have simple, flat structures that do not depend on other data entities. The outcome of each coin toss, the weight of each apple, the age of each person, etc are examples of such simple data entities. In contrast, there exist complex data entities that consist of sub-entities that are strongly related one to another. For example, a beach scene is usually composed of a blue sky on top, an ocean in the middle, and a sand beach at the bottom. In other words, beach scene is a complex entity that is composed of three sub-entities with certain spatial relations. On the other hand, in TV broadcasted baseball game videos, a typical home run event usually consists of four or more shots, which starts from a pitcher's view, followed by a panning outfield and audience view in which the video camera tracks the flying ball, and ends with a global or closeup view of the player running to home base. Obviously, a home run event is a complex data entity that is composed of a unique sequence of sub-entities.

Popular classifiers for simple data entities include Naive Bayes, Gaussian Mixture Models (GMM), Neural Networks, Support Vector Machines (SVM), etc. These classifiers all take the form of $k = g(\mathbf{x})$ to independently classify the input data $\mathbf{x}$ into one of the predefined classes k, without looking at other spatially, or temporally related data entities.

For modeling complex data entities, popular classifiers include Bayesian Networks, Hidden Markov Models (HMM), Maximum Entropy Models (MEM), Conditional Random Fields (CRF), Maximum Margin Markov Networks (M^3-nets), etc. A common character of these classifiers is that, instead of determining the class label l_i of each input data $\mathbf{x}_i$ independently, a joint probability function $P(\ldots, l_{i-1}, l_i, l_{i+1}, \ldots | \ldots, \mathbf{x}_{i-1}, \mathbf{x}_i, \mathbf{x}_{i+1}, \ldots)$ is inferred so that all spatially, temporally related data $\ldots, \mathbf{x}_{i-1}, \mathbf{x}_i, \mathbf{x}_{i+1}, \ldots$ are examined together, and the class labels $\ldots, l_{i-1}, l_i, l_{i+1}, \ldots$ of these related data are determined jointly. As illustrated in the proceeding paragraph, complex data entities are usually formed by sub-entities that possess specific spatio-temporal relationships, modeling complex data entities using the above joint probability is a very natural yet powerful way of capturing the intrinsic structures of the given problems.

Among the classifiers for modeling complex data entities, HMM has been commonly used for speech recognition, and has become a pseudo standard for modeling sequential data for the last decade. CRF and M^3-net are relatively new methods that are quickly gaining popularity for classifying sequential, or interrelated data entities. These classifiers are the ones that are particularly powerful and effective for modeling multimedia data, and will be the main focus of this book.

1.2.4 Model Identification vs. Model Prediction

Research on modern statistics has been profoundly influenced by R.A. Fisher's pioneer works conducted during the decade 1915–1925 [5]. Since then, and even now, most researchers have been following his framework for the development of statistical learning techniques. Fisher's framework models any signal Y as the sum of two components: deterministic and random:

$$Y = f(X) + \varepsilon \,. \tag{1.2}$$

The deterministic part $f(X)$ is defined by the values of a known family of functions determined by a limited number of parameters. The random part ε corresponds to the noise added to the signal, which is defined by a know density function. Fisher considered the estimation of the parameters of the function $f(X)$ as the goal of statistical analysis. To find these parameters, he introduced the maximum likelihood method.

Since the main goal of Fisher's statistical framework is to estimate the model that generates the observed signal, his paradigm in statistics can be called *Model Identification* (or inductive inference). The idea of estimating the model reflects the traditional goal of Science: To discover an existing Law of Nature. Indeed, Fisher's philosophy has attracted numerous followers, and most statistical learning methods, including many methods to be covered in this book, are formulated based on his model identification paradigm.

Despite Fisher's monumental works on modern statistics, there have been bitter controversies over his philosophy which still continue nowadays. It has been argued that Fisher's model identification paradigm belongs to the category of ill-posed problems, and is not an appropriate tool for solving high dimensional problems since it suffers from the "curse of dimensionality".

From the late 1960s, Vapnik and Chervonenkis started a new paradigm called *Model Prediction* (or predictive inference). The goal of model prediction is to predict events well, but not necessarily through the identification of the model of events. The rationale behind the model prediction paradigm is that the problem of estimating a model of events is hard (ill-posed) while the problem of finding a rule for good prediction is much easier (better-posed). It could happen that there are many different rules that predict the events well, and are very different from the model. nonetheless, these rules can still be very useful predictive tools.

To go beyond the model prediction paradigm one step further, Vapnik introduced the *Transductive Inference* paradigm in 1980s [6]. The goal of transductive inference is to estimate the values of an unknown predictive function at a given point of interest, but not in the whole domain of its definition. Again, the rationale here is that, by solving less demanding problems, one can achieve more accurate solutions. In general, the philosophy behind the paradigms of model prediction and transductive inference can be summarized by the following Imperative [7]:

Imperative: *While solving a problem of interest, do not solve a more general problem as an intermediate step. Try to get the answer that you need, but not a more general one. It is quite possible that you have enough information to solve a particular problem of interest well, but not enough information to solve a general problem.*

The Imperative constitutes the main methodological differences between the philosophy of science for simple and complex worlds. The classical philosophy of science has an ambitious goal: discovering the universal laws of nature. This is feasible in a simple world, such as physics, a world that can be described with only a few variables, but might not be practical in a complex world whose description requires many variables, such as the worlds of pattern recognition and machine intelligence. The essential problem in dealing with a complex world is to specify less demanding problems whose solutions are well-posed, and find methods for solving them.

Table 1.1 summarizes discussions on the three types of inferences, and compares their pros and cons from various view points. The development of statistical learning techniques based on the paradigms of model prediction and transductive inference (the complex world philosophy) has a relatively short history. Representative methods include neural networks, SVMs, M^3-nets, etc. In this book, we will cover SVMs and M^3-nets in Chap. 10.

1.3 Multimedia Content Analysis

During 1990s, the field of multimedia content analysis was predominated by researches on content-based image and video retrieval. The motivation behind such researches is that traditional keyword-based information retrieval

Table 1.1. Summary of three types of inferences

	inductive inference	predictive inference	transductive inference
goal	identify a model of events	discover a rule for good prediction of events	estimate values of an unknown predictive function at some points
complexity	most difficult	easier	easiest
applicability	simple world with a few variables	complex world with numerous variables	complex world with numerous variables
computation cost	low	high	highest
generalization power	low	high	highest

techniques are no longer applicable to images and videos due to the following reasons. First, the prerequisite for applying keyword-based search techniques is that we have a comprehensive content description for each image/video stored in the database. Given the state of the art of computer vision and pattern recognition techniques, by no means such content descriptions can be generated automatically by computers. Second, manual annotations of image/video contents are extremely time consuming and cost prohibiting; therefore, they can be justified only when the searched materials have very high values. Third but not the last, as there are many different ways of annotating the same image/video content, manual annotation tends to be very subjective and diverse, making the keyword-based content search even more difficult.

Given the above problems associated with keyword-based search, content-based image/video retrieval techniques strive to enable users to retrieve desired images/videos based on similarities among low level features, such as colors, textures, shapes, motions, etc [8, 9, 10]. The assumption here is that visually similar images/videos consist of similar image/motion features, which can be measured by appropriate metrics. In the past decade, great efforts have been devoted to many fundamental problems such as features, similarity measures, indexing schemes, relevance feedbacks, etc. Despite the great amount of research efforts, the success of content-based image/video retrieval systems is quite limited, mainly due to the poor performances of these systems. More than often, the use of a red car image as a query will bring back more images with irrelevant objects than the images with red cars. A main reason for the problem of poor performances is that big *semantic gaps* exist between the low level features used by the content-based image/video retrieval systems and the high level semantics expressed by the query images/videos. Users tend to judge the similarity between two images based more on the semantics than the appearances of colors and textures of the images. Therefore, a conclusion that can be drawn here is that, the key to the success of content-based image/video retrieval systems lies in the degree to which we can bridge, or reduce the semantic gaps.

A straightforward yet effective way of bridging the sematic gaps is to deepen our analysis and understanding of image/video contents. While understanding the contents of general images/videos is still unachievable now, recognizing certain classes of objects/events under certain environment settings is already within our reach. From 2003, the TREC Conference sponsored by the National Institute of Standards and Technology (NIST) and other U.S. government agencies, started the video retrieval evaluation track (TRECVID)[1] to promote research on deeper image/video content analysis. To date, TRECVID has established the following four main tasks that are open for competitions:

- **Shot boundary determination**: Identify the shot boundaries by their locations and types (cut or gradual) in the given video sequences.
- **Story segmentation**: Identify the boundary of each story by its location and type (news or miscellaneous) in the given video sequences. A story is defined as a segment of video with a coherent content focus which can be composed of multiple shots.
- **High-level feature extraction**: Detect the shots that contain various high-level semantic concepts such as "Indoor/Outdoor", "People", "Vegetation", etc.

---

[1] The official homepage of TRECVID is located at http://www-nlpir.nist.gov/projects/trecvid.

- **Search**: Given a multimedia statement of the information need (topic), return all the shots from the collection that best satisfy the information need.

Comparing the above tasks to the typical machine learning tasks described in Sect. 1.1, we can find many analogies and equivalences. Indeed, with ever increasing complexity and variability of multimedia data, machine learning techniques have become the most powerful modeling tool to analyze the contents, and gain intelligence of this kind of complex data. Traditional rule-based approaches where humans have to discover the domain knowledge and encode it into a set of programming rules are too costly and incompetent for multimedia content analysis because knowledge for recognizing high-level concepts/events could be very complex, vague, or difficult to define.

In the following chapters of this book, we intend to bring together those important machine learning techniques that are particularly powerful and effective for modeling multimedia data. We do not attempt to write a comprehensive catalog covering the entire spectrum of machine learning techniques, but rather to focus on the learning methods effective for multimedia data. To further increase the usability of this book, we include case studies in many chapters to demonstrate example applications of respective techniques to real multimedia problems, and to illustrate factors to be considered in real implementations.

Part I

Unsupervised Learning

2

Dimension Reduction

Dimension reduction is an important research topic in the area of unsupervised learning. Dimension reduction techniques aim to find a low-dimensional subspace that best represents a given set of data points. These techniques have a broad range of applications including data compression, visualization, exploratory data analysis, pattern recognition, etc.

In this chapter, we present three representative dimension reduction techniques: *Singular Value Decomposition* (SVD), *Independent Component Analysis* (ICA), and *Local Linear Embedding* (LLE). Dimension reduction based on singular value decomposition is also referred to as principal component analysis (PCA) by many papers in the literature. We start the chapter by discussing the goals and objectives of dimension reduction techniques, followed by detailed descriptions of SVD, ICA, and LLE. In the last section of the chapter, we provide a case study where the three techniques are applied to the same data set and the subspaces generated by these techniques are compared to reveal their characteristics.

2.1 Objectives

The ultimate goal of statistical machine learning is to create a model that is able to explain a given phenomenon, or to model the behavior of a given system. An observation $\mathbf{x} \in \mathbb{R}^p$ obtained from the phenomenon/system can be considered as a set of indirect measurements of an underlying source $\mathbf{s} \in \mathbb{R}^q$. Since we generally have no ideas on what measurements will be useful for modeling the given phenomemon/system, we usually attempt to measure all we can get from the target, resulting in a q that is often larger than p.

Since an observation $\mathbf{x}$ is a set of indirect measurements of a latent source $\mathbf{s}$, its elements may be distorted by noises, and may contain strong correlations or redundancies. Using $\mathbf{x}$ in analysis will not only result in poor performance accuracies, but also incur excessive modeling costs for estimating an excessive number of model parameters, some of which are redundant.

The primary goal of dimension reduction is to find a low-dimensional subspace $\mathbb{R}^{p'} \in \mathbb{R}^p$ that is optimal for representing the given data set with respect to a certain criterion function. The use of different criterion functions leads to different types of dimension reduction techniques.

Besides the above primary goal, one is often interested in inferencing the latent source $\mathbf{s}$ itself from the set of observations $\mathbf{x}_1, \ldots, \mathbf{x}_n \in \mathbb{R}^p$. Consider a meeting room with two microphones and two simultaneous talking people. The two microphones pick up two different mixtures x_1, x_2 of the two independent sources s_1, s_2. It will be very useful if we can estimate the two original speech signals s_1 and s_2 using the recorded (observed) signals x_1 and x_2. This is an example of the classical *cocktail party problem*, and independent component analysis is intended to provide solutions to blind source separations.

2.2 Singular Value Decomposition

Assume that $\mathbf{x}_1, \ldots, \mathbf{x}_n \in \mathbb{R}^p$ are a set of centered data points[1], and that we want to find a k-dimensional subspace to represent these data points with the least loss of information. Standard PCA strives to find a $p \times k$ linear projection matrix $\mathbf{V}_k$ so that the sum of squared distances from the data points $\mathbf{x}_i$ to their projections is minimized:

$$L(\mathbf{V}_k) = \sum_{i=1}^{n} ||\mathbf{x}_i - \mathbf{V}_k \mathbf{V}_k^T \mathbf{x}_i||^2. \tag{2.1}$$

In (2.1), $\mathbf{V}_k^T \mathbf{x}_i$ is the projection of $\mathbf{x}_i$ onto the k-dimensional subspace spanned by the column vectors of $\mathbf{V}_k$, and $\mathbf{V}_k \mathbf{V}_k^T \mathbf{x}_i$ is the representation of the projected vector $\mathbf{V}_k^T \mathbf{x}_i$ in the original p-dimensional space. It can be easily verified that (2.1) can be rewritten as (see Problem 2.2 at the end of the chapter):

$$\sum_{i=1}^{n} ||\mathbf{x}_i - \mathbf{V}_k \mathbf{V}_k^T \mathbf{x}_i||^2 = \sum_{i=1}^{n} ||\mathbf{x}_i||^2 - \sum_{i=1}^{n} ||\mathbf{V}_k \mathbf{V}_k^T \mathbf{x}_i||^2. \tag{2.2}$$

---

[1] A centered vector $\mathbf{x}_c$ is generated by subtracting the mean vector $\mathbf{m}$ from the original vector $\mathbf{x}$: $\mathbf{x}_c = \mathbf{x} - \mathbf{m}$, so that $\mathbf{x}_c$ is a zero-mean vector.

This means that minimizing $L(\mathbf{V}_k)$ is equivalent to maximizing the term $\sum_{i=1}^{n} \|\mathbf{V}_k \mathbf{V}_k^T \mathbf{x}_i\|^2$, which is the empirical variance of these projections. Therefore, the projection matrix $\mathbf{V}_k$ that minimizes $L(\mathbf{V}_k)$ is the one that maximizes the variance in the projected space.

The solution $\mathbf{V}_k$ can be computed by Singular Value Decomposition (SVD). Denote by $\mathbf{X}$ the $n \times p$ matrix where the i'th row corresponds to the observation $\mathbf{x}_i$. The singular value decomposition of the matrix $\mathbf{X}$ is defined as:

$$\mathbf{X} = \mathbf{UDV}^T, \tag{2.3}$$

where $\mathbf{U}$ is an $n \times p$ orthogonal matrix $(\mathbf{U}^T\mathbf{U} = \mathbf{I})$ whose column vectors $\mathbf{u}_i$ are called the *left singular vectors*, $\mathbf{V}$ is a $p \times p$ orthogonal matrix $(\mathbf{V}^T\mathbf{V} = \mathbf{I})$ whose column vectors $\mathbf{v}_j$ are called the *right singular vectors*, and $\mathbf{D}$ is a $p \times p$ diagonal matrix with the *singular values* $d_1 \geq d_2 \cdots d_p \geq 0$ as its diagonal elements.

For a given number k, the matrix $\mathbf{V}_k$ that is composed of the first k columns of $\mathbf{V}$ constitutes the *rank k* solution to (2.1). This result stems from the following famous theorem [11].

Theorem 2.1. *Let the SVD of matrix $\mathbf{X}$ be given by (2.3), $\mathbf{U} = [\mathbf{u}_1\,\mathbf{u}_2\,\cdots\,\mathbf{u}_p]$, $\mathbf{D} = \mathrm{diag}(d_1, d_2, \ldots, d_p)$, $\mathbf{V} = [\mathbf{v}_1\,\mathbf{v}_2\,\cdots\,\mathbf{v}_p]$, and $\mathrm{rank}(\mathbf{X}) = r$. Matrix $\mathbf{X}_\tau$ defined below is the closest rank-τ matrix to $\mathbf{X}$ in terms of the Euclidean and Frobenius norms.*

$$\mathbf{X}_\tau = \sum_{i=1}^{\tau} \mathbf{u}_i d_i \mathbf{v}_i^T. \tag{2.4}$$

The use of τ-largest singular values to approximate the original matrix with (2.4) has more implications than just dimension reduction. Discarding small singular values is equivalent to discarding linearly semi-dependent or practically nonessential axes of the original feature space. Axes with small singular values usually represent either non-essential features or noise within the data set. The truncated SVD, in one sense, captures the most salient underlying structure, yet at the same time removes the noise or trivial variations in the data set. Minor differences between data points will be ignored, and data points with similar features will be mapped near to each other in the τ-dimensional partial singular vector space. Similarity comparison between data points in this partial singular vector space will certainly yield better results than in the raw feature space.

The singular value decomposition in (2.3) has the following interpretations:

- Column j of the matrix $\mathbf{UD}$ (n-dimensional) corresponds to the projected values of the n data points $\mathbf{x}_i$ onto the j'th right singular vector $\mathbf{v}_j$. This is because $\mathbf{XV} = \mathbf{UD}$, $\mathbf{Xv}_j$ is the projection of $\mathbf{X}$ onto $\mathbf{v}_j$, which equals the j'th column of $\mathbf{UD}$.
- Similarly, row j of the matrix $\mathbf{DV}^T$ (p-dimensional) corresponds to the projected values of the p column vectors of $\mathbf{X}$ onto the j'th left singular vector $\mathbf{u}_j$. This is because $\mathbf{U}^T\mathbf{X} = \mathbf{DV}^T$, $\mathbf{u}_j^T\mathbf{X}$ is the projection of $\mathbf{X}$ onto $\mathbf{u}_j$, which equals the j'th row of $\mathbf{DV}^T$.
- The left singular vectors $\mathbf{u}_j$ and the diagonal elements of the matrix $\mathbf{D}^2$ are the eigenvectors and eigenvalues of the kernel matrix $\mathbf{XX}^T$ [2]. This is because

$$\mathbf{XX}^T = \mathbf{UDV}^T\mathbf{VDU}^T = \mathbf{UD}^2\mathbf{U}^T \quad \Rightarrow \quad \mathbf{XX}^T\mathbf{U} = \mathbf{UD}^2.$$

- Similarly, the right singular vectors $\mathbf{v}_j$ and the diagonal elements of the matrix $\mathbf{D}^2$ are the eigenvectors and eigenvalues of the covariance matrix $\mathbf{X}^T\mathbf{X}$ of the n data points. This is because

$$\mathbf{X}^T\mathbf{X} = \mathbf{VDU}^T\mathbf{UDV}^T = \mathbf{VD}^2\mathbf{V}^T \quad \Rightarrow \quad \mathbf{X}^T\mathbf{XV} = \mathbf{VD}^2.$$

It can be verified that for each column $\mathbf{v}_i$ of $\mathbf{V}$, the following equality holds (see Problem 2.3 at the end of the chapter):

$$\text{var}(\mathbf{Xv}_i) = d_i^2, \tag{2.5}$$

where d_i is the i'th eigenvalue. This means that the columns $\mathbf{v}_1$, $\mathbf{v}_2$, $\cdots$ of $\mathbf{V}$ correspond to the directions with the largest, second largest, $\cdots$ sample variances, which confirms that the matrix $\mathbf{V}_k$ that is composed of the first k columns of $\mathbf{V}$ does constitute the *rank k* solution to (2.1).

We use a synthetic data set to demonstrate the effect of singular value decomposition. Figure 2.1 shows two parallel Gaussian distributions in a 3-D space. These two Gaussian distributions have similar shapes, with the mass stretching mainly along one direction. Figure 2.2 shows the subspace spanned by the first two principal components found by the singular value decomposition. The horizontal and the vertical axes correspond to the first and second principal components, respectively, which are the axes with the largest, and second largest variances.

---

[2] We call $\mathbf{XX}^T$ a kernel matrix because its (i,j)'th element is dot product $\mathbf{x}_i \cdot \mathbf{x}_j$ of the data points $\mathbf{x}_i$ and $\mathbf{x}_j$.

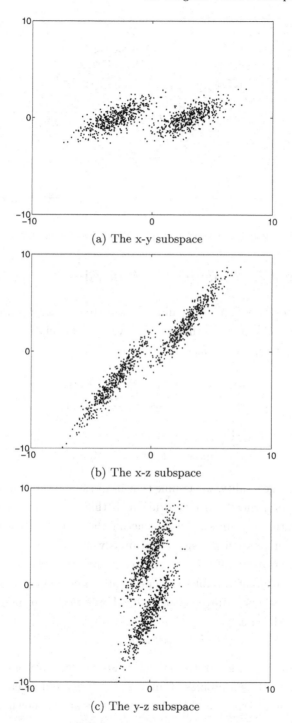

(a) The x-y subspace

(b) The x-z subspace

(c) The y-z subspace

Fig. 2.1. A synthetic data set in a 3-D space

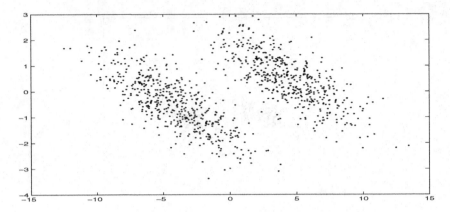

Fig. 2.2. The subspace spanned by the first two principal components

2.3 Independent Component Analysis

Independent component analysis aims to estimate the latent source from a set of observations [12]. Assume that we observe n linear mixtures of n independent components $s_1, s_2, \ldots, s_n$,

$$x_1 = a_{11}s_1 + a_{12}s_2 + \cdots + a_{1n}s_n$$
$$x_2 = a_{21}s_1 + a_{22}s_2 + \cdots + a_{2n}s_n$$
$$\vdots \qquad \quad \vdots$$
$$x_n = a_{n1}s_1 + a_{n2}s_2 + \cdots + a_{nn}s_n \,. \tag{2.6}$$

Without loss of generality, we assume that both the mixture variables and the independent components have zero mean. If this is not true, we can always center the mixture variables x_i by subtracting the sample means, which makes the independent components s_i zero mean as well.

Let $\mathbf{x}$ be the vector of the observed (mixture) variables $x_1, x_2, \ldots, x_n$, $\mathbf{s}$ the vector of the latent variables (independent components) $s_1, s_2, \ldots, s_n$, and $\mathbf{A}$ the matrix of the mixture coefficients a_{ij}. Using the vector-matrix notation, (2.6) can be written as

$$\mathbf{x} = \mathbf{As} \,. \tag{2.7}$$

The ICA model is a generative model because it describes how the observed data are generated by a process of mixing the latent components s_i. In (2.7), both the mixing matrix $\mathbf{A}$ and the latent vector $\mathbf{s}$ are unknown, and we must estimate both $\mathbf{A}$ and $\mathbf{s}$ using the observed vector $\mathbf{x}$.

It is clear from (2.7) that the ICA model is ambiguous because given any diagonal $n \times n$ matrix $\mathbf{R}$, we have

$$\mathbf{x} = \mathbf{As}$$
$$= \mathbf{AR}^{-1}\mathbf{Rs}$$
$$= \mathbf{A}^*\mathbf{s}^* . \tag{2.8}$$

To make the solution unique, we add the constraint that requires each latent variable s_i to have the unit variance: $E[s_i^2] = 1, \forall i$. Note that this constraint still leaves the ambiguity of sign: we can multiply the latent variables by -1 without affecting the model. Fortunately, this ambiguity is not a serious problem in many applications.

The key assumption for ICA is that the latent variables s_i are statistically independent, and must have non-Gaussian distributions (see Sect. 2.3.2 for explanations). The standard ICA model also assumes that the mixing matrix $\mathbf{A}$ is square, but this assumption can be sometimes relaxed, as explained in [12]. With these assumptions, the ICA problem can be formulated as: Find a matrix $\mathbf{A}$ such that the latent variables obtained by

$$\mathbf{s} = \mathbf{A}^{-1}\mathbf{x} \tag{2.9}$$

are as independent and non-Gaussian as possible.

There are several metrics that can be used to measure the degrees of independence and non-Gaussianity. Here we provide three metrics that have been widely utilized in ICA implementations [12].

Kurtosis

Kurtosis is a classical measure of non-Gaussianity. The kurtosis of a random variable y is defined by

$$\mathrm{kurt}(y) = E[y^4] - 3(E[y^2])^2 . \tag{2.10}$$

For a variable y with unit variance, $\mathrm{kurt}(y) = E[y^4] - 3$, which is simply a normalized version of the fourth moment $E[y^4]$.

Kurtosis is zero for Gaussian variables, and non-zero for most (but not all) non-Gaussian random variables. Negative kurtosis values typically correspond to spiky probabilistic distributions that have a sharp peak and a long, low-altitude tail, while positive kurtosis values typically correspond to flat probabilistic distributions that have a rather flat peak, and taper off gradually.

Kurtosis has some drawback in practice. It is very sensitive to outliers, meaning that a few data points in the tails of a distribution may largely affect its value. Therefore, kurtosis is not a robust measure of non-Gaussianity.

Negentropy

The differential entropy $H(\mathbf{y})$ of a random vector $\mathbf{y}$ is given by

$$H(\mathbf{y}) = -\int P(\mathbf{y}) \log P(\mathbf{y}) d\mathbf{y}, \qquad (2.11)$$

where $P(\mathbf{y})$ is the probabilistic density distribution of $\mathbf{y}$. Entropy is a measurement of the degree of information on a random variable. The more random (i.e. unpredictable and unstructured) the variable is, the larger its entropy. A well-known result in the information theory says that among all random variables with an equal variance, Gaussian variables have the maximum entropy. This means that entropy can be used as a measure of non-Gaussianity. Inspired by this observation, Hyvarinen and Oja introduced the negentropy $J(\mathbf{y})$ defined by [13]

$$J(\mathbf{y}) = H(\mathbf{y}_g) - H(\mathbf{y}), \qquad (2.12)$$

where $\mathbf{y}_g$ is a Gaussian random variable with the same covariance matrix as $\mathbf{y}$. Negentropy is always non-negative, and becomes zero if and only if $\mathbf{y}$ is a Gaussian variable.

Although negentropy is well justified, and has certain preferable statistical properties, its estimation, however, is problematic because it requires an estimation of the probabilistic density distribution $P(\mathbf{y})$, which is difficult to obtain for all but very simple problems.

In [13], Hyvarinen proposed a simple approximation to negentropy that can be estimated on empirical data. For a random variable $\mathbf{y}$ with zero mean and unit variance, the approximation is given by

$$J(\mathbf{y}) \approx (E[G(\mathbf{y})] - E[G(\mathbf{y}_g)])^2, \qquad (2.13)$$

where $\mathbf{y}_g$ is a Gaussian variable with zero mean and unit variable, and $G(\mathbf{y}) = \frac{1}{a} \log \cosh(a\mathbf{y})$ for $1 \leq a \leq 2$.

Mutual Information

The mutual information I between the components of a random vector $\mathbf{y} = [y_1, y_2, \ldots, y_n]^T$ is defined as

$$I(y_1, y_2, \ldots, y_n) = \sum_{i=1}^{n} H(y_i) - H(\mathbf{y}). \tag{2.14}$$

The quantity $I(y_1, y_2, \ldots, y_n)$ is equivalent to the famous Kullback-Leibler divergence between the joint density $p(\mathbf{y})$ and the product of its marginal densities $\prod_{i=1}^{n} p(y_i)$, which is an independent version of $p(\mathbf{y})$. It is always non-negative, and becomes zero if and only if the variables are statistically independent.

Mutual information can be interpreted as a metric of the code length reduction from the information theory's point of view. The terms $H(y_i)$ give the code lengths for the components y_i when they are coded separately, and $H(\mathbf{y})$ gives the code length when all the components are coded together. Mutual information shows what code length reduction is obtained by coding the whole vector instead of the separate components. If the components y_i are mutually independent, meaning that they give no information on each other, then $\sum_{i=1}^{n} H(y_i) = H(\mathbf{y})$, and there will be no code length reduction no matter whether the components y_i are coded separately or jointly.

An important property of mutual information is that, for an invertible linear transformation $\mathbf{y} = \mathbf{W}\mathbf{x}$ we have

$$I(y_1, y_2, \ldots, y_n) = \sum_{i=1}^{n} H(y_i) - H(\mathbf{x}) - \log|\det \mathbf{W}|. \tag{2.15}$$

If both $\mathbf{x}$ and $\mathbf{y}$ have the identity covariance matrix $\mathbf{I}$, then $\mathbf{W}$ is a orthogonal matrix (see the derivation of (2.17)), and $I(y_1, y_2, \ldots, y_n)$ becomes

$$I(y_1, y_2, \ldots, y_n) = \sum_{i=1}^{n} H(y_i) - H(\mathbf{x}). \tag{2.16}$$

This property implies that computation cost can be reduced if we conduct the whitening pre-processing before estimating the latent variables using (2.9) (see Sect. 2.3.1 for more descriptions).

2.3.1 Preprocessing

The most basic and necessary preprocessing is to center the observed variables $\mathbf{x}$, which means that we subtract $\mathbf{x}$ with its mean vector $\mathbf{m} = E[\mathbf{x}]$ to make $\mathbf{x}$ a zero-mean vector.

Another useful preprocessing is to first whiten the observed variables $\mathbf{x}$ before estimating $\mathbf{A}$ in (2.9). This means that we transform the observed variables $\mathbf{x}$ linearly into new variables $\tilde{\mathbf{x}} = \mathbf{B}\mathbf{x}$ such that $E[\tilde{\mathbf{x}}\tilde{\mathbf{x}}^T] = \mathbf{I}$. The whitening preprocessing transforms the mixing matrix $\mathbf{A}$ in (2.9) into an orthogonal matrix. This can be seen from

$$
\begin{aligned}
\mathbf{I} = E[\tilde{\mathbf{x}}\tilde{\mathbf{x}}^T] &= E[\mathbf{B}\mathbf{x}(\mathbf{B}\mathbf{x})^T] \\
&= E[\mathbf{B}\mathbf{A}\mathbf{s}(\mathbf{B}\mathbf{A}\mathbf{s})^T] \\
&= E[\tilde{\mathbf{A}}\mathbf{s}(\tilde{\mathbf{A}}\mathbf{s})^T] \\
&= \tilde{\mathbf{A}}E[\mathbf{s}\mathbf{s}^T]\tilde{\mathbf{A}}^T \\
&= \tilde{\mathbf{A}}\tilde{\mathbf{A}}^T ,
\end{aligned}
\tag{2.17}
$$

where $\tilde{\mathbf{A}} = \mathbf{B}\mathbf{A}$, and the last equality is derived from the assumption that the latent variables $\mathbf{s}$ are independent, have zero mean and unit variance.

Transforming the mixing matrix $\mathbf{A}$ into an orthogonal one reduces the number of parameters to be estimated. An $n \times n$ orthogonal matrix contains $n(n-1)/2$ degrees of freedom, while an arbitrary matrix of the same size contains n^2 elements (parameters). For matrixes with large dimensions, the whitening preprocessing roughly reduces the number of parameters to be estimated to half, which dramatically decreases the complexity of the problem.

The whitening preprocessing can be always accomplished using the eigenvalue decomposition of the covariance matrix $E[\mathbf{x}\mathbf{x}^T] = \mathbf{E}\mathbf{D}\mathbf{E}^T$, where $\mathbf{E}$ is the orthogonal matrix of the eigenvectors of $E[\mathbf{x}\mathbf{x}^T]$, and $\mathbf{D} = \mathrm{diag}(d_1, d_2, \ldots, d_n)$ is the diagonal matrix of its eigenvalues. It is easy to verify that the vector $\tilde{\mathbf{x}}$ given by

$$
\tilde{\mathbf{x}} = \mathbf{E}\mathbf{D}^{-1/2}\mathbf{E}^T\mathbf{x}
\tag{2.18}
$$

satisfies $E[\tilde{\mathbf{x}}\tilde{\mathbf{x}}^T] = \mathbf{I}$, and therefore, it is the whitened version of $\mathbf{x}$.

2.3.2 Why Gaussian is Forbidden

As demonstrated by (2.8), there exist certain ambiguities with the ICA formulation. The assumption of statistical independence of the latent variables $\mathbf{s}$ serves to remove these ambiguities. Intuitively, the assumption of non-correlation determines the covariances (the second-degree cross-moments) of a multivariate distribution, while the assumption of statistical independence determines all of the cross-moments. These extra moment conditions allow us to remove the ambiguities, and to uniquely identify elements of the mixing matrix

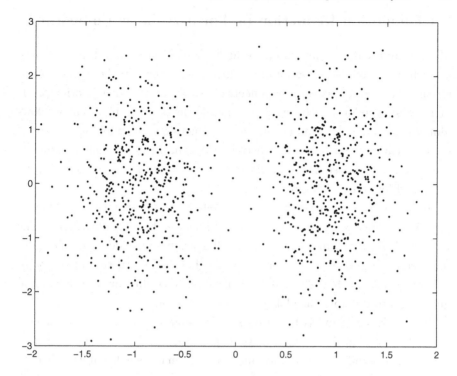

Fig. 2.3. The subspace spanned by the two independent components

A. The additional moment conditions, however, do not help Gaussian distributions because they are determined by the second-degree moments alone, and do not involve higher degree cross-moments. As a result, any Gaussian independent components can be only determined up to a rotation.

In summary, ICA aims to find a linear projection $\mathbf{A}$ of the observed data $\mathbf{x}$ such that the projected data $\mathbf{s} = \mathbf{A}^{-1}\mathbf{x}$ look as far from Gaussian, and as independent as possible. This amounts to maximizing one of the non-Gaussian, independence metrics introduced in this section. Maximizing these metrics can be achieved using the standard gradient decent algorithm and its variations. An algorithm that efficiently computes the latent variables $\mathbf{s}$ by maximizing the approximation of negentropy given by (2.13) can be found in [12].

Figure 2.3 shows the subspace obtained by applying the ICA algorithm to the synthetic data set shown in Fig. 2.1. The data distribution in the figure confirms that the two axes of this subspace correspond to the two directions that provide the maximum statistical independence.

2.4 Dimension Reduction by Locally Linear Embedding

Many complex data represented by high-dimensional spaces typically have a much more compact description. Coherent structures in the world lead to strong correlations between components of objects (such as neighboring pixels in images), generating observations that lie on or close to a smooth low-dimensional manifold. Finding such a low-dimensional manifold for the given data set can not only provide a better insight into the internal structure of the data set, but also dramatically reduce the number of parameters to be estimated for constructing reasoning models.

In this section, we present one of the latest techniques for manifold computations: dimension reduction by locally linear embedding (LLE) [14]. The LLE method strives to compute a low-dimensional embedding of the high-dimensional inputs which preserves the neighborhood structure of the original space. The method also does not have the local minimum problem, and guarantees to generate the globally optimal solution.

The LLE algorithm is based on simple geometric intuitions. Consider a manifold in a high dimensional feature space, such as the one shown in Fig. 2.4. Such a manifold can be decomposed into many small patches. If each patch is small enough, it can be approximated as a linear patch. Assume that a data set sampled from the manifold consists of N real-valued, D-dimensional vectors $\mathbf{x}_i$. If we have sufficient data points such that the manifold is well-sampled, we expect each data point and its neighbors to lie on or close to a locally linear patch of the manifold. Therefore, each data point $\mathbf{x}_i$ can be reconstructed as a linear combination of its neighbors $\mathbf{x}_j$

$$\mathbf{x}_i \approx \sum_j w_{ij} \mathbf{x}_j, \tag{2.19}$$

and the local geometry of each patch can be characterized by the linear coefficients w_{ij}. The LLE algorithm strives to find the matrix $\mathbf{W}$ of the linear coefficients w_{ij} for all the data points $\mathbf{x}_i$ by minimizing the following reconstruction error

$$E(\mathbf{W}) = \sum_i ||\mathbf{x}_i - \sum_j w_{ij} \mathbf{x}_j||^2. \tag{2.20}$$

The minimization of the reconstruction error $E(\mathbf{W})$ is conducted subject two the following two constraints:

1. Each data point $\mathbf{x}_i$ is reconstructed only from its neighbors, enforcing $w_{ij} = 0$ if $\mathbf{x}_j$ does not belong to the set of neighbors of $\mathbf{x}_i$.

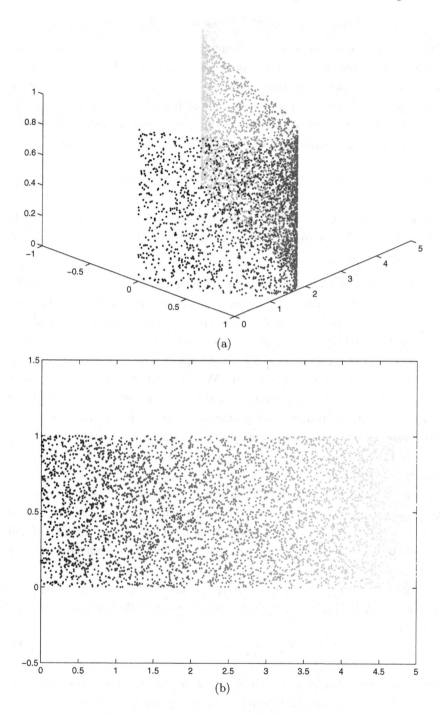

(a)

(b)

Fig. 2.4. An example of manifold. (a) shows a manifold in a 3-D space. (b) shows the projected manifold in the 2-D subspace generated by the LLE algorithm

2. The rows of the weight matrix $\mathbf{W}$ sum to one: $\sum_j w_{ij} = 1$.

The set of neighbors for each data point can be obtained either by choosing the K nearest neighbors in Euclidean distance, or by selecting data points within a fixed radius, or by using certain prior knowledge. The LLE algorithm described in [14] reconstructs each data point using its K nearest neighbors.

The optimal weights w_{ij} subject to the above two constraints can be obtained by solving a least-squares problem, and the result is given by

$$w_{ij} = \sum_k \mathbf{C}_{jk}^{-1}(\mathbf{x}_i \cdot \mathbf{x}_k + \lambda), \tag{2.21}$$

where $\mathbf{C}^{-1}$ is the inverse of the neighborhood correlation matrix $\mathbf{C} = \{c_{jk}\}$, $c_{jk} = \mathbf{x}_j \cdot \mathbf{x}_k$, $\mathbf{C}_{jk}^{-1}$ is the (j, k)'th element of the inverse matrix $\mathbf{C}^{-1}$, and $\lambda = \frac{1 - \sum_{jk} \mathbf{C}_{jk}^{-1}(\mathbf{x}_i \cdot \mathbf{x}_k)}{\sum_{jk} \mathbf{C}_{jk}^{-1}}$.

The constrained weights that minimize the reconstruction error $E(\mathbf{W})$ have the important property that for any data points, they are invariant to rotations, rescalings, and translations of the data points and their neighbors. Note that the invariance to translations is specifically enforced by the sum-to-one constraint on the rows of the weight matrix $\mathbf{W}$.

After obtaining the weight matrix $\mathbf{W}$, the next step is to find a linear mapping that maps the high-dimensional coordinates of each neighborhood to global internal coordinates on the manifold of lower dimensionality $d << D$. The linear mapping may consist of a translation, rotation, rescaling, etc. By design, the reconstruction weights w_{ij} reflect intrinsic geometric properties of the data that are invariant to exactly these transformations. Therefore, we expect their characterization of local geometry in the original data space to be equally valid for local patches on the manifold. In particular, the same weights w_{ij} that reconstruct the data point $\mathbf{x}_i$ in the original D-dimensional space should also reconstruct its embedded manifold coordinates in the lower d-dimensional space.

Based on the above idea, LLE constructs a neighborhood-preserving mapping matrix $\mathbf{Y} = [\mathbf{y}_1, \mathbf{y}_2, \ldots, \mathbf{y}_N]$ that minimizes the following embedded cost function

$$\Theta(\mathbf{Y}) = \sum_i \|\mathbf{y}_i - \sum_j w_{ij}\mathbf{y}_j\|^2, \tag{2.22}$$

where $\mathbf{y}_i$ is the global internal coordinates of the data point $\mathbf{x}_i$ on the manifold. This cost function, like (2.20), is based on locally linear reconstruction errors, but here we fix the weights w_{ij} while optimizing the mapping matrix $\mathbf{Y}$. To

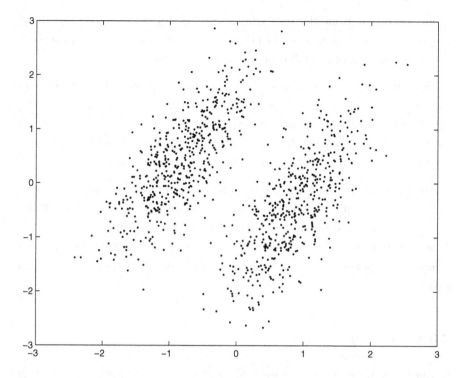

Fig. 2.5. The 2-D manifold obtained by the LLE algorithm

make the problem well-posed, the optimization is performed subject to the following two constraints:

1. The coordinates $\mathbf{y}_i$ are centered to the origin: $\sum_i \mathbf{y}_i = 0$. This is to remove the freedom that $\mathbf{y}_i$ can be translated by a constant displacement without affecting the cost $\Theta(\mathbf{Y})$.
2. The mapping matrix $\mathbf{Y}$ has an unit covariance matrix: $\mathbf{Y}\mathbf{Y}^T = \mathbf{I}$.

With the above two constraints, the optimal embedding, up to a global rotation of the embedding space, is obtained by computing the bottom $d + 1$ eigenvectors of the matrix $\mathbf{M} = [m_{ij}]$, where

$$m_{ij} = \delta_{ij} - w_{ij} - w_{ji} + \sum_k w_{ki} w_{kj}, \qquad (2.23)$$

and δ_{ij} is 1 if $i = j$ and 0 otherwise. The detailed mathematical derivations can be found in [14].

In summary, given the user's input on the number of dimensions d of the manifold and the number of neighbors K for each data point, the LLE algorithm consists of the following three major steps:

1. For each data point $\mathbf{x}_i$, choose the K nearest neighbors as its neighborhood set.
2. Use (2.21) to compute the optimal weights w_{ij}.
3. Use (2.23) to compute the matrix $\mathbf{M}$, and the embedding vectors $\mathbf{y}_i$.
4. Repeat Step $1 \sim 3$ until all the data points are processed.

Figure 2.5 shows the 2-D manifold obtained by applying the LLE algorithm to the synthetic data set shown in Fig. 2.1. The data distribution in the figure is almost identical to the one shown in Fig. 2.2 if we flip the space vertically. This indicates that the 2-D manifold is formed by preserving the first two principal components, and discarding the least important one of the original space.

2.5 Case Study

In this section, we provide a case study where the three dimension reduction techniques described in this chapter, namely SVD, ICA, and LLE, are applied to a subset of handwritten digits from the MNIST database [15]. The MNIST database has a total of 60,000 handwritten digits, each of which is normalized to a 28×28 gray-scale image with each pixel ranging in intensity from 0 to 255. Preprocessing is conducted to center each handwritten digit within the 28×28 image. Among the 60,000 handwritten digits, there are 5421 fives in the MNIST database, from which we have randomly selected 539 images to form our experimental test set.

Figure 2.6 shows the subspace generated by the singular value decomposition. In this figure, (a) shows the subspace spanned by the first two principal components, where the circled points are the projected images closest to the vertices of a square grid, and (b) displays the images corresponding to the circled points in (a). Plot (b) allows us to visualize the natures of the first two principal components. We see that the horizontal axis mainly accounts for the length of the upper and lower tails of digit five, while the vertical axis accounts for character thickness. Although there are a total of 784 possible principal components, the first 50 components account for approximately 90% of the variation in handwritten fives.

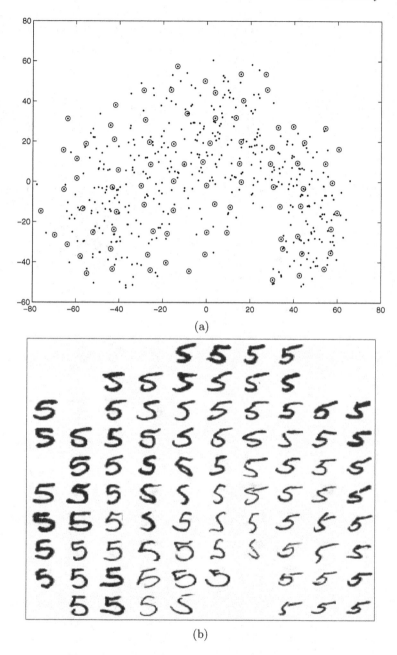

Fig. 2.6. The subspace generated by the singular value decomposition. (a) shows the subspace spanned by the first two principal components. The circled points are the projected images closest to the vertices of a square grid. (b) displays the images corresponding to the circled points in (a)

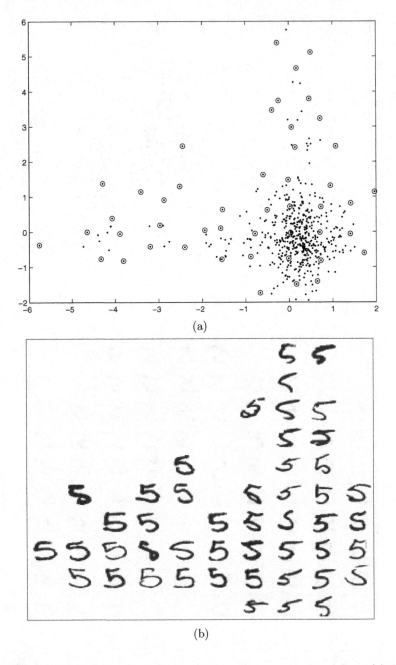

Fig. 2.7. The subspace generated by the independent component analysis. (a) shows the subspace spanned by the two independent components. The circled points are the projected images closest to the vertices of a square grid. (b) displays the images corresponding to the circled points in (a)

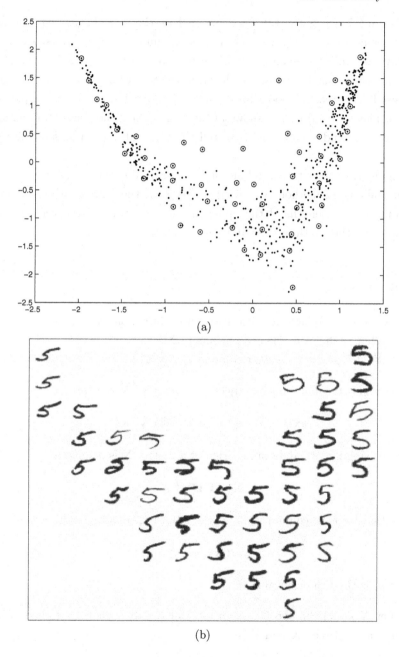

(a)

(b)

Fig. 2.8. The subspace generated by the locally linear embedding method. (a) shows the two-dimensional linear embedded space. The circled points are the projected images closest to the vertices of a square grid. (b) displays the images corresponding to the circled points in (a)

Figure 2.7 shows the subspace spanned by the two independent components. Same as Fig. 2.6, we superimpose a square grid on the space, and
display the projected images that are closest to the vertices of the grid. It is
not surprising that the subspace shown in (a) has a long-tailed distribution,
because ICA specifically looks for non-Gaussian distributions. The sample images displayed in (b) do not show salient trends along the horizontal and the
vertical axes, and we are unable to tell the physical implications of the two
axes.

Figure 2.8 shows the two-dimensional subspace generated by the locally
linear embedding method. From (b) we see that the horizontal axis mainly
accounts for the lengths of the upper and lower tails, and the vertical axis
accounts for the width of the handwritten fives.

Problems

2.1. Let $\mathbf{X} \in R^2$ follows uniform distribution in region $|X_1 + 2X_2| \le 1$.

a) What is the principle components of $\mathbf{X}$?

b) What is the independent components of $\mathbf{X}$?

2.2. For an orthogonal linear projection matrix $\mathbf{V}^T\mathbf{V} = I$, prove

$$\|\mathbf{x} - \mathbf{V}\mathbf{V}^T\mathbf{x}\|^2 = \|\mathbf{x}\|^2 - \|\mathbf{V}\mathbf{V}^T\mathbf{x}\|^2 .$$

2.3. The singular value decomposition of a matrix $\mathbf{X}$ is defined as

$$\mathbf{X} = \mathbf{U}\mathbf{D}\mathbf{V}^T .$$

Prove that for each column $\mathbf{v}_i$ of $\mathbf{V}$, the following equality holds:

$$\mathrm{var}(\mathbf{X}\mathbf{v}_i) = d_i^2 ,$$

where d_i is the i'th eigenvalue.

2.4. Let X and Y be two Gaussian random variable. Show that the mutual
information between X and Y is:

$$I(X,Y) = \frac{1}{2} \log \frac{1}{1 - \rho^2}$$

where $\rho = \frac{Cov(X,Y)}{\sqrt{Var(X)Var(Y)}}$ is the correlation coefficient between X and Y.

2.5. Let $\mathbf{A}$ be an $M \times N$ matrix, $\mathbf{w} = [w_1, w_2, \ldots, w_N]^T$ an N dimensional vector, $\mathbf{b}$ an M dimensional vector. Find the solution for the following constrained optimization problem

$$\min_{\mathbf{w}} \|\mathbf{A}\mathbf{w} - \mathbf{b}\|^2,$$

subject to constraint $\sum_i w_i = 1$.

2.6. Let $P(X, Y)$ be the joint distribution function of random variables X and Y. $f(X, Y) = \log P(X, Y)$. Assume f is twice differentiable. Prove that $\frac{\partial^2 f}{\partial x \partial y} = 0$ if and only if X and Y are independent.

2.7. Let X_1 and X_2 be two independent random variables with the distribution functions $P(X)$ and $Q(X)$. Assume $f(X) = \log P(X)$ and $g(X) = \log Q(X)$ are twice differentiable. Prove that (a) and (b) are equivalent

(a) X_1 and X_2 are two Gaussian random variables with the same variance.

(b) For any $A \in R^{2 \times 2}$ such that $AA^T = I$, $[Y_1 Y_2]^T = A[X_1 X_2]^T$ transforms X_1 and X_2 into two independent random variables Y_1 and Y_2. (Hint: Use Problem 2.6).

2.8. Show that the LLE algorithm is rotational and translational invariant, i.e., LLE will find the same result if the original data is subject to some rotation and/or translation.

2.9. Show that kernel trick can be applied to principle component analysis, i.e., the principle components can be obtained from inner products between the data vectors without the need of referring to the original vectors.

3

Data Clustering Techniques

3.1 Introduction

Data clustering, also called data segmentation, aims to partition a collection of data into a predefined number of subsets (or clusters) that are optimal in terms of some predefined criterion function. Data clustering is a fundamental and enabling tool that has a broad range of applications in many areas. Because of this, research on data clustering techniques has been the focus of considerable attention from multidisciplinary research communities such as pattern recognition, machine learning, data mining, information retrieval, bio-informatics, etc.

Generally speaking, to develop a data clustering method one needs to address the following three basic problems:

1. What is the model for modeling (or what is the assumption for the distribution of) the given data set?
2. What is the criterion function to be optimized by the clustering process?
3. What is the computation algorithm for carrying out the optimization?

The data model together with the criterion function determine the data clustering capability, while the computation algorithm determines how effectively the designated clustering result can be obtained. Good clustering results are those that correspond well to human perceptions, and such results should be obtained by using computationally effective algorithms. Therefore, a good data clustering method can be defined as the one that constantly produces clustering results that correspond well to human perceptions, using a computationally effective algorithm.

A great variety of clustering methods have been developed using various data models and criterion functions. Among them, K-means and hierarchical clustering are the two most famous and long-standing data clustering methods. K-means produces a cluster set that minimizes the sum of squared distances between the data points and the cluster centers through an iterative assignment-reassignment process [16]. Hierarchical clustering groups the data points into a hierarchical tree structure, or a dendrogram, using either the bottom-up or the top-down approach [17, 18]. The bottom-up approach starts by placing each data point into a distinct cluster and then iteratively merges the two most similar clusters into one parent cluster, while the top-down approach starts by forming the root cluster with the entire data set and then iteratively splits the cluster with the largest variation into child clusters.

Early generation data clustering methods, represented by K-means and hierarchical clustering, suffer from various drawbacks due to the following reasons. First, many methods either do not have an explicit data model, or are based on a model that makes harsh simplifying assumptions on data distributions. Second, the criterion functions adopted by some methods are too simple to handle complicated data distributions. Third, many clustering methods do not have efficient algorithms to compute the optimal solutions for the employed criterion functions. For example, the criterion function used by K-means favors the creation of compact, spherical clusters, and its iterative assignment-reassignment process is very prone to a local minimum solution. For data sets with elongated or spiral distributions, K-means often generates very poor clustering results. On the other hand, the hierarchical clustering has a computation complexity of $O(n^2 \log n)$, where n is the number of data points in the data set. Because of the quadratic order of complexity, it could become computationally prohibitive for handling a data set with millions of data points.

In recent years, two classes of new data clustering techniques: spectral clustering based on graph partitioning theories and data clustering based on Non-Negative Matrix Factorization (NMF), have emerged as the most powerful and promising alternative approaches. Spectral clustering methods are known for their powerful optimization algorithms that are guaranteed to compute globally optimal data clustering results, while NMF-based methods are characterized by the adoption of a more general model that makes an unique assumption (non-negative) on data distributions. Despite their superiorities, there is yet a text book that provides a systematic coverage on these state-of-the-art techniques.

In this chapter, instead of providing a comprehensive coverage on all kinds of data clustering methods, we focus our descriptions on the spectral clustering and NMF-based clustering techniques mentioned above. In the first half of this chapter, we provide a systematic coverage on four representative spectral clustering techniques from the aspects of problem formulation, objective functions, and solution computations. We also reveal the characteristics of these spectral clustering techniques through analytical examinations of their objective functions. In the second half of the chapter, we describe two NMF-based data clustering techniques, which stem from our original works in recent years. At the end of this chapter, we provide a case study where the spectral and NMF clustering techniques are applied to the text clustering task, and their performance comparisons are conducted through experimental evaluations.

3.2 Spectral Clustering

Spectral clustering techniques model a given data set using an undirected graph, and the data clustering task is accomplished by finding the best cuts of the graph that optimize certain predefined criterion functions. The optimization of the criterion functions usually leads to the computation of the top eigenvectors of certain graph affinity matrices, and the clustering result can be derived from the obtained eigenvector space.

3.2.1 Problem Formulation and Criterion Functions

Given an input data set $\mathcal{D}$ with a total of N data points, spectral clustering techniques represent the data set $\mathcal{D}$ using an undirected graph $\mathcal{G}(\mathbf{V}, \mathbf{E}, \mathbf{A})$, where $\mathbf{V}$, $\mathbf{E}$, $\mathbf{A}$ denote the vertex set, the edge set, and the graph affinity matrix, respectively. In graph $\mathcal{G}$, each vertex $V_i \in \mathbf{V}$ represents a data point $i \in \mathcal{D}$, each edge $(i, j) \in \mathbf{E}$ is assigned an affinity score a_{ij} to reflect the similarity between data points i and j, and each affinity score a_{ij} is used to form the (i, j)'th element of the graph affinity matrix $\mathbf{A} = [a_{ij}]$, $i, j = 1, \ldots, N$.

Once the data set $\mathcal{D}$ is represented by the undirected graph $\mathcal{G}(\mathbf{V}, \mathbf{E}, \mathbf{A})$, the data clustering task can then be transformed into the problem of finding the best cuts of the graph that optimize a predefined criterion function. Many criterion functions can be considered here, but not all of them, however, can lead to an efficient algorithm for computing the optimal clustering solution. In the following, we introduce four representative criterion functions for which there exit efficient optimization algorithms.

Let K denote the number of clusters to be generated, $\mathbf{S}_i$, $\mathbf{S}_j$ denote two vertex subsets (clusters) of $\mathbf{V}$, and $W(\mathbf{S}_i, \mathbf{S}_j)$ denote the sum of similarities between $\mathbf{S}_i$ and $\mathbf{S}_j$:

$$W(\mathbf{S}_i, \mathbf{S}_j) = \sum_{u \in \mathbf{S}_i, v \in \mathbf{S}_j} a_{uv} , \tag{3.1}$$

where a_{uv} is the (u, v)'th element of the graph affinity matrix $\mathbf{A}$. The four popular criterion functions employed by spectral clustering techniques are:

Average Weight (AW)

$$\mathcal{F}_{AW} = \sum_{c=1}^{K} \frac{W(\mathbf{S}_c, \mathbf{S}_c)}{|\mathbf{S}_c|} , \tag{3.2}$$

where $|\mathbf{S}_c|$ is the size of cluster $\mathbf{S}_c$. Spectral clustering technique using this criterion function is commonly called *Average Weight* (or *Average Association*). This naming convention also applies to other spectral clustering techniques in this book. Average Weight strives to generate a cluster set that maximizes the within-cluster similarities normalized by the cluster sizes.

Ratio Cut (RC)

$$\mathcal{F}_{RC} = \sum_{c=1}^{K} \frac{W(\mathbf{S}_c, \overline{\mathbf{S}}_c)}{|\mathbf{S}_c|} , \tag{3.3}$$

where $\overline{\mathbf{S}}_c$ denotes the vertex subset $\mathbf{V} - \mathbf{S}_c$. *Ratio Cut* [19], which is also referred to as *Average Cut*, aims to generate a cluster set that minimizes the between-cluster similarities normalized by the cluster sizes.

Normalized Cut (NC)

$$\mathcal{F}_{NC} = \sum_{c=1}^{K} \frac{W(\mathbf{S}_c, \overline{\mathbf{S}}_c)}{W(\mathbf{S}_c, \mathbf{V})} . \tag{3.4}$$

Normalized Cut [20] adopts a criterion function that replaces the denominator in (3.3) with $W(\mathbf{S}_c, \mathbf{V})$. This denominator can be considered as a measure for compactness of the entire data set. Therefore, Normalized Cut attempts to create a cluster set that minimizes the between-cluster similarities normalized by the compactness of the data set.

Minimum Maximum Cut (MMC)

$$\mathcal{F}_{MMC} = \sum_{c=1}^{K} \frac{W(\mathbf{S}_c, \overline{\mathbf{S}}_c)}{W(\mathbf{S}_c, \mathbf{S}_c)} . \tag{3.5}$$

Using this criterion function, *Minimum Maximum Cut* [21] tries to minimize the between-cluster similarities and to maximize the within-cluster similarities simultaneously.

It is noteworthy that the widely used K-means algorithm can be proven to be equivalent to the Average Weight spectral clustering method. The criterion function used by K-means is:

$$\mathcal{F}_{KM} = \sum_{c=1}^{K} \sum_{\mathbf{x} \in \mathbf{S}_c} \|\mathbf{x} - \boldsymbol{\mu}_c\|^2 \tag{3.6}$$

where $\boldsymbol{\mu}_c$ is the center of cluster $\mathbf{S}_c$. If the similarity measure used by $\mathcal{F}_{KM}$ is the dot product of feature vectors of two data points, then we have:

$$
\begin{aligned}
\mathcal{F}_{KM} &= \sum_{c=1}^{K} \frac{1}{2|\mathbf{S}_c|} \sum_{\mathbf{x}_1, \mathbf{x}_2 \in \mathbf{S}_c} \|\mathbf{x}_1 - \mathbf{x}_2\|^2 \\
&= \sum_{c=1}^{K} \frac{1}{2|\mathbf{S}_c|} \sum_{\mathbf{x}_1, \mathbf{x}_2 \in \mathbf{S}_c} (\|\mathbf{x}_1\|^2 + \|\mathbf{x}_2\|^2 - 2\mathbf{x}_1 \cdot \mathbf{x}_2) \\
&= \sum_{\mathbf{x}} \|\mathbf{x}\|^2 - \sum_{c=1}^{K} \frac{1}{|\mathbf{S}_c|} \sum_{\mathbf{x}_1, \mathbf{x}_2 \in \mathbf{S}_c} \mathbf{x}_1 \cdot \mathbf{x}_2 \\
&= \sum_{\mathbf{x}} \|\mathbf{x}\|^2 - \mathcal{F}_{AW}
\end{aligned}
\tag{3.7}
$$

Therefore, minimizing the K-means criterion function $\mathcal{F}_{KM}$ is equivalent to maximizing that of Average Weight $\mathcal{F}_{AW}$.

In the next subsection, we will show algorithms to compute the cluster set that optimizes these criterion functions.

3.2.2 Solution Computation

After defining the criterion functions in Sect. 3.2.1, the next problem is how to efficiently find the cluster set that optimizes these criterion functions. Generally, finding the exact optimal solutions (cluster sets) to these criterion functions has been proven to be an NP-hard problem [20]. The strategy taken by spectral clustering techniques is to relax some of the restrictions so that we can compute the approximate solutions using linear algebra algorithms.

Let $\mathbf{x} = [x_1, x_2, \ldots, x_N]^T$ be the indication vector of a cluster $\mathbf{S}$ where each element x_i takes a binary value to indicate if the i'th data point belongs to $\mathbf{S}$ or not. Using the indication vector $\mathbf{x}$, we can easily derive the following identities:

$$|\mathbf{S}| = \mathbf{x}^T\mathbf{x} \tag{3.8}$$

$$W(\mathbf{S}_1, \mathbf{S}_2) = \mathbf{x}_1^T\mathbf{A}\mathbf{x}_2 \tag{3.9}$$

$$W(\mathbf{S}, \mathbf{V}) = \mathbf{x}^T\mathbf{D}\mathbf{x} \tag{3.10}$$

$$W(\mathbf{S}, \overline{\mathbf{S}}) = \mathbf{x}^T(\mathbf{D} - \mathbf{A})\mathbf{x} \tag{3.11}$$

where $\mathbf{A}$ is the graph affinity matrix, $\mathbf{D}$ is the diagonal matrix such that $\mathbf{D}\mathbf{1} = \mathbf{A}\mathbf{1}$, and $\mathbf{1} = [1, 1, \ldots, 1]^T$. In other words, each diagonal element d_{ii} of the matrix $\mathbf{D}$ is the sum of all the elements in row i of the matrix $\mathbf{A}$: $d_{ii} = \sum_{j=1}^N a_{ij}$.

Using the above identities, the four criterion functions can be rewritten as:

$$\begin{aligned}
\mathcal{F}_{AW} &= \sum_{c=1}^K \frac{W(\mathbf{S}_c, \mathbf{S}_c)}{|\mathbf{S}_c|} \\
&= \sum_{c=1}^K \frac{\mathbf{x}_c^T\mathbf{A}\mathbf{x}_c}{\mathbf{x}_c^T\mathbf{x}_c} \\
&= \sum_{c=1}^K \mathbf{y}_c^T\mathbf{A}\mathbf{y}_c
\end{aligned} \tag{3.12}$$

where $\mathbf{y}_c = \mathbf{x}_c/\|\mathbf{x}_c\|$.

$$\begin{aligned}
\mathcal{F}_{RC} &= \sum_{c=1}^K \frac{W(\mathbf{S}_c, \overline{\mathbf{S}}_c)}{|\mathbf{S}_c|} \\
&= \sum_{c=1}^K \frac{\mathbf{x}_c^T(\mathbf{D} - \mathbf{A})\mathbf{x}_c}{\mathbf{x}_c^T\mathbf{x}_c}
\end{aligned}$$

$$= \sum_{c=1}^{K} \mathbf{y}_c^T (\mathbf{D} - \mathbf{A}) \mathbf{y}_c \qquad (3.13)$$

where $\mathbf{y}_c$ is the same as above.

$$\begin{aligned}
\mathcal{F}_{NC} &= \sum_{c=1}^{K} \frac{W(\mathbf{S}_c, \overline{\mathbf{S}}_c)}{W(\mathbf{S}_c, \mathbf{V})} \\
&= \sum_{c=1}^{K} \frac{\mathbf{x}_c^T (\mathbf{D} - \mathbf{A}) \mathbf{x}_c}{\mathbf{x}_c^T \mathbf{D} \mathbf{x}_c} \\
&= K - \sum_{c=1}^{K} \frac{\mathbf{x}_c^T \mathbf{A} \mathbf{x}_c}{\mathbf{x}_c^T \mathbf{D} \mathbf{x}_c} \\
&= K - \sum_{c=1}^{K} \frac{\mathbf{x}_c^T \mathbf{D}^{\frac{1}{2}} \mathbf{D}^{-\frac{1}{2}} \mathbf{A} \mathbf{D}^{-\frac{1}{2}} \mathbf{D}^{\frac{1}{2}} \mathbf{x}_c}{\mathbf{x}_c^T \mathbf{D}^{\frac{1}{2}} \mathbf{D}^{\frac{1}{2}} \mathbf{x}_c} \\
&= K - \sum_{c=1}^{K} \mathbf{y}_c^T \mathbf{D}^{-\frac{1}{2}} \mathbf{A} \mathbf{D}^{-\frac{1}{2}} \mathbf{y}_c \qquad (3.14)
\end{aligned}$$

where $\mathbf{y}_c = \mathbf{D}^{\frac{1}{2}} \mathbf{x}_c / \|\mathbf{D}^{\frac{1}{2}} \mathbf{x}_c\|$.

$$\begin{aligned}
\mathcal{F}_{MMC} &= \sum_{c=1}^{K} \frac{W(\mathbf{S}_c, \overline{\mathbf{S}}_c)}{W(\mathbf{S}_c, \mathbf{S}_c)} \\
&= \sum_{c=1}^{K} \frac{\mathbf{x}_c^T (\mathbf{D} - \mathbf{A}) \mathbf{x}_c}{\mathbf{x}_c^T \mathbf{A} \mathbf{x}_c} \\
&= -K + \sum_{c=1}^{K} \frac{\mathbf{x}_c^T \mathbf{D} \mathbf{x}_c}{\mathbf{x}_c^T \mathbf{A} \mathbf{x}_c} \\
&= -K + \sum_{c=1}^{K} \frac{1}{\mathbf{y}_c^T \mathbf{D}^{-\frac{1}{2}} \mathbf{A} \mathbf{D}^{-\frac{1}{2}} \mathbf{y}_c} \qquad (3.15)
\end{aligned}$$

where $\mathbf{y}_c$ is the same as in (3.14).

The vectors $\mathbf{y}_c$ in the above equations all satisfy: $\mathbf{y}_c \cdot \mathbf{y}_{c'} = 0$, $\mathbf{y}_c \cdot \mathbf{y}_c = 1$. In other words, they are orthonormal vectors (see Problem 3.1 at the end of this chapter). This orthonormal property is important because it enables us to apply the Rayleigh Quotient Theorem to deriving the optimization algorithm.

With the above derivations, our task of finding the cluster set that optimizes one of the above criterion functions can be turned into the following optimization problem:

Find the set of K indicator vectors $[\mathbf{x}_1, \mathbf{x}_2, \ldots, \mathbf{x}_K]$ *with binary-valued elements that minimizes (or maximizes) the predefined criterion function.*

Generally, solving this optimization problem in its original form has been proven to be NP-hard. However, if we relax all the elements of each indicator vector $\mathbf{x}_i$ from binary values to real values, the above optimization problem can be easily solved by applying the following *Rayleigh Quotient Theorem* [20].

Theorem 3.1. *Let* $\mathbf{A}$ *be a real symmetric matrix. Under the constraint that* $\mathbf{x}$ *is orthogonal to the* $j - 1$ *smallest eigenvectors* $\mathbf{x}_1, \ldots, \mathbf{x}_{j-1}$, *the quotient* $\frac{\mathbf{x}^T \mathbf{A} \mathbf{x}}{\mathbf{x}^T \mathbf{x}}$ *is minimized by the next smallest eigenvector* $\mathbf{x}_j$, *and its minimum value is the corresponding eigenvalue* λ_j.

Applying this theorem to the above four criterion functions, we obtain the following solutions.

Average Weight

$$\mathcal{F}_{AW} \leq \lambda_1 + \ldots + \lambda_K \tag{3.16}$$

where $\lambda_1, \ldots, \lambda_K$ are the K largest eigenvalues of $\mathbf{A}$, and the maximum is achieved when $\mathbf{y}_c$'s in (3.12) are the eigenvectors of the largest eigenvalues.

Ratio Cut

$$\mathcal{F}_{RC} \geq \lambda_N + \ldots + \lambda_{N-K+1} \tag{3.17}$$

where $\lambda_N, \ldots, \lambda_{N-K+1}$ are the K smallest eigenvalues of $\mathbf{D} - \mathbf{A}$, and the minimum is achieved when $\mathbf{y}_c$'s in (3.13) are the eigenvectors of the smallest eigenvalues.

Normalized Cut

$$\mathcal{F}_{NC} \geq K - (\lambda_1 + \ldots + \lambda_K) \tag{3.18}$$

where $\lambda_1, \ldots, \lambda_K$ are the K largest eigenvalues of $\mathbf{D}^{-\frac{1}{2}} \mathbf{A} \mathbf{D}^{-\frac{1}{2}}$, and the minimum is achieved when $\mathbf{y}_c$'s in (3.14) are the eigenvectors of the largest eigenvalues.

Minimum Maximum Cut

Zha, *et al.* [22] proved that

$$\mathcal{F}_{MMC} \geq -K + \frac{K^2}{\lambda_1 + \ldots + \lambda_K} \tag{3.19}$$

The minimum is achieved when $\mathbf{y}_1, \ldots, \mathbf{y}_K$ in (3.15) are the orthonormal basis of the subspace spanned by the eigenvectors of the K largest eigenvalues of $\mathbf{D}^{-\frac{1}{2}}\mathbf{A}\mathbf{D}^{-\frac{1}{2}}$ and further satisfy

$$\mathbf{y}_c^T \mathbf{D}^{-\frac{1}{2}}\mathbf{A}\mathbf{D}^{-\frac{1}{2}}\mathbf{y}_c = \frac{\lambda_1 + \ldots + \lambda_K}{K}. \tag{3.20}$$

In other words, the vector set that minimizes $\mathcal{F}_{MMC}$ can be obtained by rotating the K largest eigenvectors of $\mathbf{D}^{-\frac{1}{2}}\mathbf{A}\mathbf{D}^{-\frac{1}{2}}$ within the derived eigenspace. Therefore, the solution to $\mathcal{F}_{MMC}$ is equivalent to the one for $\mathcal{F}_{NC}$, with the only difference lying in a rotation between the two vector sets.

The four criterion functions and the corresponding eigen-problems are summarized in Table 3.1.

Table 3.1. Summary of representative spectral clustering techniques

Method	Average Weight	Ratio Cut	Normalized Cut	Min-Max Cut
Criterion	$\sum_c \frac{W(\mathbf{S}_c, \mathbf{S}_c)}{\|\mathbf{S}_c\|}$	$\sum_c \frac{W(\mathbf{S}_c, \overline{\mathbf{S}}_c)}{\|\mathbf{S}_c\|}$	$\sum_c \frac{W(\mathbf{S}_c, \overline{\mathbf{S}}_c)}{W(\mathbf{S}_c, \mathbf{V})}$	$\sum_c \frac{W(\mathbf{S}_c, \overline{\mathbf{S}}_c)}{W(\mathbf{S}_c, \mathbf{S}_c)}$
Matrix Form	$\sum_c \frac{\mathbf{x}_c^T \mathbf{A} \mathbf{x}_c}{\mathbf{x}_c^T \mathbf{x}_c}$	$\sum_c \frac{\mathbf{x}_c^T (\mathbf{D}-\mathbf{A}) \mathbf{x}_c}{\mathbf{x}_c^T \mathbf{x}_c}$	$\sum_c \frac{\mathbf{x}_c^T (\mathbf{D}-\mathbf{A}) \mathbf{x}_c}{\mathbf{x}_c^T \mathbf{D} \mathbf{x}_c}$	$\sum_c \frac{\mathbf{x}_c^T (\mathbf{D}-\mathbf{A}) \mathbf{x}_c}{\mathbf{x}_c^T \mathbf{A} \mathbf{x}_c}$
Eigen Prob.	$\mathbf{A}\mathbf{y} = \lambda\mathbf{y}$ $\mathbf{y}_c = \frac{\mathbf{x}_c}{\|\mathbf{x}_c\|}$	$(\mathbf{D}-\mathbf{A})\mathbf{y} = \lambda\mathbf{y}$ $\mathbf{y}_c = \frac{\mathbf{x}_c}{\|\mathbf{x}_c\|}$	$\mathbf{A}\mathbf{y} = \lambda\mathbf{D}\mathbf{y}$ $\mathbf{y}_c = \frac{\mathbf{D}^{\frac{1}{2}}\mathbf{x}_c}{\left\|\mathbf{D}^{\frac{1}{2}}\mathbf{x}_c\right\|}$	$\mathbf{A}\mathbf{y} = \lambda\mathbf{D}\mathbf{y}$ $\mathbf{y}_c = \frac{\mathbf{D}^{\frac{1}{2}}\mathbf{x}_c}{\left\|\mathbf{D}^{\frac{1}{2}}\mathbf{x}_c\right\|}$
Bound	$\leq \sum_{i=1}^{K} \lambda_i$	$\geq \sum_{i=1}^{K} \lambda_{N-i+1}$	$\geq \sum_{i=1}^{K} (1 - \lambda_i)$	$\geq -K + \frac{K^2}{\sum_{i=1}^{K} \lambda_i}$

Note: $\lambda_1, \lambda_2, \ldots$ represent the eigen vectors of the largest, second largest, $\ldots$ eigen values.

The K eigenvectors $\mathbf{y}_1, \cdots, \mathbf{y}_K$ obtained above encode the cluster membership information for the given data set $\mathbf{V}$. However, since these eigenvectors take real values for their elements, they do not directly indicate the cluster membership for each data point i. A common approach for deriving the final cluster set is to project each data point into the eigen-space spanned by the K eigenvectors, and apply the K-means algorithm within this eigen-space.

Let $\mathbf{Y}$ be the $N \times K$ matrix comprising the K eigenvectors, and $\mathbf{u}_i$ be the $K \times 1$ vector comprising elements i of all the K eigenvectors:

$$\mathbf{Y} = [\mathbf{y}_1, \mathbf{y}_2, \ldots, \mathbf{y}_K] = \begin{bmatrix} \mathbf{u}_1^T \\ \vdots \\ \mathbf{u}_N^T \end{bmatrix} = \begin{bmatrix} a_1 \tilde{\mathbf{u}}_1^T \\ \vdots \\ a_n \tilde{\mathbf{u}}_N^T \end{bmatrix}, \tag{3.21}$$

where $a_i = \|\mathbf{u}_i\|$ and $\tilde{\mathbf{u}}_i = \mathbf{u}_i / \|\mathbf{u}_i\|$. In the eigen-space spanned by the K eigenvectors, each data point i is represented by the vector $\mathbf{u}_i$ (or the normalized vector $\tilde{\mathbf{u}}_i$). It has been proven by Ng and Zha [23, 22] that if the given data set has exactly K separable clusters, then these K clusters can be well separated in the space of $\tilde{\mathbf{u}}_i$'s. Thus a further step of applying a simple data clustering algorithm such as K-means will be sufficient to obtain the final cluster set.

In summary, the general procedure for spectral clustering techniques can be described as follows:

1. Represent the given data set using the undirected graph $\mathcal{G}(\mathbf{V}, \mathbf{E}, \mathbf{A})$.
2. Solve the eigen problem to find the K largest/smallest eigenvectors $\mathbf{Y} = [\mathbf{y}_1, \mathbf{y}_2, \ldots, \mathbf{y}_k]$ according to Table 3.1.
3. Compute $\tilde{\mathbf{u}}_i$'s according to (3.21).
4. Recover the cluster membership from the eigen-space by performing K-means algorithm on $\tilde{\mathbf{u}}_i$'s.

3.2.3 Example

We use a simple, small data set to illustrate data distributions in the eigen-spaces derived by the respective spectral clustering methods. The data set was composed by mixing three document classes from the TDT2 document corpus, which consist of 12, 37, and 54 documents, respectively. Each document was represented by a 996-dimensional feature vector, with each dimension indicating the occurrence frequency of a specific keyword in the document (see

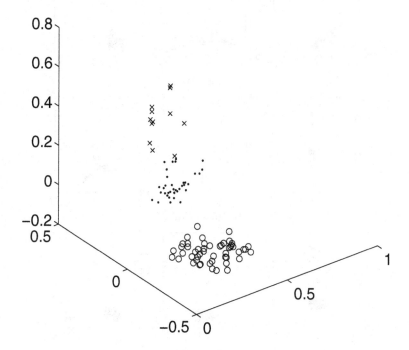

Fig. 3.1. Data distribution in the original feature subspace. The figure is created by finding the three most important axes of the original feature space using principal component analysis, and then plotting the data set into the subspace spanned by these three axes

Sect. 3.5 for detailed descriptions on TDT2, and feature vectors for document representation).

Figure 3.1 shows the distribution of the given data set in the original feature subspace. Because the original feature space consists of 996 dimensions, it can not be directly shown using a 2-D or 3-D graph. Figure 3.1 was created by finding the three most important axes of the original feature space using principal component analysis, and then plotting the data set into the subspace spanned by these three axes. Data points belonging to the same cluster are depicted using the same symbol.

Applying the spectral clustering techniques to the given data set, we obtain the eigen-spaces spanned by three eigenvectors. Fig. 3.2(a), (b), (c) depict the

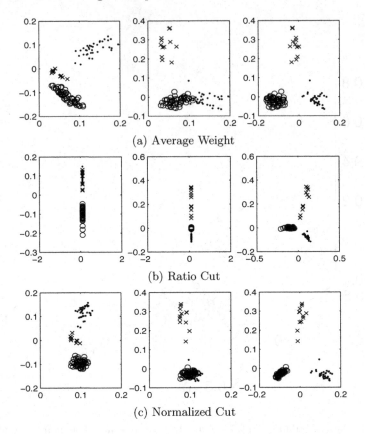

(a) Average Weight

(b) Ratio Cut

(c) Normalized Cut

Fig. 3.2. Data distributions in the subspaces of u_1-u_2, u_1-u_3, and u_2-u_3, respectively. (a), (b), (c) depict the subspaces derived by the Average Weight, Ratio Cut, and Normalized Cut, respectively. Documents belonging to the same cluster are depicted by the same symbol

eigen-spaces derived by the Average Weight, Ratio Cut, and Normalized Cut, respectively. Each group of three graphs depict the data distributions in the subspaces of u_1-u_2, u_1-u_3, and u_2-u_3, respectively. In these figures, data points belonging to the same cluster are depicted using the same symbol. Since the Minimum Maximum Cut is essentially the same as the Normalized Cut except for the rotations of eigenvectors, we omit its graphs here, and will not conduct further evaluations on it in subsequent sections.

For comparisons, We also show the data distributions in the subspaces of $\tilde{u}_1$-$\tilde{u}_2$, $\tilde{u}_1$-$\tilde{u}_3$, and $\tilde{u}_2$-$\tilde{u}_3$ derived by the three spectral clustering techniques (Fig. 3.3). From these two figures, we can clearly make the following observations:

- Spectral clustering techniques essentially project the given data set of a high dimension into an eigen-space of a much lower dimension where the data set can be easily separated.
- The eigen-space derived by the Normalized Cut has the data distribution that is the easiest to separate.
- The axes spanning each eigen-space do not directly indicate the cluster membership for each data point, and an additional step of applying a

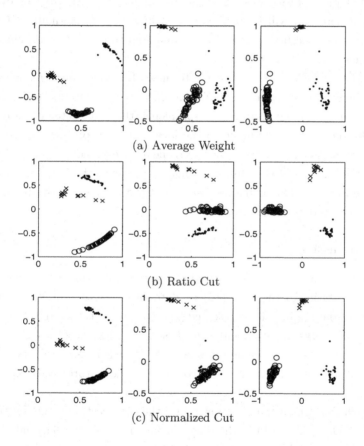

(a) Average Weight

(b) Ratio Cut

(c) Normalized Cut

Fig. 3.3. Data distributions in the subspaces of $\tilde{u}_1$-$\tilde{u}_2$, $\tilde{u}_1$-$\tilde{u}_3$, and $\tilde{u}_2$-$\tilde{u}_3$, respectively. (a), (b), (c) depict the subspaces derived by the Average Weight, Ratio Cut, and Normalized Cut, respectively. Documents belonging to the same cluster are depicted by the same symbol

simple data clustering algorithm such as K-means is necessary to obtain the final cluster set.

- Data distributions in the normalized eigen-spaces $\tilde{\mathbf{u}}_1$-$\tilde{\mathbf{u}}_2$-$\tilde{\mathbf{u}}_3$ are more compact than those in the corresponding eigen-spaces $\mathbf{u}_1$-$\mathbf{u}_2$-$\mathbf{u}_3$, so that applying K-means in the normalized eigen-spaces is expected to generate better final clustering results.

In fact, the above observations are true for most data sets. Indeed, Fig. 3.2 and 3.3 provide us with the insight on why spectral clustering techniques are generally better than traditional data clustering methods which mostly conduct data clustering operations in the original data space. Moreover, as witnessed here and will be further proven in Sect. 3.5, Normalized Cut always generates the best performances compared to other spectral clustering techniques.

Another advantage of spectral clustering techniques, which can not be observed directly from the above figures, is that because data clustering results are derived by solving certain eigen-problems, they guarantee globally optimal solutions, and are immune to the local optimum problem. In contrast, traditional clustering methods such as K-means are prone to local optimums, even if they use a criterion function that is similar to those of spectral clustering techniques. This is mainly because of the ad hoc algorithms used for computing the optimal solutions.

3.2.4 Discussions

We study the reason why Normalized Cut always performs better than other spectral clustering methods. Consider a data set with a total of N data points, where each data point i is represented by a feature vector $\mathbf{x}_i$. If we define the affinity score between data points i and j as $a_{ij} = (\mathbf{x}_i \cdot \mathbf{x}_j)$, then the graph affinity matrix for the data set becomes $\mathbf{A} = \mathbf{X}^T\mathbf{X}$, where $\mathbf{X} = [\mathbf{x}_1, \mathbf{x}_2, \ldots, \mathbf{x}_N]$ is the feature–data matrix in which column i is the feature vector $\mathbf{x}_i$ of data point i.

Normalized Cut attempts to compute the eigenvectors of $\mathbf{D}^{-\frac{1}{2}}\mathbf{A}\mathbf{D}^{-\frac{1}{2}} = \mathbf{D}^{-\frac{1}{2}}\mathbf{X}^T\mathbf{X}\mathbf{D}^{-\frac{1}{2}}$, where $\mathbf{D}$ is the diagonal matrix with the diagonal element $d_{ii} = \sum_{j=1}^{N} a_{ij} = \sum_{j=1}^{N}(\mathbf{x}_i \cdot \mathbf{x}_j)$. This is equivalent to finding the singular vectors for $\mathbf{X}\mathbf{D}^{-\frac{1}{2}}$. In contrast, Average Weight attempts to find the singular vectors for $\mathbf{X}$. Therefore, what distinguishes Normalized Cut from other spectral clustering methods is that Normalized Cut applies weight $1/d_{ii}$ to the feature vector $\mathbf{x}_i$ of data point i while others do not!

What does the weighting scheme employed by Normalized Cut mean? A closer examination on this weighting scheme reveals the following:

- If a data point i belongs to a large cluster, which means the feature vector $\mathbf{x}_i$ is similar to many other feature vectors $\mathbf{x}_j$, $j \neq i$, then the weight $1/d_{ii}$ becomes very small. Therefore, the weight to $\mathbf{x}_i$ serves to reduce the importance of data point i.
- On the other hand, if the data point i belongs to a small cluster, which means $\mathbf{x}_i$ is similar to only few feature vectors $\mathbf{x}_j$, then the weight $1/d_{ii}$ becomes very large, and therefore, serves to increase the important of data point i.

This kind of weighting scheme is particularly useful for data sets with unbalanced clusters. For unbalanced data sets, without an appropriate weighting, the derived eigenvectors will be predominated by large clusters, and will contain little information about small clusters. If we can give more weights to the data points belonging to small clusters, then the derived eigenvectors would be more useful for data clustering purposes. The ideal weighting scheme would be the one that the sum of the weights in each cluster is the same. Without the knowledge of the cluster membership of each data point, how can this be achieved? Indeed, the weighting scheme employed by Normalized Cut is an approximation to this ideal weighting scheme. It is really a smart, and best weighting scheme without knowing the cluster membership of each data point.

3.3 Data Clustering by Non-Negative Matrix Factorization

Data clustering techniques based on Non-Negative Matrix Factorization (NMF) tackle the data clustering problem from the concept factorization point of view. The model used by these techniques considers each cluster of a data set as the embodiment of a coherent concept (or topic for document corpora), and each data point as a linear combination of all the concepts (the cluster centers). Because it is more natural to consider each data point as an additive rather than subtractive mixture of the underlying concepts, the linear combination coefficients should all take non-negative values. Furthermore, it is also quite common that the concepts comprising a data set are not completely independent of each other, and there are some overlaps among them.

In such cases, the axes of the semantic space that capture these concepts are not necessarily orthogonal.

Using the model described above, the data clustering problem becomes the problem of computing the linear combination coefficients for each data point which meet the above constraints, and then deriving the clustering result from the computed coefficients. This can be efficiently accomplished by non-negative matrix factorization of a certain feature matrix of the given data set. In this section, we describe two NMF-based data clustering techniques, which stem from our original works in recent years [24, 25].

3.3.1 Single Linear NMF Model

Assume that the given data set contains a total of N data points that form K clusters, and that each data point i is represented by an M-dimensional feature vector $\mathbf{x}_i = [x_{1i}, x_{2i}, \ldots, x_{Mi}]^T$. Further assume that $\mathbf{u}_k = [u_{1k}, u_{2k}, \ldots, u_{Mk}]$ is an M-dimensional vector representing the k'th cluster center (or concept), and that $\mathbf{v}_i = [v_{i1}, v_{i2}, \ldots, v_{iK}]^T$ is a K-dimensional vector containing the linear combination coefficients for data point i. The single linear model models each cluster center $\mathbf{u}_k$ as the embodiment of a coherent concept, and each data point $\mathbf{x}_i$ as a linear combination of all the concepts [24]. Translating this statement into mathematics, we have

$$\mathbf{x}_i \approx v_{i1}\mathbf{u}_1 + v_{i2}\mathbf{u}_2 + \cdots + v_{iK}\mathbf{u}_K \ . \tag{3.22}$$

Writing (3.22) in matrix form, we have

$$\mathbf{X} \approx \mathbf{U} \cdot \mathbf{V}^T \ , \tag{3.23}$$

where $\mathbf{X}$ is the $M \times N$ feature–data matrix $\mathbf{X} = [\mathbf{x}_1, \mathbf{x}_2, \ldots, \mathbf{x}_N]$ in which column i is the feature vector $\mathbf{x}_i$ of data point i, $\mathbf{U}$ is the $M \times K$ non-negative matrix $\mathbf{U} = [\mathbf{u}_1, \mathbf{u}_2, \ldots, \mathbf{u}_K]$, and $\mathbf{V}^T$ is the $K \times N$ non-negative matrix $\mathbf{V}^T = [\mathbf{v}_1, \mathbf{v}_2, \ldots, \mathbf{v}_N]$. The goal here is to factorize $\mathbf{X}$ into two non-negative matrixes $\mathbf{U}, \mathbf{V}$ that minimize the following criterion function

$$J = \frac{1}{2}\|\mathbf{X} - \mathbf{U}\mathbf{V}^T\|^2 \tag{3.24}$$

where $\| \cdot \|^2$ denotes the squared sum of all the elements in the matrix.

The criterion function (3.24) can be easily minimized using existing non-negative matrix factorization algorithms. The following describes the one used in our implementation.

Equation (3.24) can be re-written as:

$$J = \frac{1}{2}\text{trace}((\mathbf{X} - \mathbf{UV}^T)(\mathbf{X} - \mathbf{UV}^T)^T)$$

$$= \frac{1}{2}\text{trace}(\mathbf{XX}^T - 2\mathbf{XVU}^T + \mathbf{UV}^T\mathbf{VU}^T)$$

$$= \frac{1}{2}(\text{trace}(\mathbf{XX}^T) - 2\text{trace}(\mathbf{XVU}^T) + \text{trace}(\mathbf{UV}^T\mathbf{VU}^T)) \quad (3.25)$$

where the second step of the above derivations uses the matrix properties $\text{trace}(\mathbf{AB}) = \text{trace}(\mathbf{BA})$, $\text{trace}(\mathbf{A}) = \text{trace}(\mathbf{A}^T)$. Let $\mathbf{U} = [u_{ij}]$, $\mathbf{V} = [v_{ij}]$. The above minimization problem can be restated as follows:

Minimize J with respect to $\mathbf{U}$ and $\mathbf{V}$ under the constraints of $u_{ij} \geq 0$, $v_{xy} \geq 0$, where $0 \leq i \leq M$, $0 \leq j \leq K$, $0 \leq x \leq N$, and $0 \leq y \leq K$.

This is a typical conditional minimization problem, and can be solved using the Lagrange multiplier algorithm [26]. Let α_{ij} and β_{ij} be the Lagrange multipliers for constraints $u_{ij} \geq 0$ and $v_{ij} \geq 0$, respectively, and $\boldsymbol{\alpha} = [\alpha_{ij}]$, $\boldsymbol{\beta} = [\beta_{ij}]$. The Lagrange L is:

$$L = J + \text{trace}(\boldsymbol{\alpha}\mathbf{U}^T) + \text{trace}(\boldsymbol{\beta}\mathbf{V}^T) . \quad (3.26)$$

The derivatives of L with respect to $\mathbf{U}$ and $\mathbf{V}$ are:

$$\frac{\partial L}{\partial \mathbf{U}} = -\mathbf{XV} + \mathbf{UV}^T\mathbf{V} + \boldsymbol{\alpha} \quad (3.27)$$

$$\frac{\partial L}{\partial \mathbf{V}} = -\mathbf{X}^T\mathbf{U} + \mathbf{VU}^T\mathbf{U} + \boldsymbol{\beta} \quad (3.28)$$

Using the Kuhn-Tucker conditions $\alpha_{ij}u_{ij} = 0$ and $\beta_{ij}v_{ij} = 0$, we get the following equations for u_{ij} and v_{ij}:

$$(\mathbf{XV})_{ij}u_{ij} - (\mathbf{UV}^T\mathbf{V})_{ij}u_{ij} = 0 \quad (3.29)$$

$$(\mathbf{X}^T\mathbf{U})_{ij}v_{ij} - (\mathbf{VU}^T\mathbf{U})_{ij}v_{ij} = 0 \quad (3.30)$$

where $(\mathbf{A})_{ij}$ denotes the element (i, j) of matrix $\mathbf{A}$. These equations lead to the following updating formulas:

$$u_{ij} \leftarrow u_{ij}\frac{(\mathbf{XV})_{ij}}{(\mathbf{UV}^T\mathbf{V})_{ij}} \quad (3.31)$$

$$v_{ij} \leftarrow v_{ij}\frac{(\mathbf{X}^T\mathbf{U})_{ij}}{(\mathbf{VU}^T\mathbf{U})_{ij}} \quad (3.32)$$

It is proven by Lee [27] that the objective function J is non-increasing under the above iterative updating rules, and that the convergence of the iteration is guaranteed. Notice that the solution to minimizing the criterion function J is not unique. If $\mathbf{U}$ and $\mathbf{V}$ are the solution to J, then, $\mathbf{UD}$, $\mathbf{VD}^{-1}$ will also form a solution for any positive diagonal matrix $\mathbf{D}$. To make the solution unique, we further require that the Euclidean length of column vectors in matrix $\mathbf{U}$ is one. This requirement of normalizing $\mathbf{U}$ can be achieved by[1]:

$$v_{ij} \leftarrow v_{ij}\sqrt{\sum_i u_{ij}^2} \tag{3.33}$$

$$u_{ij} \leftarrow \frac{u_{ij}}{\sqrt{\sum_i u_{ij}^2}} \tag{3.34}$$

There is an analogy to the Singular Value Decomposition (SVD) in interpreting the meaning of the two non-negative matrices $\mathbf{U}$ and $\mathbf{V}$. From the data clustering model described at the beginning of this section, it is clear that each element v_{ij} of matrix $\mathbf{V}$ indicates the degree to which data point i belongs to cluster j. If data point i solely belongs to cluster j, then v_{ij} will take on a large value while rest of the elements in the i'th column vector $\mathbf{v}_i$ of matrix $\mathbf{V}^T$ will take on a small value close to zero. Furthermore, as the k'th column vector $\mathbf{u}_k$ of matrix $\mathbf{U}$ represents the k'th cluster center, each of its elements u_{ik} can be interpreted as the degree to which feature i belongs to cluster k. Therefore, from the two non-negative matrices $\mathbf{U}$ and $\mathbf{V}$, we can derive the data clustering result directly without additional clustering steps.

In summary, the single linear model conducts the data clustering task using the following steps:

1. Given a data set, construct the feature–data matrix $\mathbf{X}$ in which column i represents the feature vector $\mathbf{x}_i$ of data point i.
2. Perform NMF on $\mathbf{X}$ to obtain the two non-negative matrices $\mathbf{U}$ and $\mathbf{V}$ using (3.31) and (3.32).
3. Normalize $\mathbf{U}$ and $\mathbf{V}$ using (3.34) and (3.33).
4. Use matrix $\mathbf{V}$ to determine the cluster label of each data point. More precisely, examine each column vector $\mathbf{v}_i$ of matrix $\mathbf{V}^T$, and assign data point i to cluster c if $c = \arg\max_j v_{ij}$.

---

[1] When normalizing matrix $\mathbf{U}$, matrix $\mathbf{V}$ needs to be adjusted accordingly so that $\mathbf{UV}^T$ does not change.

3.3.2 Bilinear NMF Model

Section 3.3.1 described the single linear model using non-negative matrix factorization. However, the single linear NMF model has the following limitations. First, it requires that all cluster centers be non-negative. Although this is not a severe constraint for text documents, it is not desirable for many other data involving negative numbers. Second, because of the non-negative constraint on cluster centers, the optimization algorithm has to be performed in the original feature space of the data points, so that the powerful kernel method cannot be applied here to further improve clustering accuracies. We refer readers to [28] for an introduction to kernel based algorithms.

In this subsection, we present a bilinear NMF model that strives to address the problems while inheriting all the strengths of the single linear NMF model [25]. This new model models each cluster center as a linear combination of all the data points, and each data point as a linear combination of all the cluster centers. With this model, the data clustering task is accomplished by computing the two sets of linear combination coefficients which define the degrees of association between each pair of cluster and data point. Because it is more natural to consider that a concept (or a data point) is formed by additions rather than subtractions of the underlying data points (or concepts), in analogy to the single linear model, we demand that the two sets of coefficients be positive.

Let $\mathbf{x}_i$ be an M-dimensional feature vector representing data point i where $i = 1, \ldots, N$, $\mathbf{r}_c$ be the c'th cluster center where $c = 1, \ldots, K$. Translating the above statement into mathematics, we have

$$\mathbf{r}_c = \sum_{i=1}^{N} w_{ic} \mathbf{x}_i \qquad (3.35)$$

$$\mathbf{x}_i \approx \sum_{c=1}^{K} v_{ic} \mathbf{r}_c \qquad (3.36)$$

where w_{ic} is the non-negative association weight indicating to which degree data point i is related to concept $\mathbf{r}_c$, and v_{ic} is a non-negative number showing the projection value of $\mathbf{x}_i$ onto each concept (cluster center) $\mathbf{r}_c$. Replacing $\mathbf{r}_c$ in (3.36) with (3.35), we have

$$\mathbf{x}_i \approx \sum_{c=1}^{K} v_{ic} \mathbf{r}_c = \sum_{c=1}^{K} v_{ic} \sum_{j=1}^{N} \mathbf{x}_j w_{jc} . \qquad (3.37)$$

We form the $M \times N$ feature–data matrix $\mathbf{X} = [\mathbf{x}_1, \mathbf{x}_2, \ldots, \mathbf{x}_N]$ using the feature vector of data point i as the i'th column, the $N \times K$ association matrix $\mathbf{W} = [w_{ic}]$ using the association weights w_{ic}, and the $N \times K$ projection matrix $\mathbf{V} = [v_{ic}]$ using the projection values v_{ic}. From (3.37) we have

$$\mathbf{X} \approx \mathbf{XWV}^T \tag{3.38}$$

Equation (3.38) can be interpreted as the approximation of the original data set $\mathbf{X}$ using the clustering result defined by the matrices $\mathbf{W}$ and $\mathbf{V}$. The bilinear model attempts to find a data cluster set that minimizes the following criterion function:

$$J = \frac{1}{2}\|\mathbf{X} - \mathbf{XWV}^T\|^2 . \tag{3.39}$$

where $\| \cdot \|^2$ denotes the squared sum of all the elements in the matrix. The algorithm for computing the optimal solution to (3.39) is provided below.

Define $\mathbf{K} = \mathbf{X}^T\mathbf{X}$, and use the property $\|\mathbf{A}\|^2 = \text{trace}(\mathbf{A}^T\mathbf{A})$, we have

$$
\begin{aligned}
J &= \frac{1}{2}\text{trace}((\mathbf{X} - \mathbf{XWV}^T)^T(\mathbf{X} - \mathbf{XWV}^T)) \\
&= \frac{1}{2}\text{trace}((\mathbf{I} - \mathbf{WV}^T)^T\mathbf{K}(\mathbf{I} - \mathbf{WV}^T)) \\
&= \frac{1}{2}\text{trace}(\mathbf{K} - 2\mathbf{VW}^T\mathbf{K} + \mathbf{VW}^T\mathbf{KWV}^T) \\
&= \frac{1}{2}(\text{trace}(\mathbf{K}) - 2\text{trace}(\mathbf{W}^T\mathbf{KV}) + \text{trace}(\mathbf{W}^T\mathbf{KWV}^T\mathbf{V})) \quad (3.40)
\end{aligned}
$$

where the last step of the above derivations has used the matrix properties $\text{trace}(\mathbf{AB}) = \text{trace}(\mathbf{BA})$ and $\text{trace}(\mathbf{A}) = \text{trace}(\mathbf{A}^T)$.

In (3.40), fixing $\mathbf{V}$, J becomes a quadratic form of $\mathbf{W}$ which is denoted as $J(\mathbf{W})$. Similarly, fixing $\mathbf{W}$, we get a quadratic form of $\mathbf{V}$ denoted as $J(\mathbf{V})$. Since quadratic form minimization/maximization is a well studied problem, the strategy here is to optimize $\mathbf{W}$ and $\mathbf{V}$ alternatively so that we can leverage on existing quadratic programming algorithms. In [29], Sha et al derived a multiplicative update algorithm that computes the non-negative solution for minimizing the general quadratic form.

Theorem 3.2. *Define the non-negative general quadratic form as*

$$F(\mathbf{y}) = \frac{1}{2}\mathbf{y}^T\mathbf{Ay} + \mathbf{b}^T\mathbf{y} \tag{3.41}$$

where $\mathbf{y} = [y_i]$ is an $M \times 1$ vector in which each element y_i satisfies $y_i \geq 0$, $\mathbf{A}$ is an arbitrary $M \times M$ symmetric semi-positive definite matrix, and $\mathbf{b} = [b_i]$

is an arbitrary $M \times 1$ vector. Let $\mathbf{A} = \mathbf{A}^+ - \mathbf{A}^-$, where $\mathbf{A}^+$ and $\mathbf{A}^-$ are two symmetric matrices whose elements are all positive. Then the solution $\mathbf{y}$ that minimizes $F(\mathbf{y})$ can be obtained by the following iterative update

$$y_i \leftarrow y_i \left[\frac{-b_i + \sqrt{b_i^2 + 4(\mathbf{A}^+\mathbf{y})_i(\mathbf{A}^-\mathbf{y})_i}}{2(\mathbf{A}^+\mathbf{y})_i} \right] \tag{3.42}$$

where $(\mathbf{x})_i$ denotes the i'th element of vector $\mathbf{x}$.

To apply the above theorem to minimize the criterion function J, we need to identify the corresponding $\mathbf{A}$ and $\mathbf{b}$ terms in (3.40). Fixing $\mathbf{V}$, the two co-efficients for the quadratic form $J(\mathbf{W})$ can be obtained by taking the second order derivative with respect to $\mathbf{W}$, and by taking the first order derivative with respect to $\mathbf{W}$ at $\mathbf{W} = 0$, respectively. Let $\mathbf{K} = \mathbf{K}^+ - \mathbf{K}^-$ where $\mathbf{K}^+$ and $\mathbf{K}^-$ are the symmetric matrices whose elements are all positive, the compu-tation of the two coefficients becomes

$$\frac{\partial^2 J}{\partial w_{ij} \partial w_{kl}} = k_{ik}^+ (\mathbf{V}^T\mathbf{V})_{lj} - k_{ik}^- (\mathbf{V}^T\mathbf{V})_{lj} \tag{3.43}$$

$$\left. \frac{\partial J}{\partial w_{ij}} \right|_{\mathbf{W}=0} = -(\mathbf{KV})_{ij} \tag{3.44}$$

where the two terms at the right hand side of (3.43) corresponds to $\mathbf{A}^+$ and $\mathbf{A}^-$ in (3.42) respectively. By substituting $\mathbf{A}$ and b_i in (3.42) using the right-hand side of the above two equations, we obtain the multiplicative updating equation for computing each element w_{ij} of $\mathbf{W}$:

$$w_{ij} \leftarrow w_{ij} \frac{(\mathbf{KV})_{ij} + \sqrt{(\mathbf{KV})_{ij}^2 + 4\mathbf{P}_{ij}^+\mathbf{P}_{ij}^-}}{2\mathbf{P}_{ij}^+} \tag{3.45}$$

where $\mathbf{P}^+ = \mathbf{K}^+\mathbf{W}\mathbf{V}^T\mathbf{V}$ and $\mathbf{P}^- = \mathbf{K}^-\mathbf{W}\mathbf{V}^T\mathbf{V}$. For the case that matrix $\mathbf{K}$ is comprised of all positive elements (i.e. $\mathbf{K}^- = 0$), we get a compact equation as follows:

$$w_{ij} \leftarrow w_{ij} \frac{(\mathbf{KV})_{ij}}{\mathbf{P}_{ij}} \tag{3.46}$$

Similarly, we can compute each element v_{ij} of $\mathbf{V}$ by applying the above the-orem to the quadratic form $J(\mathbf{V})$. Fixing $\mathbf{W}$, we get

$$\frac{\partial^2 J}{\partial v_{ij} \partial v_{kl}} = \delta_{ik}((\mathbf{W}^T\mathbf{K}^+\mathbf{W})_{lj} - (\mathbf{W}^T\mathbf{K}^-\mathbf{W})_{lj}) \tag{3.47}$$

$$\left. \frac{J}{\partial v_{ij}} \right|_{\mathbf{V}=0} = -(\mathbf{KW})_{ij} \tag{3.48}$$

where δ_{ik} is equal to 1 if $i = k$ and equal to 0 otherwise. The update rule for $\mathbf{V}$ is:

$$v_{ij} \leftarrow v_{ij} \frac{(\mathbf{KW})_{ij} + \sqrt{(\mathbf{KW})_{ij}^2 + 4Q_{ij}^+ Q_{ij}^-}}{2Q_{ij}^+} \tag{3.49}$$

where $\mathbf{Q}^+ = \mathbf{VW}^T \mathbf{K}^+ \mathbf{W}$ and $\mathbf{Q}^- = \mathbf{VW}^T \mathbf{K}^- \mathbf{W}$. The the compact form of the update rule in the case of non-negative $\mathbf{K}$ is:

$$v_{ij} \leftarrow v_{ij} \frac{(\mathbf{KW})_{ij}}{Q_{ij}^+} \tag{3.50}$$

Notice that the solution to minimizing the criterion function J is not unique. If $\mathbf{W}$ and $\mathbf{V}$ are the solution to J, then, $\mathbf{WD}$, $\mathbf{VD}^{-1}$ will also form a solution for any positive diagonal matrix $\mathbf{D}$. To make the solution unique, we further require that $\|\mathbf{r}_c\| = 1$. This requirement of normalizing $\mathbf{W}$ can be achieved by[2]:

$$\mathbf{V} \leftarrow \mathbf{V}[\mathrm{diag}(\mathbf{W}^T \mathbf{KW})]^{1/2} \tag{3.51}$$

$$\mathbf{W} \leftarrow \mathbf{W}[\mathrm{diag}(\mathbf{W}^T \mathbf{KW})]^{-1/2} \tag{3.52}$$

The above algorithm is derived with the standard kernel matrix $\mathbf{K} = \mathbf{X}^T \mathbf{X}$. In fact each element k_{ij} of $\mathbf{K}$ is nothing but the inner product $(\mathbf{x}_i \cdot \mathbf{x}_j)$ between the feature vectors of data points i and j. In addition to the standard kernel matrix, the bilinear model can be readily applied to any kernel matrix $\mathbf{K}$ in which k_{ij} is defined by an arbitrary kernel function $k_{ij} = \mathcal{K}(\mathbf{x}_i, \mathbf{x}_j)$. Employing a kernel function amounts to performing the algorithm in a high-dimensional (or even infinite-dimensional) space defined by the kernel function. This capability of using any kernel functions for defining the kernel matrix $\mathbf{K}$, as will be demonstrated in Sect. 3.5, remarkably increases the power of the bilinear model for achieving high data clustering accuracies for certain data sets.

The immediate outcome from the bilinear NMF model is the two sets of coefficients $\mathbf{W}$ and $\mathbf{V}$. Each column vector $\mathbf{w}_c$ of $\mathbf{W}$ indicates the association degrees of all the data points to cluster c, while each column vector $\mathbf{v}_i$ of $\mathbf{V}^T$ indicates the projection values of data point i on all the cluster centers. Because of such semantic meanings possessed by the two coefficient sets, it is expected that the cluster label of each data point can be directly derived from either $\mathbf{W}$ or $\mathbf{V}$. For example, if the data set has a clear cluster structure

---

[2] When normalizing matrix $\mathbf{W}$, matrix $\mathbf{V}$ needs to be adjusted accordingly so that $\mathbf{WV}^T$ does not change.

(i.e., there is only one obvious way to cluster it and there is no overlap among the clusters), usually only one coefficient in each $\mathbf{v}_i$ is significantly different from zero and this coefficient corresponds to the cluster to which data point i belongs to.

Although both $\mathbf{W}$ and $\mathbf{V}$ can be used to derive the cluster label for each data point, it is preferable to use $\mathbf{V}$ because of the following reason. Consider the case that a data point i happens to overlap the center of a particular cluster c. Then the coefficient w_{ic} could take a large value, while coefficients w_{jc} for all other data points $j \neq i$ could be close to zero. Obviously this makes the identification of cluster labels of other data points difficult if $\mathbf{W}$ is to be used.

In summary, the bilinear NMF model is composed of the following steps:

1. Given a data set, construct the data–feature matrix $\mathbf{X}$ in which column $\mathbf{x}_i$ represents the feature vector of data point i.
2. Construct the kernel matrix $\mathbf{K}$ using an appropriate kernel function $\mathcal{K}(\mathbf{x}_i, \mathbf{x}_j)$.
3. Fixing $\mathbf{V}$, update matrix $\mathbf{W}$ to decrease the quadratic form $J(\mathbf{W})$ using (3.45).
4. Fixing $\mathbf{W}$, update matrix $\mathbf{V}$ to decrease the quadratic form $J(\mathbf{V})$ using (3.49).
5. Normalize $\mathbf{W}$ and $\mathbf{V}$ using (3.52) and (3.51), respectively.
6. Repeat Step 3, 4 and 5 until the result converges.
7. Use matrix $\mathbf{V}^T$ to determine the cluster label of each data point. More precisely, examine each column $\mathbf{v}_i$ of matrix $\mathbf{V}^T$. Assign data point i to cluster x if $x = \arg\max_c (v_{ic})$.

3.4 Spectral vs. NMF

In Sections 3.2 and 3.3, we provided detailed descriptions of spectral and NMF-based clustering techniques, respectively. To further gain insights into these two types of clustering techniques, in this section, we illustrate their characteristics and differences using examples. To make more focused discussions, we choose the Normalized Cut and the bilinear NMF model to represent each type of clustering techniques. We apply the two methods to a data set that consists of three clusters (the same data set as shown in Fig. 3.1), and plot the data set in the spaces derived by them, respectively.

Figure 3.4 (a) and (b) show the data distributions in the two spaces where data points belonging to the same cluster are depicted by the same symbol. The three graphs in (a) show the data points in the subspaces of $\mathbf{u}_1$–$\mathbf{u}_2$, $\mathbf{u}_1$–$\mathbf{u}_3$, and $\mathbf{u}_2$–$\mathbf{u}_3$, respectively, where $\mathbf{u}_1, \mathbf{u}_2, \mathbf{u}_3$ are the three axes derived by the Normalized Cut. Similarly, the three graphs in (b) show the data points in the subspaces of $\mathbf{v}_1$–$\mathbf{v}_2$, $\mathbf{v}_1$–$\mathbf{v}_3$, and $\mathbf{v}_2$–$\mathbf{v}_3$, respectively, where $\mathbf{v}_1, \mathbf{v}_2, \mathbf{v}_3$ are the three column vectors of $\mathbf{V}^T$ from the bilinear NMF model. From Fig. 3.4 we can make the following observations:

- The three clusters are well separated in both spaces.
- In the $\mathbf{v}_1$-$\mathbf{v}_2$-$\mathbf{v}_3$ space, every data point takes non-negative values in all three directions, while in the $\mathbf{u}_1$-$\mathbf{u}_2$-$\mathbf{u}_3$ space, each data point may take negative values in some of the directions.
- In the $\mathbf{v}_1$-$\mathbf{v}_2$-$\mathbf{v}_3$ space, each axis corresponds to a cluster, and all the data points belonging to the same cluster spread along the same axis. Determining the cluster label for a data point is as simple as finding the axis with which the data point has the largest projection value.
- In the $\mathbf{u}_1$-$\mathbf{u}_2$-$\mathbf{u}_3$ space, there is no direct relationship between the axes and the clusters. Traditional data clustering methods such as K-means have to be applied in this space to identify the final data clusters.

The differences between the two clustering techniques can be further illustrated by Fig. 3.5. Spectral clustering techniques strive to find the latent semantic structure of the given data set by computing eigenvectors of certain graph affinity matrices. The derived latent semantic space is orthogonal, and each data point can take negative values in some directions in the space.

In contrast, NMF-based methods do not require the derived latent semantic space to be orthogonal, and it is guaranteed that each data point takes only non-negative values in all the latent semantic directions. These two characteristics make the NMF-based methods more likely to capture the latent semantic directions of a data set than the spectral clustering methods, because it is quite common that the concepts comprising a data set are not orthogonal, and there are some overlaps among them. Indeed, Fig. 3.4 (a) and (b) do serve as a good evidence that the NMF-based methods have done a better job in capturing the latent semantic directions of the given data set. As the direct benefit of these NMF characteristics, the cluster membership of each data point can be easily identified from the axes derived by NMF, while the axes derived by spectral clustering techniques do not provide a direct indication of data partitions.

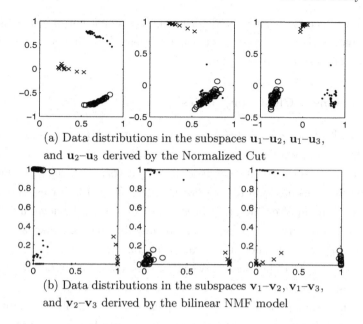

(a) Data distributions in the subspaces $\mathbf{u}_1$–$\mathbf{u}_2$, $\mathbf{u}_1$–$\mathbf{u}_3$,
and $\mathbf{u}_2$–$\mathbf{u}_3$ derived by the Normalized Cut

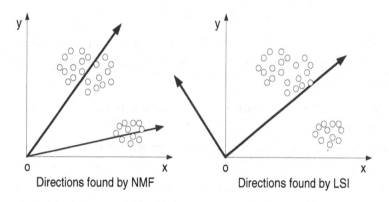

(b) Data distributions in the subspaces $\mathbf{v}_1$–$\mathbf{v}_2$, $\mathbf{v}_1$–$\mathbf{v}_3$,
and $\mathbf{v}_2$–$\mathbf{v}_3$ derived by the bilinear NMF model

Fig. 3.4. Data distributions in the spaces derived by the Normalized Cut and the bilinear NMF model

Fig. 3.5. Illustration of the differences between Spectral and NMF Clustering techniques

3.5 Case Study: Document Clustering Using Spectral and NMF Clustering Techniques

In this section, we provide a case study where the spectral and NMF clustering techniques are applied to the document clustering task. We briefly explain the document clustering basics, describe the document corpora used for the performance evaluations, and unveil the document clustering accuracies of the two types of clustering techniques.

3.5.1 Document Clustering Basics

For the task of document clustering, each document i is commonly represented by a term-frequency vector $\mathbf{x}_i = [x_{1i}, x_{2i}, \ldots, x_{Ni}]$, where N is the total number of keywords in the given document corpus, and x_{ji} is the number of occurrences of keyword j in document i. Keywords correspond to the words that remain after the pre-processing of stop-words removal and words stemming. Stop-words are those that are mainly used to make a sentence grammatically correct, such as *a, the, from, to,* etc. Words stemming aims to eliminate trivial differences between two words, such as *take* and *takes, different* and *difference,* by keeping only the stems of the words.

In many real applications, term-frequency vector is often weighted by various weighting schemes [30]. The weighted term-frequency vector $\mathbf{a}_i = [a_{1i}, a_{2i}, \ldots, a_{Ni}]$ is defined as

$$a_{ji} = L(x_{ji})G(x_{ji}) \tag{3.53}$$

where $L(x_{ji})$ is the local weighting for term j in document i, and $G(x_{ji})$ is the global weighting for term j. Local weighting $L(i)$ includes the following four possible alternatives:

1. No weight: $L(i) = \text{tf}(i)$ where $\text{tf}(i)$ is the number of times term i occurs in the document.
2. Binary weight: $L(i) = 1$ if term i appears at least once in the document; otherwise, $L(i) = 0$.
3. Augmented weight: $L(i) = 0.5 + 0.5 \cdot (\text{tf}(i)/\text{tf}(max))$ where $\text{tf}(max)$ is the frequency of the most frequently occurring term in the document.
4. Logarithm weight: $L(i) = \log(1 + \text{tf}(i))$.

Possible global weighting $G(i)$ includes:

1. No weight: $G(i) = 1$ for any term i.
2. Inverse document frequency (idf): $G(i) = \log(N/n(i))$ where N is the total number of documents in the document corpus, and $n(i)$ is the number of documents that contain term i.

When the weighted term-frequency vector $\mathbf{a}_i$ of a document i is created using one of the above local and global weighting schemes, we further have the choice of

1. Normalization: which normalizes $\mathbf{a}_i$ by its length $|\mathbf{a}_i|$.
2. No normalization: which uses $\mathbf{a}_i$ with its original form.

Therefore, for creating the vector $\mathbf{a}_i$ of a document i, we have a total of $4 \times 2 \times 2 = 16$ combinations of the possible weighting schemes.

In this case study, we used the tf-idf weighting scheme (i.e., no local weighting, and the idf global weighting), and normalized each feature vector $\mathbf{a}_i$ to the unit length.

For NMF-based clustering, the input to the methods is simply the normalized data–feature matrix $\mathbf{X} = [\mathbf{x}_1, \mathbf{x}_2, \ldots, \mathbf{x}_N]$ where column vector $\mathbf{x}_i$ is the normalized feature vector of document i. For spectral clustering, we need to create the graph affinity matrix $\mathbf{A} = [a_{ij}]$ where a_{ij} is an affinity score to reflect the similarity between documents i and j. Many similarity measures can be used to define a_{ij}, and some popular choices are shown below:

1. Cosine similarity:

$$a_{ij} = \cos(\mathbf{x}_i, \mathbf{x}_j) = \frac{\mathbf{x}_i^T \cdot \mathbf{x}_j}{\|\mathbf{x}_i\| \|\mathbf{x}_j\|} \ . \tag{3.54}$$

2. Cosine square similarity:

$$a_{ij} = \cos^2(\mathbf{x}_i, \mathbf{x}_j) \ . \tag{3.55}$$

3. Radius-based similarity:

$$a_{ij} = \exp\left(-\frac{\|\mathbf{x}_i - \mathbf{x}_j\|^2}{\sigma_{\mathbf{x}}}\right) \ . \tag{3.56}$$

In the experimental evaluations, we used both the cosine and cosine square similarities for creating the graph affinity matrix $\mathbf{A}$. Since using higher order similarity functions are analogous to creating kernel matrixes using kernel functions, in this book, we use the term *kernel spectral clustering* to refer to the spectral clustering methods using higher order similarity functions.

3.5.2 Document Corpora

We used two document corpora in the case study: the TDT2 [3] and the Reuters-21578 [4]. These two document corpora have been among the ideal test sets for document clustering purposes because documents in the corpora have been manually clustered based on their topics, and each document has been assigned one or more labels indicating which topic/topics it belongs to. The TDT2 corpus consists of 100 document classes, each of which reports a major news event occurred in 1998. It contains a total of 64527 documents from six news agencies such as ABC, CNN, VOA, NYT, PRI and APW, among which 7803 documents have a unique category label. The number of documents for different news events is very unbalanced, ranging from 1 to 1485. In our experiments, we excluded those events with less than 5 documents, which left us with a total of 56 events. The final test set is still very unbalanced, with some large clusters more than 100 times larger than some small ones.

On the other hand, Reuters-21578 corpus contains 21578 documents which are grouped into 135 classes. Compared with TDT2 corpus, the Reuters corpus is more difficult for clustering. In TDT2, each document has a unique category label, and the content of each class is narrowly defined, whereas in Reuters, many documents have multiple category labels, and documents in each class have a broader variety of content. In our test, we discarded documents with multiple category labels, and removed the classes with less than 5 documents. This has lead to a data set that consists of 51 classes with a total of 9494 documents. Table 3.2 provides the statistics of the two document corpora.

3.5.3 Evaluation Metrics

We use the normalized mutual information as our evaluation metric. Given the two sets of document clusters $\mathcal{C}, \mathcal{C}'$, their mutual information metric $\mathrm{MI}(\mathcal{C}, \mathcal{C}')$ is defined as:

$$\mathrm{MI}(\mathcal{C}, \mathcal{C}') = \sum_{c_i \in \mathcal{C}, c_j' \in \mathcal{C}'} p(c_i, c_j') \cdot \log_2 \frac{p(c_i, c_j')}{p(c_i) \cdot p(c_j')} \tag{3.57}$$

---

[3] Nist Topic Detection and Tracking corpus at http://www.nist.gov/speech/tests/tdt/tdt98/index.htm

[4] Reuters-21578 distribution 1.0 at http://kdd.ics.uci.edu/databases/reuters21578/reuters21578.html

Table 3.2. Statistics of TDT2 and Reuters corpora

	TDT2	Reuters
No. documents	64527	21578
No. docs. used	7803	9494
No. clusters	100	135
No. clusters used	56	51
Max. cluster size	1485	3945
Min. cluster size	5	5
Med. cluster size	48	30
Avg. cluster size	137	186

where $p(c_i)$, $p(c_j')$ denote the probabilities that a document randomly selected from the data set belongs to the clusters c_i and c_j', respectively, and $p(c_i, c_j')$ denotes the joint probability that this randomly selected document belongs to both clusters c_i and c_j' at the same time. $\text{MI}(\mathcal{C}, \mathcal{C}')$ takes values between zero and $\max(\text{H}(\mathcal{C}), \text{H}(\mathcal{C}'))$, where $\text{H}(\mathcal{C})$ and $\text{H}(\mathcal{C}')$ are the entropies of $\mathcal{C}$ and $\mathcal{C}'$, respectively. It reaches the maximum $\max(\text{H}(\mathcal{C}), \text{H}(\mathcal{C}'))$ when the two sets of document clusters are identical, whereas it becomes zero when the two sets are completely independent. Another important character of $\text{MI}(\mathcal{C}, \mathcal{C}')$ is that, for each $c_i \in \mathcal{C}$, it does not need to find the corresponding counterpart in $\mathcal{C}'$, and the value keeps the same for all kinds of permutations. To simplify comparisons between different pairs of cluster sets, instead of using $\text{MI}(\mathcal{C}, \mathcal{C}')$, we use the following normalized metric $\widehat{\text{MI}}(\mathcal{C}, \mathcal{C}')$ which takes values between zero and one:

$$\widehat{\text{MI}}(\mathcal{C}, \mathcal{C}') = \frac{\text{MI}(\mathcal{C}, \mathcal{C}')}{\max(\text{H}(\mathcal{C}), \text{H}(\mathcal{C}'))} \tag{3.58}$$

3.5.4 Performance Evaluations and Comparisons

We have applied the spectral clustering, the NMF-based clustering techniques, and their variations to the same document corpora, and conducted intensive experimental evaluations to reveal their performances. The algorithms that we evaluated include:

1. Traditional K-means (KM).
2. Spectral clustering based on the Average Weight criterion (AW).
3. Spectral clustering based on the Ratio Cut criterion (RC).
4. Spectral clustering based on the Normalized Cut criterion (NC).
5. Clustering based on single linear NMF model (NMF).

6. Clustering based on bilinear NMF model (BiNMF).

Table 3.3. Performance comparisons using TDT2 corpus

K	2	3	4	5	6	7	8	9	10	avg.
KM	0.866	0.804	0.810	0.760	0.743	0.731	0.696	0.717	0.711	0.760
KM-NCW	**0.943**	**0.909**	0.893	0.893	0.824	0.834	0.785	0.798	0.805	0.854
AW	0.834	0.754	0.743	0.696	0.663	0.679	0.624	0.662	0.656	0.701
RC	0.817	0.713	0.692	0.679	0.628	0.592	0.594	0.626	0.618	0.662
NC	0.954	0.890	0.846	0.802	0.761	0.756	0.695	0.732	0.736	0.797
NMF	0.855	0.778	0.784	0.733	0.702	0.706	0.653	0.681	0.680	0.730
NMF-NCW	**0.973**	**0.931**	0.907	0.866	0.826	0.810	0.771	0.802	0.805	0.855
BiNMF	0.859	0.773	0.789	0.745	0.702	0.703	0.652	0.691	0.682	0.733
BiNMF-NCW	**0.973**	**0.934**	0.912	0.890	0.830	0.824	0.778	0.799	0.812	0.861
following are kernel version of each algorithm with cosine square kernel function										
KM	0.500	0.544	0.594	0.581	0.592	0.622	0.587	0.619	0.616	0.584
KM-NCW	0.364	0.362	0.429	0.454	0.498	0.540	0.534	0.578	0.603	0.485
AW	0.815	0.811	0.771	0.739	0.713	0.716	0.677	0.680	0.712	0.737
RC	0.779	0.768	0.782	0.755	0.748	0.723	0.739	0.793	0.770	0.762
NC	**0.934**	**0.912**	**0.963**	**0.931**	**0.915**	**0.904**	0.876	0.876	0.902	0.912
BiNMF	0.836	0.836	0.809	0.775	0.763	0.747	0.714	0.727	0.744	0.772
BiNMF-NCW	**0.953**	**0.917**	**0.952**	**0.930**	**0.935**	**0.922**	**0.913**	**0.919**	**0.927**	**0.930**

In addition to their original forms, we have also applied the weighting scheme underpinning the Normalized Cut method to the above algorithms whenever this weighting scheme is applicable. As discussed in Sect. 3.2.4, the Normalized Cut Weighting scheme (NCW) has the effect of automatically balancing clusters with very different sizes so as to help a clustering algorithm to achieve a better result when dealing with unbalanced data set. The weighted variation of BiNMF is derived in Appendix A.

For the algorithms to which the kernel method can be applied, (i.e. KM, NC, AW, RC and BiNMF), we have also implemented their kernel versions and tested their performances using the cosine square similarity as the kernel.

The evaluations were conducted for the cluster numbers ranging from 2 to 10. For each given cluster number K, 50 test runs were conducted on different clusters randomly chosen from the corpus, and the final performance scores were obtained by averaging the scores from the 50 test runs. For algorithms whose result is affected by initialization (i.e. KM, NMF and BiNMF), each

Table 3.4. Performance comparisons using Reuters-215768 corpus

K	2	3	4	5	6	7	8	9	10	avg.
KM	0.404	0.402	0.461	0.525	0.561	0.548	0.583	0.597	0.618	0.522
KM-NC	0.438	0.462	0.525	0.554	0.592	0.577	0.594	0.607	0.618	0.552
AW	**0.443**	0.415	0.488	0.531	0.571	0.542	0.587	0.594	0.611	0.531
RC	0.417	0.381	0.505	0.460	0.485	0.456	0.548	0.484	0.495	0.470
NC	**0.484**	0.461	0.555	0.592	0.617	0.594	0.640	0.634	0.643	0.580
NMF	**0.480**	0.426	0.498	0.559	0.591	0.552	0.603	0.601	0.623	0.548
NMF-NCW	**0.494**	**0.500**	**0.586**	**0.615**	0.637	**0.613**	**0.654**	**0.659**	0.658	0.602
BiNMF	**0.480**	0.429	0.503	0.563	0.592	0.556	0.613	0.609	0.629	0.553
BiNMF-NCW	**0.496**	**0.505**	**0.595**	**0.616**	**0.644**	**0.615**	**0.660**	**0.660**	**0.665**	**0.606**
following are kernel version of each algorithm with cosine square kernel function										
KM	0.249	0.205	0.243	0.272	0.302	0.312	0.325	0.330	0.356	0.288
KM-NCW	0.258	0.147	0.198	0.209	0.232	0.228	0.253	0.254	0.270	0.228
AW	0.326	0.342	0.384	0.433	0.498	0.482	0.524	0.559	0.559	0.456
RC	**0.467**	0.453	**0.554**	0.517	0.518	0.516	0.577	0.574	0.573	0.528
NC	**0.485**	**0.478**	**0.587**	0.586	0.597	0.582	0.633	0.633	0.642	0.580
BiNMF	0.325	0.332	0.369	0.441	0.484	0.469	0.502	0.542	0.548	0.446
BiNMF-NCW	**0.454**	**0.472**	**0.582**	0.569	0.579	**0.602**	0.612	0.627	0.628	0.569

test run consists of 10 sub-runs among which the result of the best sub-run is selected. Tables 3.3 and 3.4 show the evaluation results using the TDT2 and the Reuters corpus, respectively. For each k, the performance values that are within 2x of the standard deviation of the best one are shown in bold font.

The findings from the two tables can be summarized as follows.

- Regardless of the document corpora, the Ratio Cut has the worst performance, whereas the traditional K-means clustering method is the worst in its kernel form.
- BiNMF-NCW always has the best performance both in its original and kernel form.
- The use of Normalized Cut weighting usually improves the clustering performance (NC vs. AW, KM-NCW vs. KM, BiNMF-NCW vs. BiNMF) with the kernel K-means as the only exception. The improvement becomes more obvious for the TDT2 than the Reuters.
- For the TDT2 corpus, using the cosine square kernel function improves the clustering performance for AW, RC, NC, BiNMF and BiNMF-NCW by at least 5%, whereas it works negatively for the Reuters corpus. Cosine

square has the effect that brings little change to small distances while amplifying large distances.

The results show that the kernel K-means performs very poorly compared to other kernel clustering algorithms. This is particularly strange because the spectral clustering algorithms based on the criterion function similar to the K-means (i.e. AW and NC) all perform reasonably well. We hypothesize that the poor performance of the kernel K-means is caused by the fact that it is very prone to local optimal solutions. To test this hypothesis, we used the correct clustering result as the initial partition. With such initial condition, the final result of the kernel K-means improves dramatically. On the other hand, although theoretically BiNMF could have the same problem of local optima as K-means, in practice, its performance is quite good.

These experimental results verify the fact that clusters in TDT2 are more compact and focused than clusters in Reuters. For such a simple data set as TDT2, any data clustering method can produce a reasonably good result. The difference becomes more remarkable with a complex data set such as Reuters, and both the Normalized Cut and the NMF-based clustering techniques show clear advantages over the traditional K-means method. The results also show that the use of different kernels can lead to significantly different results and suggest that higher order kernel functions are effective for the data sets that consist of narrowly-defined clusters, while lower order kernel functions should be used for the data sets that consist of clusters with a broader variety of contents.

Problems

3.1. Prove that the vectors $\mathbf{y}_c$ defined in (3.12)$\sim$ (3.15) all satisfy the following identities:

(a) $\mathbf{y}_c \cdot \mathbf{y}_{c'} = 0$,

(b) $\mathbf{y}_c \cdot \mathbf{y}_c = 1$.

3.2. Let $\lambda_1, \cdots \lambda_n$ be the eigenvalues of an $n \times n$ matrix $\mathbf{A}$. Verify the following identities:

(a) $\text{trace}(\mathbf{A}) = \sum_{i=1}^{n} \lambda_i$,

(b) $|\mathbf{A}| = \prod_{i=1}^{n} \lambda_i$.

3.3. The differential $dy(x)$ can be approximated by the first-order term $y(x + dx) - y(x)$, which is linear in dx. Using this approximation, verify the following identities

(a) $d(AB) = dAB + AdB$,

(b) $dA^{-1} = -A^{-1}dAA^{-1}$,

(c) $d\log|A| = \text{trace}(A^{-1}dA)$.

3.4. Let $\mathbf{A}$ be a symmetric matrix. Prove that $\hat{\mathbf{x}} = \max_{\mathbf{x}:\|\mathbf{x}\|=1} \mathbf{x}^T\mathbf{A}\mathbf{x}$ is the eigenvector corresponding to the largest eigenvalue of $\mathbf{A}$.

3.5. Low-rank matrix factorization. The best low rank factorization of an $m \times n$ matrix $\mathbf{X}$ can be defined as:

$$\arg\min_{\mathbf{U},\mathbf{V}} \|\mathbf{X} - \mathbf{U}\mathbf{V}^{\mathbf{T}}\|^2,$$

where $\mathbf{U}$ and $\mathbf{V}$ are $m \times k$ and $n \times k$ matrices, respectively. Show that the solution can be found using singular value decomposition.

3.6. Connection between Normalized-Cut and K-Means. Considering a weighted version of a K-means cost function where each data point $\mathbf{x}_i$ is weighted by γ_i

$$J = \sum_k \sum_{i \in C_k} \gamma_i \|\mathbf{x}_i - \mu_k\|^2.$$

Show that with carefully chosen γ_i, the above cost function is equivalent to the Normalized-Cut cost function.

3.7. Sometimes it is desirable to encourage sparse solution for NMF. One way of doing this is to add L-1 regularization terms for $\mathbf{U}$ and $\mathbf{V}$ to the cost function. Develop the corresponding update rules for the modified cost function.

3.8. Show that for BiNMF, without the non-negative constraints, the solution can be found using SVD.

3.9. Word-document relationship can be represented as a bipartite graph. Examine how normalized-cut can be applied to this graph.

3.10. Local minima of standard K-means algorithm. Write a program to generate a set of 5000-dimensional data from a mixture of two Gaussians with unit variance. The means of the two Gaussians are $[-5, 0, \cdots, 0]^T$ and $[5, 0, \cdots, 0]^T$, respectively. Use standard K-means to do the clustering. Check if K-means can separate the two Gaussians starting from an initial random partition.

3.11. With the same data set as Problem 3.10, partition the data set according to the sign of the first principal component. Compare the clustering result with Problem 3.10.

Part II

Generative Graphical Models

4

Introduction of Graphical Models

One of the main goals of multimedia content analysis is to detect objects inside an image, or to recognize events contained in a video sequence. Such detection and recognition tasks have been tackled increasingly using supervised classification methods in recent years. Supervised classification methods aim to learn from given training samples a function that assigns labels to arbitrary objects. More precisely, given a set of labeled instances $\mathcal{S} = \{(\mathbf{x}^{(i)}, y^{(i)})\}_{i=1}^{n}$, where $\mathbf{x}^{(i)}$ is the feature vector of the i'th instance, and $y^{(i)}$ is a label assigned to the instance by a trusted source, the goal is to learn a function $f : \mathbf{x} \mapsto y$, where $f(\mathbf{x}, \boldsymbol{\alpha})$ is often selected from some parametric family, and is determined by the parameter set $\boldsymbol{\alpha}$.

An important characteristic of multimedia content analysis is that multimedia objects exhibit much richer structures than simple objects. In some cases, we might need to label a set of inter-related instances altogether because determining the class label of an object depends on the class labels of spatially, temporally related objects. For example, the part-of-speech tagging, also called grammatical tagging, is the process of automatically determining the grammatical role (or attribute) of each word in a text. This is a typical problem that can not be solved without examining both the word itself and the neighboring words in the same sentence, because many words in natural languages can represent more than one part of speech at different times. On the other hand, detecting "home run" events from a baseball video program is another typical problem that requires a joint labeling of a sequence of frames, because such a event is composed of a sequence of actions that span over many video frames. The label of each frame can not be determined without examining both its visual content and its context within the sequence.

The above two examples are typical multi-label, multi-class classification problems. In contrast to the single-label classification problems, here the task becomes to learn a function $f : \mathbf{x} \mapsto \mathbf{y}$ from a set of labeled instances, where $\mathbf{x} = [x_1, x_2, \ldots, x_m]$ is the feature vector for a sequence of m instances, with x_i the feature vector of instance i, $\mathbf{y} = [y_1, y_2, \ldots, y_m]$ is the labels for the m instances, and $y_i \in \{l_1, l_2, \ldots, l_k\}$. Probabilistic graphical models are powerful statistical tools for multi-label, multi-class classification problems. The advantage of graphical models is that they are able to exploit correlations and dependencies among different instances, often resulting in significant improvements in accuracy over approaches that classify instances independently. The modeling of correlations and dependencies is generally achieved by defining a graph $G = (V, E)$ that explicitly reflects the problem structure. Here V and E are the vertex set and the edge set of graph G, respectively, and are defined in such a way that each vertex $v \in V$ represents a random variable of the target problem, and each edge $(v_i, v_j) \in E$, either directed or undirected, represents a correlation/dependency between the random variables v_i and v_j. If all the edges of graph G are associated with directions, the graph is called a *directed graphical model*; otherwise, it is called an *undirected graphical model*. Directed graphical models are also called Bayesian Networks or Belief Networks, while undirected graphical models are also referred to as Markov Random Fields in the literature. Undirected graphical models are a preferred choice in the physics and pattern recognition communities, while directed models are more popular in the AI and statistics communities.

Among the random variables in V, some random variables are unobservable (i.e. their values are unknown), and hence are called hidden variables. Graphical models aim to define and learn a joint probability distribution over the set of hidden and observable random variables V. The learned joint probability distribution can be used either to estimate the probability that a hidden variable takes on certain values given the values of the observable ones, or to conduct various joint labeling/classification tasks.

4.1 Directed Graphical Model

We use a simple example to illustrate the concept of directed graphical models. Assume that we wish to model a home security system that consists of burglar intrusion sensors, earthquake sensors, alarms, and the emergency call function. The activation of either a burglar sensor or an earthquake sensor can trigger an alarm, which will in turn trigger an emergency call to the central monitoring station. For this problem, we can define a graphical model shown in Fig. 4.1, where each node represents a component of the home security system, and each directed edge represents a conditional dependency between two corresponding components. As each edge of the graph has a direction, the model is a directed graphical model. Because burglar sensors and earthquake sensors are independent of each other, there is no link between the two nodes. Moreover, since burglar and earthquake sensors influence emergency calls only indirectly through alarms, we say that the emergency call is conditionally independent of the burglar and earthquake sensors given the alarm, and there are no edges linking the emergency call node with the burglar sensor and the earthquake sensor nodes.

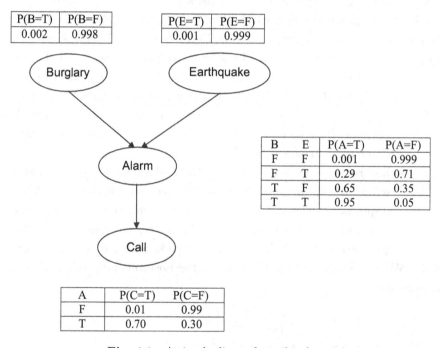

P(B=T)	P(B=F)
0.002	0.998

P(E=T)	P(E=F)
0.001	0.999

B	E	P(A=T)	P(A=F)
F	F	0.001	0.999
F	T	0.29	0.71
T	F	0.65	0.35
T	T	0.95	0.05

A	P(C=T)	P(C=F)
F	0.01	0.99
T	0.70	0.30

Fig. 4.1. A simple directed graphical model

By the chain rule of probability, the joint probability of all the nodes in the graph can be calculated as follows

$$P(B, E, A, C) = P(B)P(E|B)P(A|B, E)P(C|A, B, E), \qquad (4.1)$$

where each node is represented using the first letter of its name. By using the conditional independence relationships defined by the graph, we can rewrite this equation as

$$P(B, E, A, C) = P(B)P(E)P(A|B, E)P(C|A), \tag{4.2}$$

which is a more compact representation of the joint probability.

To completely define a graphical model, in addition to the graph structure, it is also necessary to specify the parameters of the model. For a directed graphical model, we must specify the Conditional Probability Distribution (CPD) for each node. If the variables are discrete, this can be represented as a table (Conditional Probability Table (CPT)), which lists the probability that a node takes on each of its different values for each combination of its parents' values. Consider the same example shown in Fig. 4.1, where all the nodes have two possible values, which we will denote by T (true) and F (false). We see that the event "alarm is on" (A=T) has two possible causes: either a burglar intrusion sensor is on (B=T) or an earthquake sensor is on (E=T). The strength of this relationship is shown in the table. For example, we see that $P(A = T \mid B = T, E = T) = 0.95$ (last row), and hence, $P(A = F \mid B = T, E = T) = 1 - 0.95 = 0.05$, since each row must add up to one. Because both the B and E nodes have no parents, their CPTs specify the prior probability of a burglar intrusion or an earthquake occurrence.

Once the structure and the parameters of a graphical model are completely defined, we can perform various probabilistic inferences using the model. Consider the graphical model shown in Fig. 4.1, and assume that we observe the event that an emergency call is dispatched. There are two possible causes for this: a burglar intruded the house, or an earthquake occurred. Which is more likely? We can use Bayes' rule to compute the posterior probability of each explanation

$$
\begin{aligned}
P(B = T|C = T) &= \frac{P(B = T, C = T)}{P(C = T)} \\
&= \frac{\sum_{e,a \in \{T,F\}} P(B = T, E = e, A = a, C = T)}{P(C = T)} \\
&= \frac{\sum_{e,a \in \{T,F\}} P(B = T)P(E = e)P(A = a|B = T, E = e)P(C = T|A = a)}{P(C = T)} \\
&= \frac{917.2 \times 10^{-6}}{11784.6 \times 10^{-6}} = 0.0778, \tag{4.3}
\end{aligned}
$$

where

$$P(C = T) = \sum_{b,e,a \in \{T,F\}} P(B = b, E = e, A = a, C = T) = 11784.6 \times 10^{-6} \,.$$

Similarly,

$$\begin{aligned}
P(E = T | C = T) &= \frac{P(E = T, C = T)}{P(C = T)} \\
&= \frac{\sum_{b,a \in \{T,F\}} P(B = b, E = T, A = a, C = T)}{P(C = T)} \\
&= \frac{\sum_{b,a \in \{T,F\}} P(B = b) P(E = T) P(A = a | B = b, E = T) P(C = T | A = a)}{P(C = T)} \\
&= \frac{210.8 \times 10^{-6}}{11784.6 \times 10^{-6}} = 0.0179 \,.
\end{aligned}$$
(4.4)

Therefore, for the graphical model given in Fig. 4.1, when an emergency call is dispatched, it is more likely that the call is caused by a burglar intrusion than an earthquake.

It is clear from the above example that, once we have computed the joint probability over all the random variables, we can compute conditional probabilities of values of any variables, given the observed values of other variables.

4.2 Undirected Graphical Model

Figure 4.2 shows two examples of undirected graphical models. For undirected graphical models, the vertex pairs (u, v) and (v, u) are considered to be the same pair. A clique, which is an important concept unique to undirected graphical models, is defined as a set of vertices S that for every two vertices $\forall u, v \in S$, there exists an edge connecting u and v. In other words, the subgraph induced by a clique is a complete graph. In the graph shown in Fig. 4.2(a), vertices (1,2,3), (2,3,4,5), and (5,6) form three different cliques because each vertex has an edge to all the others within each set. The size of a clique is the number of vertices the clique contains. A maximal clique is the one to which no more vertices can be added. Finding whether there is a clique of a given size in a graph (the clique problem) is an NP-complete problem.

For an undirected graph $G = (V, E)$, the joint probability distribution is generally defined as a product of a set of potential functions $\Psi_C(\mathbf{x}_C)$

$$P(\mathbf{x}) = \frac{1}{Z} \prod_C \Psi_C(\mathbf{x}_C),$$
(4.5)

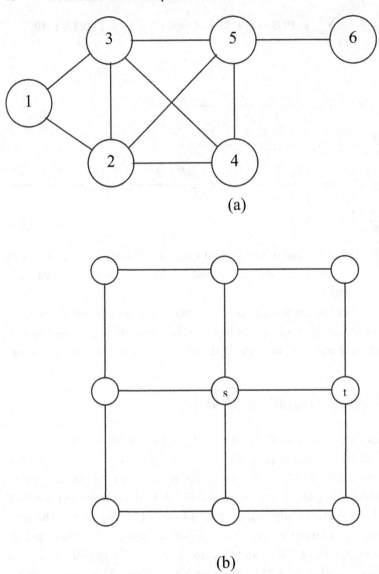

(a)

(b)

Fig. 4.2. Two undirected graphical models

where $\mathbf{x}$ denotes the entire set of random variables defined over the vertex set V, $\mathbf{x}_C$ is the subset of random variables defined over clique C, $\Psi_C(\mathbf{x}_C)$ is a potential function of $\mathbf{x}_C$, and Z is a normalizing factor that ensures $\sum_{\mathbf{x}} P(\mathbf{x}) = 1$. The potential functions $\Psi_C(\mathbf{x}_C)$ are defined to reflect interactions among neighboring vertices (random variables), and can take any form of functions.

Fig. 4.2(b) shows the undirected graph used by the Ising model to explain ferromagnetic materials. Here, each vertex (random variable) represents a ferromagnetic molecule, and takes values of $+1$ or -1. There exist two types of cliques, singleton and 2-element clique, which are denoted by $\{s\}$, $\{s,t\}$, respectively, where $s,t \in V$, and s,t are two adjacent vertices in the graph. The potential functions for the two types cliques are defined as

$$\Psi_{\{s\}} \left(\mathbf{x}_{\{s\}} \right) = \exp \left(\frac{H}{k} x(s) \right) , \tag{4.6}$$

$$\Psi_{\{s,t\}} \left(\mathbf{x}_{\{s,t\}} \right) = \exp \left(\frac{J}{k} x(t)x(s) \right) , \tag{4.7}$$

where k is the Boltzmann constant, H is the external magnetic field, and J is the internal energy of an element magnetic dipole. The joint probability distribution of the Ising model is defined as

$$\begin{aligned} P(\mathbf{x}) &= \prod_{s \in V} \Psi_{\{s\}} \left(\mathbf{x}_{\{s\}} \right) \cdot \prod_{\{s,t\}} \Psi_{\{s,t\}} \left(\mathbf{x}_{\{s,t\}} \right) \\ &= \prod_{s \in V} \exp \left(\frac{H}{k} x(s) \right) \cdot \prod_{\{s,t\}} \exp \left(\frac{J}{k} x(s)x(t) \right) . \end{aligned} \tag{4.8}$$

In defining an undirected graphical model, one can define arbitrary potential functions on cliques of arbitrary sizes. However, large cliques with fully-parameterized potential functions are problematic both for computational and statistical reasons, because the inference complexity is exponential to the clique size, and the estimation of large number of parameters requires a large amount of training data. Therefore, in real applications, it is more practical to use cliques of small sizes with potentials of reduced parameters.

4.3 Generative vs. Discriminative

Besides directed and undirected graphical models, we can also categorize graphical models as either generative or discriminative. Generative models aim to model the joint probability distribution $P(\mathbf{x}, \mathbf{y})$ over the sets of observed and hidden variables $\mathbf{x}, \mathbf{y}$, while discriminative models attempt to learn the conditional probability $P(\mathbf{y}|\mathbf{x})$ of the hidden variable set $\mathbf{y}$ given the observed variable set $\mathbf{x}$. Generative models generally seek to model both the observed and the hidden variables, often resulting in excessive modeling efforts that are more than necessary for regular classification tasks. In contrast, discriminative models try to confine the modeling efforts to the hidden variables only without the attempt to modeling the observed variables, and this often leads to less modeling efforts and better data modeling performances.

4.4 Content of Part II

Part II of this book is dedicated to the descriptions of representative generative graphical models. We first present Markov chains in Chap. 5, which are the most fundamental and long-standing directed graphical model in the literature. In Chap. 6, we present Markov Random Fields (MRFs) that are a representative undirected graphical model, and are widely used in various pattern recognition applications. In Chap. 7, we provide detailed descriptions of Hidden Markov Models (HMMs) that are extensions of Markov chains to allow more model freedoms while avoiding a substantial complication to the basic structure of Markov chains. In Chap. 8, we describe general graphical models and related algorithms for learning and inferences. This chapter serves as a summary of generative graphical models that can be considered as an umbrella of many kinds of graphical models.

Markov Chains and Monte Carlo Simulation

In this chapter, we present Markov chains that are the most fundamental and long-standing graphical model for modeling dependencies among data entities. We start by introducing various definitions, terminologies, and important properties of Markov chains, followed by describing the stationary distribution and associated theorems. At the end of this chapter, we present the Markov Chain Monte Carlo simulation (MCMC) that is one of the most important applications of Markov chains for probabilistic data sampling and model estimations.

5.1 Discrete-Time Markov Chain

A sequence $\{X_n\}_{n\geq0}$ of random variables with values in a set S is called a *discrete-time stochastic process* with state space S. To simplify the notations and descriptions, in this book we assume a discrete state space S whose elements are countable, and can be denoted by $i,j,k,\cdots$. However, this assumption does not cause a dramatic loss in generality, and most contents provided in this chapter are applicable to a continuous state space in a straightforward way. For a discrete-time stochastic process with a discrete state space, the notation $X_n = i$ means that the process is in state i at time n, or visits state i at time n.

A discrete-time stochastic process describes a system that constantly undergoes a transition between states at each discrete time instant (see Fig. 5.1). At any time $t = n$, the process stays in one of the states $i \in S$. At the next discrete time instant $t = n + 1$, the process undergoes a change of state (possibly back to the same state) according to a set of probabilities associated

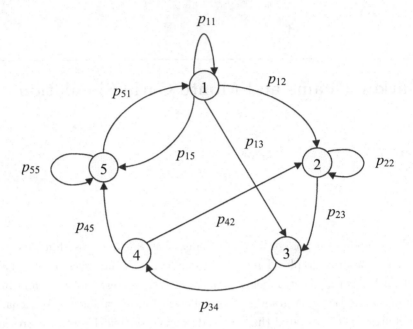

Fig. 5.1. A homogenous Markov chain with five states and selective state transitions

with the state i. If nothing more is said, then a full probabilistic description of this stochastic process can be obtained by the following Bayes' formula

$$P(X_0 = i_0, X_1 = i_1, \ldots, X_n = i_n)$$
$$= \prod_{k=0}^{n} P(X_k = i_k \mid X_{k-1} = i_{k-1}, X_{k-2} = i_{k-2}, \ldots, X_0 = i_0) . \quad (5.1)$$

In general, this equation requires the specification of the current state X_k, as well as all the predecessor states: $P(X_k = i_k \mid X_{k-1} = i_{k-1}, X_{k-2} = i_{k-2}, \ldots, X_0 = i_0)$. If for all discrete time instants $k \geq 0$ and all states $i_0, i_1, \ldots, i_k$, the following equation holds,

$$P(X_k = i_k \mid X_{k-1} = i_{k-1}, X_{k-2} = i_{k-2}, \ldots, X_0 = i_0)$$
$$= P(X_k = i_k \mid X_{k-1} = i_{k-1}) \quad (5.2)$$

then, this stochastic process is called a *Markov Chain*. It is called a *homogeneous Markov Chain* (HMC) if in addition, both sides of (5.2) are independent of k. Since HMC is independent of time, we can define the set of state transition probabilities p_{ij} as follows:

$$p_{ij} = P(X_k = j \,|\, X_{k-1} = i), \quad i, j \in S \,. \tag{5.3}$$

The matrix $\mathbf{P} = \{p_{ij}\}$, $i, j \in S$, is called a transition matrix of the HMC. Since its entries are probabilities, and a transition from any sate i must be to some state, it follows that

$$p_{ij} \geq 0, \quad \sum_{k \in S} p_{ik} = 1 \tag{5.4}$$

for all states i, j.

The random variable X_0 is called the *initial state*, and its probability distribution $\boldsymbol{\pi}_0 = \{\pi_{0i}\}$, $i \in S$, is called the *initial state distribution*, where

$$\pi_{0i} = P(X_0 = i) \,. \tag{5.5}$$

A homogeneous Morkov chain is uniquely determined by the following three components:

1. A state space S.
2. An initial state distribution $\boldsymbol{\pi}_0$.
3. A state transition matrix $\mathbf{P} = \{p_{ij}\}$, where $i, j \in S$.

Given these three components, the probability of observing a given state sequence from the HMC can be computed as follows

$$P(X_0 = i_0, X_1 = i_1, \ldots, X_n = i_n) = \prod_{k=0}^{n} P(X_k = i_k \,|\, X_{k-1} = i_{k-1})$$
$$= \pi_{0i_0} P_{i_0 i_1} \cdots P_{i_{k-1} i_k} \tag{5.6}$$

where the first and second equalities in the above derivation used the HMC property (5.2) and the state transition probabilities (5.3), respectively. A Markov chain is a generative model because it describes how the observed data sequence is generated by a process of state transitions. Furthermore, a Markov chain is a stochastic process with one-step (or order-one) memory, since the transition probabilities are dependent only on the preceding state. It is noteworthy that this one-step memory restriction is no serious limitation because processes with arbitrary finite memory length k can be modeled by order-one Markov chains on the product space S^k.

Denote the state distribution at time n by vector $\mathbf{v}_n = \{v_{ni}\}$, where $v_{ni} = P(X_n = i)$. From Bayes's rule of exclusive and exhaustive causes,

$$v_{n+1j} = \sum_{i \in S} v_{ni} \, p_{ij} \,. \tag{5.7}$$

Writing (5.7) in matrix form, we have

$$\mathbf{v}_{n+1}^T = \mathbf{v}_n^T \mathbf{P} . \tag{5.8}$$

Iteration of this equality yields

$$\mathbf{v}_n^T = \boldsymbol{\pi}_0^T \mathbf{P}^n . \tag{5.9}$$

The matrix $\mathbf{P}^n$ is called the *n-step transition matrix* because its general term is

$$p_{ij}(n) = P(X_{k+n} = j \,|\, X_k = i) . \tag{5.10}$$

Using the Bayes's chain rule and the Markov property, each entry $p_{ij}(n)$ can be computed as

$$p_{ij}(n) = \sum_{i_1,\ldots,\,i_{m-1} \in S} p_{ii_1} p_{i_1 i_2} \cdots p_{i_{m-1} j} . \tag{5.11}$$

The Markov property (5.2) can be extended to

$$P\left(X_{n+1} = j_1, \ldots, X_{n+k} = j_k \,|\, X_n = i, X_{n-1} = i_{n-1}, \ldots, X_0 = i_0\right)$$
$$= P(X_{n+1} = j_1, \ldots, X_{n+k} = j_k \,|\, X_n = i) \tag{5.12}$$

for all $i_0, \ldots, i_{n-1}, i, j_1, \ldots, j_k$. Writing $A = \{X_{n+1} = j_1, \ldots, X_{n+k} = j_k\}$, $B = \{X_0 = i_0, \ldots, X_{n-1} = i_{n-1}\}$, (5.12) can be written as

$$P(A \,|\, X_n = i, B) = P(A \,|\, X_n = i) \tag{5.13}$$
$$P(A \cap B \,|\, X_n = i) = P(A \,|\, X_n = i) P(B \,|\, X_n = i) \tag{5.14}$$

Stating these two equations in words, it becomes that the future at time n and the past at time n are conditionally independent given the present state $X_n = i$. This shows in particular that the Markov property is independent of the direction of time.

5.2 Canonical Representation

In real applications, it is often necessary to determine if a stochastic process is a homogenous Markov chain or not. The following theorem is very useful and convenient for this purpose.

Theorem 5.1. *Let $\{Z_n\}_{n\geq 1}$ be an i.i.d sequence of random variables with values in an arbitrary space F. Let S be a countable state space, and $f : S \times F \to S$ be some function. Let X_0 be a random variable with values in S, independent of $\{Z_n\}_{n\geq 0}$. The recurrent equation*

$$X_{n+1} = f(X_n, Z_{n+1}) \tag{5.15}$$

then defines an HMC.

Proof: Iteration of the recurrent equation (5.15) yields

$$X_{n+1} = f(X_n, Z_{n+1}) = f(f(X_{n-1}, Z_n), Z_{n+1}) =$$
$$= f(f(f(X_{n-2}, Z_{n-1}), Z_n), Z_{n+1}) = \cdots$$
$$= g_n(X_0, Z_1, Z_2, \cdots, Z_{n+1}) \tag{5.16}$$

for all $n \geq 1$. From (5.16), it follows that the state sequence $\{X_0 = i_0, \ldots, X_{n-1} = i_{n-1}, X_n = i\}$ is expressible in terms of $X_0, Z_1, \ldots, Z_n$, and therefore, is independent of Z_{n+1}. From this independence statement, we have

$$P(X_{n+1} = j \,|\, X_n = i, X_{n-1} = i_{n-1}, \ldots, X_0 = i_0)$$
$$= P(f(i, Z_{n+1}) = j \,|\, X_n = i, X_{n-1} = i_{n-1}, \ldots, X_0 = i_0)$$
$$= P(f(i, Z_{n+1}) = j) \tag{5.17}$$

Similarly,

$$P(X_{n+1} = j \,|\, X_n = i) = P(f(i, Z_{n+1}) = j) \tag{5.18}$$

Therefore, we have a Markov chain, and it is homogeneous since the right-hand side of the above two equations do not depend on n. (proof-end).

We use the following examples to illustrate applications of the above theorem and the HMC to some real problems.

Example 5.1. 1-D Random Walk

Let X_0 be a random variable with values in $\mathbb{Z}$. Let $\{Z_n\}_{n\geq 1}$ be a sequence of i.i.d random variables independent of X_0, that take the values $+1$ or -1 with the probability distribution $P(Z_n = +1) = p$, where $p \in (0, 1)$. The process $\{X_n\}_{n\geq 1}$ defined by

$$X_{n+1} = X_n + Z_{n+1} \tag{5.19}$$

is called the *random walk* on $\mathbb{Z}$. According to Theorem 5.1, the process is an HMC.

Example 5.2. Gambler's Ruin [31]

Consider the following gamble game problem: Two players A and B play bets on "heads or tails" of a coin. A bets \$1 on heads, and B bets \$1 on tails at each toss. The game ends when a player looses all his fortune. Assume that the initial fortunes of A and B are a and b, respectively, and that heads occur with a probability $p \in (0,1)$, we would like to compute the probability of A winning the game, and the average duration of the game.

Denote by X_n the fortune of player A at time n. Then the process $\{X_n\}_{n \geq 0}$ can be defined as a random walk $X_{n+1} = X_n + Z_{n+1}$ on the state space $S = \{0, \ldots, a, a+1, \ldots, a+b\}$, where $Z_{n+1} = +1$ (or $Z_{n+1} = -1$) with probability p (or $q = 1-p$), and $\{Z_n\}_{n \geq 1}$ is i.i.d independent of X_0. According to Theorem 5.1, the process $\{X_n\}_{n \geq 0}$ forms an HMC.

The game duration T can be defined as the first time n at which $X_n = 0$ or $a+b$. The probability of A winning the game is

$$u(a) = P(X_T = a+b \,|\, X_0 = a).$$

Instead of computing $u(a)$ alone, we first compute

$$u(i) = P(X_T = a+b \,|\, X_0 = i)$$

for all states $i \in [0, a+b]$ to generate a recurrent equation for $u(i)$. If $X_0 = i \in [1, a+b-1]$, then $X_1 = i+1$ (or $X_1 = i-1$) with probability p (or q). The probability of A winning the game with A's initial fortune $i+1$ (or $i-1$) is $u(i+1)$ (or $u(i-1)$). Therefore, for $i \in [1, a+b-1]$, we have

$$u(i) = pu(i+1) + qu(i-1) \tag{5.20}$$

with the boundary conditions $u(0) = 0$, $u(a+b) = 1$.

In order to compute $u(i)$, we rewrite (5.20) as follows:

$$p(u(i+1) - u(i)) - q(u(i) - u(i-1)) = 0 \,.$$

Defining $y_i = u(i) - u(i-1)$, we have

$$0 = py_{i+1} - qy_i \,, \tag{5.21}$$

$$u(i) = y_i + u(i-1)$$

$$= y_i + y_{i-1} + u(i-2)$$

$$= \cdots$$

$$= y_1 + y_2 + \cdots + y_i \,. \tag{5.22}$$

Consider a fair coin where $p = q = \frac{1}{2}$. From (5.21) we have

$$0 = \frac{1}{2}y_2 - \frac{1}{2}y_1$$
$$0 = \frac{1}{2}y_3 - \frac{1}{2}y_2$$
$$\vdots$$
$$0 = \frac{1}{2}y_i - \frac{1}{2}y_{i-1}$$

Summing up the left and right-hand sides of the above equations obtains the equation

$$0 = \frac{1}{2}y_i - \frac{1}{2}y_1 \ .$$

That is, for $i \in [1, a+b-1]$,

$$y_i = y_1 \ .$$

Reporting this expression in (5.22), and observing that $y_1 = u(1) - u(0) = u(1)$, we have

$$u(i) = iu(1) \ . \tag{5.23}$$

The boundary condition $u(a+b) = 1$ yields $u(a+b) = (a+b)u(1) = 1$, and therefore gives

$$u(i) = iu(1) = \frac{i}{a+b} \ .$$

The above derivation can be applied to compute the average duration of the game as well. The average duration $m(i) = E[T \mid X_0 = i]$ of the game when the initial fortune of player A is i satisfies the recurrent equation

$$m(i) = 1 + pm(i+1) + qm(i-1) \tag{5.24}$$

for $i \in [1, a+b-1]$. The boundary conditions are $m(0) = 0$, $m(a+b) = 0$. Assume that $p = q = \frac{1}{2}$, and use the same derivation for deriving (5.23), we have

$$m(i) = im(1) - i(i-1) \ . \tag{5.25}$$

The boundary condition $m(a+b) = 0$ gives

$$m(a+b) = im(1) - (a+b)(a+b-1) \ .$$

Combining this equation with (5.25) yields

$$m(i) = i(a+b-i) \ .$$

5.3 Definitions and Terminologies

To prepare for the theorems in the following sections, we introduce necessary concepts and terminologies here.

Communication and Communication Class

State j is said to be *accessible* from state i if there exists $M > 0$ such that $p_{ij}(M) > 0$. States i and j are said to *communicate* if i is accessible from j and j is accessible from i, and this is denoted by $i \leftrightarrow j$.

Given a set of states C, if one can get to any state from any other states with one or more steps, i.e. $i \leftrightarrow j$, $\forall i, j \in C$, then the set of states is said to form a *communication class*.

Figure 5.2 shows a transition graph with seven states. It can be easily verified that there are two groups of states, $\{1, 2, 3, 4\}$ and $\{5, 6, 7\}$, where each pair of states within the same group communicate to each other, but any two states belonging to different groups do not. Therefore, according to the definitions given above, this transition graph is composed of two communications classes.

Irreducible

If there exists only one communication class, then the chain, its transition matrix, and its transition graph, are said to be *irreducible*.

Figure 5.3 shows another seven-state transition graph. It is clear that any state in the graph can be accessed from any other states with one or more steps. Therefore, the entire transition graph forms only one communication class, and according to the definition, it is irreducible.

Period

For any irreducible Markov chain, one can find a unique partition of the chain into d classes $C_0, C_1, \ldots, C_{d-1}$ such that

$$\forall k, \ i \in C_k, \ \sum_{j \in C_{k+1}} p_{ij} = 1,$$

where $C_d = C_0$, and d is maximal. The number $d \geq 1$ is called the *period* of the chain (see Fig. 5.4).

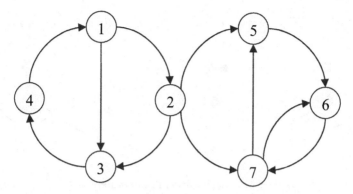

(a) A transition graph with seven states

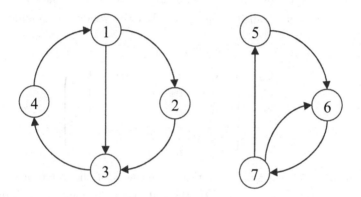

(b) Two communication classes

Fig. 5.2. A transition graph with two communication classes

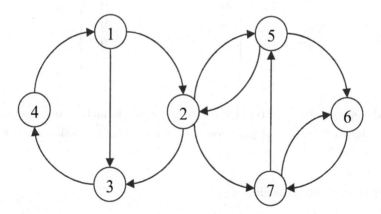

Fig. 5.3. An irreducible transition graph

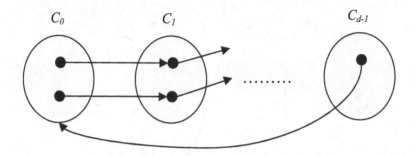

Fig. 5.4. A transition graph of period d

Given an irreducible Markov chain of period d with the cyclic classes $C_0, C_1, \ldots, C_{d-1}$, its transition matrix takes the following canonical block structure:

$$\mathbf{P} = \begin{array}{c} \\ C_0 \\ C_1 \\ C_2 \\ \vdots \\ C_{d-1} \end{array} \begin{array}{c} \begin{array}{ccccc} C_0 & C_1 & C_2 & \cdots & C_{d-1} \end{array} \\ \left(\begin{array}{ccccc} 0 & A_0 & 0 & \cdots & 0 \\ 0 & 0 & A_1 & \cdots & 0 \\ 0 & 0 & 0 & \cdots & 0 \\ \vdots & \vdots & \vdots & \ddots & \vdots \\ A_{d-1} & 0 & 0 & \cdots & 0 \end{array} \right) \end{array}.$$

It can be proven with generality that, regardless of the value of d and the entries of the block matrixes in $\mathbf{P}$, $\mathbf{P}^d$ will always become a block-diagonal matrix as follows:

$$\mathbf{P}^d = \begin{array}{c} \\ C_0 \\ C_1 \\ C_2 \\ \vdots \\ C_{d-1} \end{array} \begin{array}{c} \begin{array}{ccccc} C_0 & C_1 & C_2 & \cdots & C_{d-1} \end{array} \\ \left(\begin{array}{ccccc} E_0 & 0 & 0 & \cdots & 0 \\ 0 & E_1 & 0 & \cdots & 0 \\ 0 & 0 & E_2 & \cdots & 0 \\ \vdots & \vdots & \vdots & \ddots & \vdots \\ 0 & 0 & 0 & \cdots & E_{d-1} \end{array} \right) \end{array}.$$

The d-step transition matrix $\mathbf{P}^d$ is also a stochastic matrix, and each of the cyclic classes $C_0, C_1, \ldots, C_{d-1}$ forms a different communication class, as the diagonal block structure suggests.

Recurrence and Transience

Let T_i be the time between two successive visits to state $i \in S$. State i is called *recurrent* if

$$P(T_i < \infty) = 1 , \tag{5.26}$$

and is called *transient* otherwise. A recurrent state i is called *positive recurrent* if

$$E[T_i] < \infty , \tag{5.27}$$

and is called *null recurrent* otherwise.

By the above definitions, an irreducible HMC is positive recurrent when any given state is visited infinitely often and moreover, when the average time between two successive visits to this state is finite.

Ergodic

An homogenous Markov chain is called *ergodic* if it is aperiodic, irreducible, and positive recurrent.

It is noteworthy that recurrence and transience are the class properties in the sense that if states i and j communicate, then they are either both recurrent or both transient (see Problem 5.12 at the end of this chapter). Therefore, an irreducible Markov Chain has all its states possessing the same nature: transient, positive recurrent, or null recurrent. To determine the category of each state of a chain, it suffices to study only one state, and one can study the state that is the easiest to infer.

5.4 Stationary Distribution

A probability distribution π on the state space S satisfying the following equation

$$\pi^T = \pi^T \mathbf{P} \tag{5.28}$$

is called a *stationary distribution* of the transition matrix $\mathbf{P}$, or of the corresponding HMC. Iterating (5.28) for n times, we have

$$\pi^T = \pi^T \mathbf{P}^n \tag{5.29}$$

for all $n \geq 0$. What means by this equation is that, if the initial distribution of the HMC is π, it keeps the same distribution forever. In this sense we say that the chain is *stationary*, in *steady state*, or in *equilibrium*.

Stationary distribution is a very important concept that has many useful properties. The following Detailed Balance Theorem provides a sufficient condition for a distribution π to be a stationary distribution.

Theorem 5.2 (Detailed Balance). *Assume that* **P** *is a transition matrix for an HMC with the state space* S, *and that* π *is a probability distribution on* S. *If for all* $i, j \in S$,

$$\pi(i)p_{ij} = \pi(j)p_{ji} , \qquad (5.30)$$

then π *is a stationary distribution of* **P**.

Proof: For fixed $i \in S$, summing both sides of (5.30) with respect to $j \in S$ yields

$$\sum_{j \in S} \pi(i)p_{ij} = \sum_{j \in S} \pi(j)p_{ji} .$$

Since the left-hand side is

$$\sum_{j \in S} \pi(i)p_{ij} = \pi(i) \sum_{j \in S} p_{ij} = \pi(i) ,$$

we have

$$\pi(i) = \sum_{j \in S} \pi(j)p_{ji}$$

for all $i \in S$. (proof-end).

The theorem below provides us with some insight into the physical meaning of a stationary distribution. The proof of the theorem is can be found in [31].

Theorem 5.3. *Let* **P** *be the transition matrix of an irreducible recurrent HMC* $\{X_n\}_{n\geq 0}$, *and* T_0 *be the return time to state* 0. *Define for all* $i \in S$

$$x_i = E_0 \left[\sum_{1 \leq n \leq T_0} \delta(X_n = i) \right] , \qquad (5.31)$$

where $E_0[U]$ *is the expectation of random variable* U *(the subscript* 0 *is used here because this expectation is computed given the parameter* T_0*). Then, for all* $i \in S$,

$$x_i \in (0, \infty), \quad x_i = \sum_{j \in S} x_j \, p_{ji} . \qquad (5.32)$$

In the above theorem, $\delta(\text{cond})$ is the delta function that equals one if the argument cond is true, and equals zero otherwise. x_i is called an *invariant measure* of the HMC, and is essentially the expected number of visits to state i before returning to state 0. Note that for time instant $n \in [1, T_0]$, $X_n = 0$ if and only if $n = T_0$. Therefore,

$$x_0 = 1 . \qquad (5.33)$$

Additionally, by summing up both sides of (5.31) with respect to $i \in S$, and with some derivations, we obtain the following equalities:

$$\sum_{i \in S} x_i = E_0 \left[\sum_{i \in S} \sum_{1 \leq n \leq T_0} \delta(X_n = i) \right]$$

$$= E_0 \left[\sum_{1 \leq n \leq T_0} \left\{ \sum_{i \in S} \delta(X_n = i) \right\} \right]$$

$$= E_0 \left[\sum_{1 \leq n \leq T_0} 1 \right]$$

$$= E_0[T_0] \tag{5.34}$$

Equality (5.34) and the definition of positive recurrence directly give the following theorem.

Theorem 5.4. *An irreducible recurrent HMC is positive recurrent if and only if its invariant measures x_i satisfy*

$$\sum_{i \in S} x_i < \infty . \tag{5.35}$$

From the invariant measures x_i, we can easily create a stationary distribution π of the HMC using the following equation:

$$\pi(i) = \frac{x_i}{\sum_{j \in S} x_j} . \tag{5.36}$$

In particular, for $i = 0$, using (5.33) and (5.34), we have

$$\pi(0) = \frac{x_0}{\sum_{j \in S} x_j} = \frac{1}{E_0[T_0]} .$$

Since state 0 does not play a special role in the analysis, this equality is true for all $i \in S$. Therefore, the above analysis yields the following theorem.

Theorem 5.5 (Mean Return Time). *Let π be the stationary distribution of an irreducible positive recurrent chain, and let T_i be the time between two successive visits to state i. Then*

$$\pi(i)E_i[T_i] = 1 . \tag{5.37}$$

The Mean Return Time Theorem provides a clear interpretation on the physical meaning of a stationary distribution: it is the reciprocal of the mean return time to each state of an ergodic HMC. From this interpretation, and with some other analysis, one can easily arrive at the following theorem (see Problem 5.13 at the end of this chapter).

Theorem 5.6. *An irreducible homogeneous Markov chain is positive current if and only if there exists a stationary distribution. When the stationary distribution exists, it is unique and positive.*

5.5 Long Run Behavior and Convergence Rate

Given a homogenous Markov chain and an arbitrary initial distribution $\boldsymbol{\mu}$, what is the long-run behavior of the chain? Will the chain converge to its stationary distribution? Under what conditions will the chain converge to its stationary distribution? If it converges, what is the convergence speed? The answers to these questions form the central notion of the HMC stability theory, and are the basis for Gibbs sampling and Monte Carlo simulation. Gibbs sampling and Mote Carlo simulation are the powerful statistical tools that have been widely used for probabilistic inferences and model estimations.

In this section, we present several important theorems that address the above important questions. The following theorem provides a sufficient condition for an HMC to converge to the stationary distribution.

Theorem 5.7 (Convergence to Stationary Distribution). *Let $\mathbf{P}$ be the transition matrix of an ergodic (i.e., aperiodic, irreducible positive recurrent) Markov chain with the countable state space S and the stationary distribution $\boldsymbol{\pi}$. For any arbitrary probability distributions $\boldsymbol{\mu}$ on S,*

$$\lim_{n\to\infty} |\boldsymbol{\mu}^T \mathbf{P}^n - \boldsymbol{\pi}^T| = 0 . \tag{5.38}$$

The proof of this theorem requires the understanding of the coupling theory that is out of the scope of this book. Interested readers are directed to the book [32] for additional information and historical comments.

We use the following example to verify the correctness of the above theorem.

Example 5.3. Convergence to Stationary Distribution
Consider a five-state ergodic Markov chain depicted in Fig. 5.5. Its transition matrix $\mathbf{P}$ is defined as follows:

$$\mathbf{P} = \begin{pmatrix} 0 & 0.3 & 0.2 & 0 & 0.5 \\ 0.5 & 0 & 0.5 & 0 & 0 \\ 0 & 0.5 & 0.2 & 0.3 & 0 \\ 0 & 0 & 0.7 & 0 & 0.3 \\ 0.3 & 0 & 0.2 & 0.5 & 0 \end{pmatrix}.$$

We conduct experiments using the following three initial distributions on the state space:

$$\mu_1 = [1, 0, 0, 0, 0], \quad \mu_2 = [0.5, 0, 0.5, 0, 0] \ , \mu_3 = [0.2, 0.2, 0.2, 0.2, 0.2] \ .$$

Figure 5.6 shows how each state distribution μ_i, $i = 1, 2, 3$, evolves after each iteration of state transitions. In the figure, the i'th column in the n'th row corresponds to $\mu_i^T(n) = \mu_i^T(n-1)\mathbf{P}$, for $n \geq 2$. It is clear from the figure that no matter with which initial distribution the chain starts, it converges to the same stationary distribution with no exception. In this example, the stationary distribution is $\pi = [0.15, 0.22, 0.35, 0.17, 0.12]$.

Theorem 5.7 has addressed the problem of under what conditions a Markov chain converges to a stationary distribution. When applying this theorem to statistical simulation problems, one is concerned about the speed of convergence to the stationary distribution, because it determines the "burn-in" time

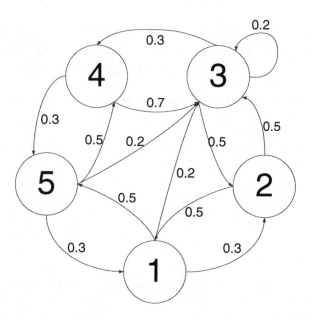

Fig. 5.5. An ergodic transition graph

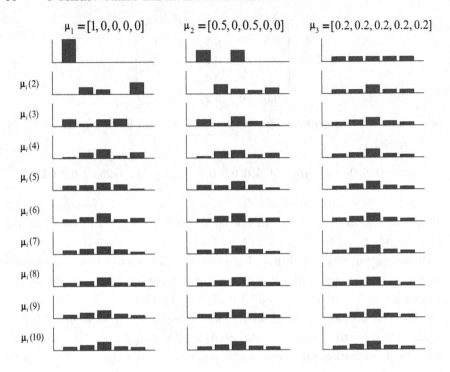

Fig. 5.6. Convergence to the stationary distribution

of the simulation for getting an accurate estimation result. Indeed, the speed of convergence depends on the eigenstructure of the transition matrix $\mathbf{P}$, and the Perron-Frobenius theorem provides the answer to this problem.

Theorem 5.8 (Perron-Frobenius Theorem). *Let* $\mathbf{A}$ *be a nonnegative[1] primitive[2] $r \times r$ matrix. Then*

- *There exists a real-valued eigenvalue λ_1 of $\mathbf{A}$ such that $\lambda_1 > 0$, and $\lambda_1 > |\lambda_j|$ for any other eigenvalues λ_j.*

---

[1] A matrix $\mathbf{A}$ is called nonnegative (or positive) if all its entries are nonnegative (or positive).

[2] A nonnegative square matrix $\mathbf{A}$ is primitive if and only if there exists an integer k such that $\mathbf{A}^k > 0$ element-wise.

- The eigenvalue λ_1 is simple. In other words, both its algebraic[3] and geometric multiplicity[4] are equal to one.
- The associated left and right eigenvectors $\mathbf{u}_1$, $\mathbf{v}_1$ are both positive.
- Let $\lambda_2, \lambda_3, \ldots, \lambda_r$ be the other eigenvalues of $\mathbf{A}$ ordered in such a way that

$$\lambda_1 > |\lambda_2| \geq \cdots \geq |\lambda_r| . \tag{5.39}$$

Then

$$\mathbf{A}^n = \lambda_1^n \mathbf{v}_1 \mathbf{u}_1^T + O(n^{m_2-1}|\lambda_2|^n) . \tag{5.40}$$

where m_2 is the algebraic multiplicity of λ_2.
- If in addition, $\mathbf{A}$ is stochastic, then $\lambda_1 = 1$.

Furthermore, if $\mathbf{A}$ is not nonnegative primitive but satisfies the following conditions, we have

- If $\mathbf{A}$ is stochastic and irreducible with period $d > 1$, then there are exactly d distinct eigenvalues of modulus[5] 1, and all other eigenvalues have modulus strictly less than 1.
- If $\mathbf{A}$ is stochastic but not irreducible, then the algebraic and geometric multiplicities of the eigenvalue 1 are equal to the number of communication classes.

The proof of the theorem can be found in [33, 34].

In the Perron-Frobenius theorem, (5.40) can be loosely verified using simple linear algebra and rest of the results in the Theorem. Since matrix $\mathbf{A}$ is a nonnegative primitive $r \times r$ matrix, there exists a nonsingular matrix $\mathbf{D}$ of the same dimension such that

$$\mathbf{DAD}^{-1} = \Lambda \tag{5.41}$$

where $\Lambda = diag(\lambda_1, \ldots, \lambda_r)$, and $\lambda_1, \ldots, \lambda_r$ are the eigenvalues of $\mathbf{A}$. Let $\mathbf{U}^T = D$, and $\mathbf{V} = \mathbf{D}^{-1}$, it follows from (5.41) that

$$\mathbf{U}^T \mathbf{A} = \Lambda \mathbf{U}^T \tag{5.42}$$

$$\mathbf{AV} = \mathbf{V}\Lambda \tag{5.43}$$

---

[3] An eigenvalue λ of a matrix $\mathbf{A}$ has algebraic multiplicity k if $(x-\lambda)^k$ is the highest power of $(x - \lambda)$ that divides the matrix characteristic polynomial $det(\mathbf{A} - \lambda\mathbf{I})$.
[4] The geometric multiplicity of an eigenvalue λ of a matrix $\mathbf{A}$ is the dimension of the subspace of vectors $\mathbf{x}$ for $\mathbf{Ax} = \lambda\mathbf{x}$.
[5] The modulus of a eigenvalue λ is its absolute value $|\lambda|$.

Therefore, the i'th row of $\mathbf{U}^T$ is a left eigenvector, and the i'th column of $\mathbf{V}$ is a right eigenvector associated with the eigenvalue λ_i. Also, a simple manipulation on (5.41) yields

$$\mathbf{A} = \mathbf{D}^{-1}\mathbf{\Lambda}\mathbf{D} = \mathbf{V}\mathbf{\Lambda}\mathbf{U}^T \tag{5.44}$$

$$\mathbf{A}^n = \mathbf{V}\mathbf{\Lambda}^n\mathbf{U}^T = \sum_{i=1}^{r} \lambda_i^n \mathbf{v}_i \mathbf{u}_i^T \tag{5.45}$$

If $\mathbf{A}$ is the transition matrix of a Markov chain, it follows from the Perron-Frobenium Theorem that

$$1 = \lambda_1 > |\lambda_2| \geq \cdots \geq |\lambda_r| . \tag{5.46}$$

From (5.45), (5.46), we reach the following equation:

$$\mathbf{A}^n = \lambda_1^n \mathbf{v}_1 \mathbf{u}_1^T + \lambda_2^n \mathbf{v}_2 \mathbf{u}_2^T + \cdots$$
$$= \lambda_1^n \mathbf{v}_1 \mathbf{u}_1^T + O(|\lambda_2|^n) ,$$

which is a loose version of (5.40).

If $\mathbf{A}$ is the transition matrix of an irreducible and aperiodic Markov chain, then as Theorem 5.6 stipulates, the chain has a stationary distribution $\boldsymbol{\pi}$ that satisfies:

$$\boldsymbol{\pi}^T \mathbf{A} = \boldsymbol{\pi}^T .$$

Additionally, since $\mathbf{A}$ is a stochastic matrix, it further satisfies

$$\mathbf{A}\mathbf{1} = \mathbf{1} .$$

where $\mathbf{1}$ is the vector with all the entries equal to one. Clearly, $\boldsymbol{\pi}$ and $\mathbf{1}$ are the left and right eigenvectors of the eigenvalue $\lambda_1 = 1$ respectively, and therefore, $\mathbf{A}^T$ can be written as:

$$\mathbf{A}^n = \mathbf{1}\boldsymbol{\pi}^T + O(n^{m_2-1}|\lambda_2|^n) .$$

The conclusions of the Perron-Frobenium theorem can be illustrated by the following example.

Example 5.4.
Consider the ergodic Markov chain described in **Example 5.3**. Its transition matrix $\mathbf{P}$ has the following five eigenvalues:

$$\lambda_1 = 1.0, \quad \lambda_2 = -0.65 + 0.12i, \quad \lambda_3 = -0.65 - 0.12i,$$
$$\lambda_4 = 0.25 + 0.19i, \quad \lambda_5 = 0.25 - 0.19i.$$

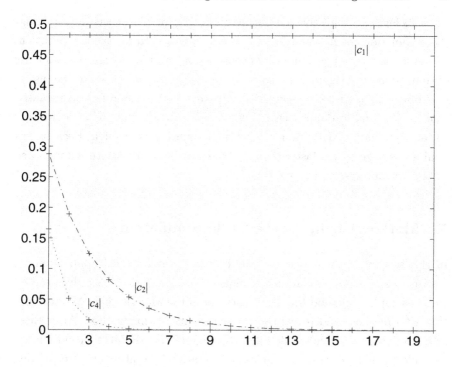

Fig. 5.7. Plots of $|c_1|$, $|c_2|$, and $|c_4|$ as functions of n

Because matrix $\mathbf{P}$ is primitive and stochastic, as predicted by the Perron-Frobenium theorem, its largest eigenvalue λ_1 is real-valued, simple, and equals to one. The rest of eigenvalues satisfy:

$$1 = \lambda_1 > |\lambda_2| = |\lambda_3| > |\lambda_4| = |\lambda_5| \, .$$

Because $\mathbf{P}$ has the period $d = 1$, all the eigenvalues except λ_1 have modules strictly less than 1. Note that λ_2, λ_3, and λ_4, λ_5 are the two pairs of complementary eigenvalues.

To examine how quickly an arbitrary initial distribution $\boldsymbol{\mu}$ converges to the stationary distribution, we compute the following quantity,

$$\boldsymbol{\mu}^T \mathbf{P}^n = \boldsymbol{\mu}^T \mathbf{1} \boldsymbol{\pi}^T + \sum_{i=2}^{5} \lambda_i^n \boldsymbol{\mu}^T \mathbf{v}_i \mathbf{u}_i^T$$

$$= c_1 \boldsymbol{\pi}^T + \sum_{i=2}^{5} c_i \mathbf{u}_i^T \, ,$$

where $\boldsymbol{\pi}$ is the stationary distribution, $\mathbf{u}_i$, $\mathbf{v}_i$ are the left and right eigenvectors of λ_i, $c_1 = \boldsymbol{\mu}^T \mathbf{1}$, $c_i = \lambda_i^n \boldsymbol{\mu}^T \mathbf{v}_i$ are some scalar numbers that can be considered as coefficients of respective left eigenvectors. Figure 5.7 depicts $|c_1|$, $|c_2|$, and $|c_4|$ as functions of n, where $\boldsymbol{\mu} = [1, 0, 0, 0, 0]$ was used for the computation. We omit the plots of $|c_3|$ and $|c_5|$ because λ_2, λ_3, and λ_4, λ_5 are the two pairs of complementary eigenvalues, so that $|c_2| = |c_3|$, $|c_4| = |c_5|$. From the figure, it is obvious that when n increases, $|c_1|$ stays at the same level constantly, whereas $|c_2|$ and $|c_4|$ approach to zero rapidly. As a result, $\boldsymbol{\mu}^T \mathbf{P}^n$ converges to the stationary distribution $\boldsymbol{\pi}$ when n becomes large enough. Because $|c_4|$ diminishes to zero even faster than $|c_2|$, the speed of convergence is dominated by $|c_2|$, or more precisely, by $O(|\lambda_2|^n)$.

5.6 Markov Chain Monte Carlo Simulation

In this section, we first describe the objectives and typical applications of statistical sampling/simulation techniques. Then, we briefly introduce the rejection sampling method that is an ancestor of the Morkov chain Monte Carlo (MCMC) method, and reveal the characteristics of this method. After these introductions, we provide a detailed coverage of the MCMC method and an example to demonstrate its real implementation. We also compare MCMC with rejection sampling, and discuss the pros and cons of the two methods.

5.6.1 Objectives and Applications

In statistical modeling and inference, there are many complex problems for which one can not obtain closed-form descriptions of their probability distributions $P(X)$. In most cases, one can define a function $f(X)$ that computes $P(X)$ up to a normalizing constant

$$P(X) = \frac{f(X)}{Z} ,$$

where $Z = \int_{x \in S} f(x) dx$ can not be computed either because $f(X)$ is too complex, or because the state space S is too large to compute the integral. In such circumstances, statistical sampling and simulation techniques become valuable and important tools for getting fair samples from target probability distributions. In general, statistical sampling and simulation techniques can be used to fulfill the following tasks.

1. **Simulation:** Draw typical (fair) samples from a probability that governs a system:

$$x \sim P(X) . \tag{5.47}$$

For many complex systems, their states are governed by some probability models, and the probability models are too complex to be described using closed-form equations. The fair samples generated by statistical sampling will show us what states are *typical* of the underlying system.

2. **Integration/estimation:** Compute integrals in very high dimensional spaces or estimate the expectations of certain quantities by empirical means:

$$E_P[f(X)] = \int_S f(x)P(x)dx = \lim_{n \to \infty} \frac{1}{n} \sum_{i=1}^{n} f(x_i) , \tag{5.48}$$

where S is the state space of the system, $(x_1, \ldots, x_n)$ are a finite set of samples drawn from the probability density function $P(X)$. Equation (5.48) is called the *law of large numbers*, and is a powerful means for computing an approximation of an integral or expectation when the exact integral is difficult to compute either due to a high dimensionality of the space, or due to an insufficient knowledge about the probability density function $P(X)$.

3. **Optimization:** Identify the most probable state of the underlying system governed by the probability model $P(X)$:

$$x^* = \arg\max P(x) . \tag{5.49}$$

Optimization is a problem of great interest in statistical inferences because it can be used to compute the most probable interpretation for an input given the underlying probability model.

4. **Learning:** Acquire the parameters θ that give the maximum likelihood estimation of the probability model $P(X; \theta)$ governing the target system. Statistical sample and simulation techniques are commonly used for probability model estimations when the models are too complex to make analytic estimations.

5.6.2 Rejection Sampling

Rejection sampling is an early statistical sampling method that is considered as an ancestor of the MCMC method. It aims to draw independent samples from a probability distribution $P(X) = f(X)/Z$. The assumption here is that we do not know the normalizing constant Z, but can evaluate $f(X)$ at any position x we choose. It is noteworthy that this sampling method, as well

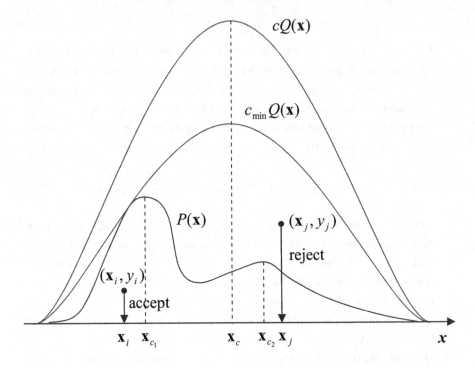

Fig. 5.8. Illustration of the rejection sampling algorithm

as the following MCMC method, can be applied to $P(X)$ that either gives probabilities for discrete X or is a probability density function over continuous X.

The main ingredient of rejection sampling is that, instead of sampling directly from $P(X)$, we use a distribution $Q(X)$ from which sampling is easier. The only restriction for $Q(X)$ is that we must be able to identify a constant $c > 1$ for which $f(X) \leq cQ(X)$ for all x. Furthermore, the constant c should be as small as possible in order to achieve an efficient sampling process.

With the above settings, the rejection sampling algorithm can be described as follows:

1. Draw a sample x_i from $Q(X)$.
2. Draw a sample y_i from an uniform distribution with the range $[0, \ cQ(x_i)]$.
3. if $y_i \leq f(x_i)$, accept x_i as a sample from $P(X)$; otherwise, reject the sample.
4. Repeat Step 1 $\sim$ 3 until the number of samples reaches the predefined value.

The rejection sampling algorithm can be justified using the following simple derivations (see Fig. 5.8). The cumulative distribution $P(a \leq X \leq b)$ on interval $[a, b]$ is defined as

$$P(a \leq X \leq b) = \int_{x=a}^{x=b} P(x)dx .$$ (5.50)

Following the rejection sampling algorithm described above, the computation of (5.50) becomes as follows:

$$
\begin{aligned}
P(a \leq X \leq b) &= P(a \leq X \leq b \mid Y \leq f(X)) \\
&= \frac{P(a \leq X \leq b, Y \leq f(X))}{P(Y \leq f(X))} \\
&= \frac{P(a \leq X \leq b, Y \leq f(X))}{P(-\infty < X < \infty, Y \leq f(X))} \\
&= \frac{\int_{x=a}^{x=b} \int_{y=0}^{y=f(x)} 1 \, dy dx}{\int_{x=-\infty}^{x=\infty} \int_{y=0}^{y=f(x)} 1 \, dy dx} \\
&= \frac{\int_{x=a}^{x=b} f(x)dx}{\int_{x=-\infty}^{x=\infty} f(x) \, dx} .
\end{aligned}
$$ (5.51)

Clearly, the unknown normalizing constant Z is canceled out in (5.51), and independent samples from the target probability distribution $P(X)$ are obtained via the rejection sampling process.

In addition to the above mathematical derivations, a more intuitive interpretation of the rejection sampling algorithm can be given as follows (see Fig. 5.8). Samples are drawn from the instrumental distribution $Q(X)$ instead of the target distribution $P(X)$. At each location $x_i \sim Q(X)$, $cQ(x_i)$ is evaluated and a random height $y_i \sim U[0, cQ(x_i)]$ is drawn, where $U[0, cQ(x_i)]$ denotes an uniform distribution with the range $[0, cQ(x_i)]$. Here, y_i gives a random position drawn uniformly from under the curve $cQ(x_i)$. By accepting only x_i for which $y_i \leq f(x_i)$ and rejecting others, we end up with points drawn uniformly from the area under the curve $f(X)$, equivalent to drawing samples from the target distribution $P(X)$.

The probability that a point x_i is accepted is simply the ratio of the areas underneath $f(X)$ and $cQ(X)$. As a function of c, this probability can be written as

$$P_{acpt}(c) = \frac{Z}{c} ,$$ (5.52)

where we assume that the instrumental distribution $Q(X)$ is normalized so that $\int_{-\infty}^{\infty} Q(x)dx = 1$. Thus the number of samples from $Q(X)$ required for a single sample from $P(X)$ follows a geometric distribution with mean $\frac{c}{Z}$, and this explains why the constant c should be chosen as small as possible in order to achieve an efficient sampling.

From the above discussions it is clear that with the rejection sampling algorithm, one needs to use an instrumental distribution $Q(X)$ that is similar to the target distribution $P(X)$ in order for the sampling process to be efficient. Using an instrumental distribution $Q(X)$ that is quite different from $P(X)$ will result in a smaller P_{acpt}, which means that one needs to draw many samples from $Q(X)$ to get one accepted sample.

Another characteristic of rejection sampling is the complete independence between samples generated by the process. While sample independence is good for obtaining i.i.d. sample sets, it is another main cause for the inefficiency of the rejection sampling algorithm. Take Fig. 5.8 as an example. The instrumental distribution $Q(X)$ used in this example is a Gaussian distribution centered at x_c, while the target distribution $P(X)$ has two peaks centered at x_{c_1}, x_{c_2}, respectively. The instrumental distribution $Q(X)$ tends to generate most samples around the neighborhood of x_c, and few samples in the vicinities of x_{c_1}, x_{c_2}. Because the sampling process generates each sample without being influenced by the location of the previous sample, after it happens to visit the vicinity of x_{c_1}, for example, the process will be very likely to jump back to the neighborhood of x_c again, generating the next sample from there, which is likely to be rejected with a high probability. As a result, most samples drawn from $Q(X)$ (a Gaussian distribution) are rejected, and only a small percentage of samples are accepted as the output. If the number of samples drawn from the sampling process is not large enough, one may not get a sample set that is unbiased, and typical of the target distribution $P(X)$.

5.6.3 Markov Chain Monte Carlo

Same as rejection sampling, Markov Chain Monte Carlo can generate samples from a complex probability function $P(X)$ that is defined over either continuous or discrete X. Again, for description simplicity, we present the technique for discrete probability functions in this section. As will be revealed later, the Makovian characteristic of the MCMC method makes it much more efficient than the rejection sampling and other sampling techniques for drawing fair samples from complex distributions, especially when the state space is very large and high dimensional.

The basic idea of the MCMC algorithm is to find an ergodic transition matrix $\mathbf{P}$ on the state space S so that its stationary distribution $\boldsymbol{\pi}$ is the target distribution. Since $\mathbf{P}$ is ergodic, it follows from Theorem 5.7 that for any initial distribution $\boldsymbol{\mu}$, the chain is guaranteed to converge to its stationary distribution $\boldsymbol{\pi}$:

$$\lim_{n \to \infty} |\boldsymbol{\mu}^T \mathbf{P}^n - \boldsymbol{\pi}^T| = 0 \ .$$

Knowing the fact that an ergodic Markov chain will converge to the stationary distribution $\boldsymbol{\pi}$ regardless of its initial distribution $\boldsymbol{\mu}$, now the problem becomes: how can we find such an ergodic transition matrix $\mathbf{P}$ that its stationary distribution $\boldsymbol{\pi}$ is the target distributon? The most common practice is that we first construct an ergodic transition matrix $\mathbf{Q}$, called the *candidate generating matrix*, that has some good properties (e.g. fast convergence rate, simple structure, etc), and then twist $\mathbf{Q}$ a bit so that the stationary distribution of the new matrix equals the target distribution $\boldsymbol{\pi}$. More precisely, from Theorem 5.2 we know that $\boldsymbol{\pi}$ is the stationary distribution of $\mathbf{Q}$ if for all $i, j \in S$,

$$\pi(i)q_{ij} = \pi(j)q_{ji} \ .$$

In case entries q_{ij} of $\mathbf{Q}$ do not satisfy this detailed balance test, we can insert factors α_{ij} such that

$$p_{ij} = q_{ij}\alpha_{ij} \ , \quad \pi(i)p_{ij} = \pi(j)p_{ji} \ . \tag{5.53}$$

In the literature, α_{ij} are called *candidate acceptance rates*, or *candidate acceptance probability*. There are several ways of making α_{ij} to satisfy the above condition, and we enumerates two most famous ones below [35, 36].

Metropolis Algorithm

$$\alpha_{ij} = \min\left(1, \frac{\pi(j)q_{ji}}{\pi(i)q_{ij}}\right) \ . \tag{5.54}$$

A spacial case of the Metropolis algorithm is that the candidate generating matrix $\mathbf{Q}$ is symmetric so that (5.54) becomes

$$\alpha_{ij} = \min\left(1, \frac{\pi(j)}{\pi(i)}\right) \ . \tag{5.55}$$

Barker's Algorithm

$$\alpha_{ij} = \frac{\pi(j)q_{ji}}{\pi(j)q_{ji} + \pi(i)q_{ij}} . \qquad (5.56)$$

In the special case of a symmatric candidate generating matrix $\mathbf{Q}$,

$$\alpha_{ij} = \frac{\pi(j)}{\pi(j) + \pi(i)} . \qquad (5.57)$$

One can easily verify that α_{ij}'s computed by (5.54) $\sim$ (5.57) all satisfy the detailed balance test (5.53), and therefore the target distribution π is the stationary distribution of the chain.

In summary, the MCMC algorithm can be described as follows.

1. Construct an ergodic transition matrix $\mathbf{Q} = \{q_{ij}\}$ with a fast convergence rate to its stationary distribution.
2. Start with a state i.
3. Choose the next tentative state j with probability q_{ij}.
4. Calculate α_{ij} using either of the equations (5.54) $\sim$ (5.57).
5. Accept j as the new state with probability α_{ij}; otherwise, the next state is the same state i. This operation ensures that the resulting probability of moving from state i to j is given by $p_{ij} = q_{ij}\alpha_{ij}$.
6. Repeat Step 3 to 5 until the number of sampled states reaches the predefined threshold.

In implementing the above MCMC algorithm, there are several design issues that need to be considered in order to accomplish a good performance for the simulation process. First, as the Perron-Frobenius theorem has revealed, the convergence rate depends greatly on the second largest eigen-value modulus $|\lambda_2|$ of the transition matrix. Therefore, one needs to choose a transition matrix with a small $|\lambda_2|$ to achieve a fast convergence rate of the simulation process. Second, the speed of convergence also depends on the acceptance probability a_{ij} that determines how fast we can move forward along the simulation process. In other words, we want a_{ij} to be as close to one as possible at all times so that we can keep the rejection rate for the proposed new states as low as possible. Indeed, the value of a_{ij} reflects the degree of closeness between the candidate-generating matrix $\mathbf{Q}$ and the target matrix $\mathbf{P}$. It is clear from (5.53) that the closer the two corresponding entries p_{ij} and q_{ij} are, the closer to one a_{ij} is. Therefore, to quickly move the simulation process forward, one needs to choose a candidate-generating matrix $\mathbf{Q}$ that is as close to the target matrix $\mathbf{P}$ as possible. This requires a good understanding about the target problem, as well as a certain know-how on the MCMC design.

We use the following example to demonstrate a real implementation of the MCMC algorithm for sampling a target probabilistic distribution.

Example 5.5. MCMC Implementation

Consider a 2-D probability distribution depicted in Fig. 5.9. Its density function is known up to a normalizing factor Z [6]:

$$P(\mathbf{X}) = \frac{1}{Z}\left(\exp(-U_1^4 - 16U_2^4) + \frac{1}{10}\exp(-\frac{1}{2}(X_1^2 + X_2^2))\right), \qquad (5.58)$$

where $\mathbf{X} = (X_1, X_2)^T$, and

$$\begin{pmatrix} U_1 \\ U_2 \end{pmatrix} = \left[\begin{pmatrix} X_1 \\ X_2 \end{pmatrix} - \begin{pmatrix} 5 \\ 3 \end{pmatrix}\right]^T \cdot \begin{pmatrix} 0.8 & 0.6 \\ -0.6 & 0.8 \end{pmatrix}.$$

Our task is to use the MCMC algorithm to generate a set of random samples that follow this probability distribution.

In this example, we use the following Gaussian distribution with an unit variance as the candidate-generating function:

$$P(\mathbf{X}_{n+1} = \mathbf{x}_{n+1} \mid \mathbf{X}_n = \mathbf{x}_n) = \frac{1}{2\pi}\exp\left(-\frac{1}{2}(\mathbf{x}_{n+1} - \mathbf{x}_n)^T(\mathbf{x}_{n+1} - \mathbf{x}_n)\right).$$
$$(5.59)$$

If we consider $\mathbf{X}$ as a continuous variable and want to draw real-value samples for $\mathbf{X}$, then (5.59) serves as the state transition (or candidate-generating) function, and it is impossible, and unnecessary to define the candidate-generating matrix $\mathbf{Q}$. In contrast, if $\mathbf{X}$ is considered as a discrete variable defined on a discrete state space S, then we define the candidate-generating matrix $\mathbf{Q} = \{q_{ij}\}$ as follows:

$$q_{ij} = P(\mathbf{X}_{n+1} = \mathbf{j} \mid \mathbf{X}_n = \mathbf{i}) = \frac{1}{2\pi}\exp\left(-\frac{1}{2}(\mathbf{j} - \mathbf{i})^T(\mathbf{j} - \mathbf{i})\right). \qquad (5.60)$$

We start the simulation process from the state $\mathbf{x}_0 = 0$, and use the metropolis algorithm to compute the acceptance rate α_{ij} at each iteration of the process. The entire simulation algorithm for continuous variable $\mathbf{X}$ is summarized as follows (the algorithm for discrete variable is straightforward from the continuous version):

---

[6] In fact Z can be easily computed for this probability density function. The problem is trivial for the MCMC algorithm. We use the trivial problem to demonstrate a real MCMC implementation

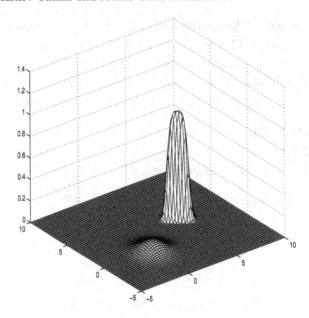

Fig. 5.9. The target probability distribution

1. Set $n = 0$, and start with $\mathbf{x}_n=0$.
2. Choose the next candidate sample $\mathbf{x}_{n+1}$ with probability $P(\mathbf{x}_{n+1}|\mathbf{x}_n)$ defined by (5.59).
3. Calculate the acceptance rate α_{ij} using (5.54), where $\pi(j)/\pi(i) = P(\mathbf{x}_{n+1})/P(\mathbf{x}_n)$ is computed using (5.58) (the unknown normalizing factor Z is canceled out in computing this fraction), and $q_{ji}/q_{ij} = P(\mathbf{x}_n|\mathbf{x}_{n+1})/P(\mathbf{x}_{n+1}|\mathbf{x}_n) = 1$ when computed using (5.59). Accept the sample $\mathbf{x}_{n+1}$ with probability α_{ij}; otherwise, the next sample is the same as $\mathbf{x}_n$.
4. Set $n = n + 1$. If $n \geq N$, where N is the user defined number, terminate the simulation process; otherwise, go to Step 2.

Figure (5.10)(a) $\sim$ (d) plot the sampling results generated by the MCMC algorithm at 2000, 10000, 20000, and 100000 iterations, respectively. It is interesting to see that the first 2000 samples capture only half (one heap) of the true distribution, and this heap has been sampled with an incorrect scale. Obviously, at this stage, the simulation process has yet to reach its stationary distribution, and the samples generated so far do not reflect the target distribution very much. When the number of iterations reaches 10000, the two heaps of the target distribution has been captured by the sampling

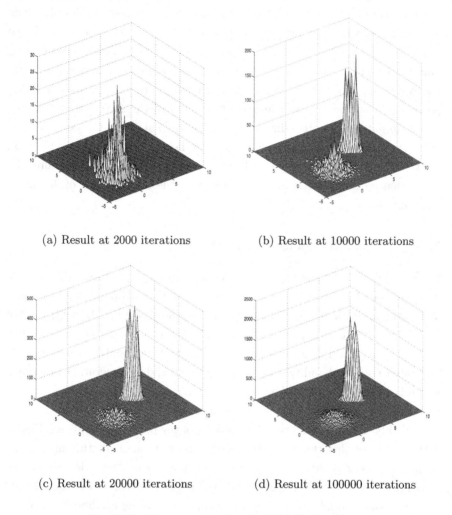

(a) Result at 2000 iterations   (b) Result at 10000 iterations

(c) Result at 20000 iterations   (d) Result at 100000 iterations

Fig. 5.10. Data sampling by the MCMC algorithm

result. When the number of iterations further increases, the sampling result becomes smoother, and closer to the true target distribution.

Note that the simulation process demonstrated in this example has a relatively slow convergence rate: it requires more than 20000 iterations to obtain a reasonable approximation of the target distribution. This is mainly because there is a big difference between the distributions of the candidate-generating function and the target function: the candidate-generating function (5.59) is a cylindrical Gaussian (with a unit variance) which spreads uniformly along all directions, while the target distribution (5.58) is composed of two heaps which are arranged along a line. Since $q_{ij} = q_{ji}$ (the candidate-generating function is symmetrical), $\alpha_{ij} = \frac{\pi(j)}{\pi(i)}$. As (5.59) tends to generate candidate states within an unit-size circular area with a high probability, the simulation process is prone to be stuck in a neighborhood of the same area for a long time before it jumps onto a different area. This explains why the sampled data at the first 2000 iterations capture only one heap of the target distribution. It takes many iterations to jump from one heap to the other, therefore, the simulation process needs a long time to capture the entire picture of the target distribution.

5.6.4 Rejection Sampling vs. MCMC

In Sect. 5.6.2, we explained that rejection sampling generates each sample independent of the previous samples, and that this sample independence is one of the main causes for the inefficiency of the algorithm. In contrast, the MCMC algorithm generates a sequence of samples using an ergodic Markov chain. When a sample $\mathbf{x}_n$ is generated, the next candidate sample $\mathbf{x}_{n+1}$ is generated with probability $P(\mathbf{x}_{n+1}|\mathbf{x}_n)$ (the candidate-generating function), which is statistically dependent on $\mathbf{x}_n$. When a Gaussian distribution is used to define $P(\mathbf{x}_{n+1}|\mathbf{x}_n)$, such as in the example 5.5, each candidate sample $\mathbf{x}_{n+1}$ will be generated in the neighborhood of the previous sample $\mathbf{x}_n$. Figure 5.11 illustrates this characteristic using a contour map. In this figure, the sampling process starts from an arbitrary point $\mathbf{x}_0$. Then, the candidate-generating Gaussian distribution is moved so as to be centered at $\mathbf{x}_0$, and the next candidate sample $\mathbf{x}_1$ is likely to be generated in the neighborhood of $\mathbf{x}_0$. If $\mathbf{x}_1$ is rejected, the center of the Gaussian distribution will stay at $\mathbf{x}_0$, and another candidate sample will be generated. If $\mathbf{x}_1$ is accepted, the center of the Gaussian distribution will be moved to $\mathbf{x}_1$, and the next candidate sample $\mathbf{x}_2$ will be generated in the vicinity of $\mathbf{x}_1$. If $\mathbf{x}_2$ happens to be in a peak area of the target distribution, it will be accepted with a high probability, and will become the next center of the Gaussian distribution. Because of this, when the sampling process happens to visit a peak area of the target distribution, it will wander in that area, and keep drawing samples from there with a high probability. Clearly, the sampling process is rubber-banded by the Markov chain, and this ensures that each sample will not be too far away from the previous one. Therefore, we can conclude that the MCMC algorithm

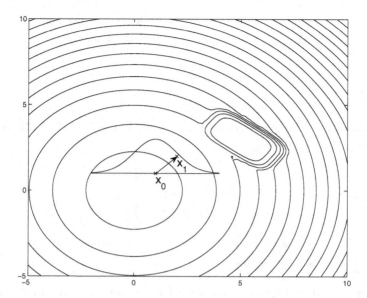

(a) The sampling process starts from an arbitrary point $\mathbf{x}_0$. Then, the center of the candidate-generating Gaussian distribution is moved to $\mathbf{x}_0$, and the next candidate sample $\mathbf{x}_1$ is generated in the neighborhood of $\mathbf{x}_0$

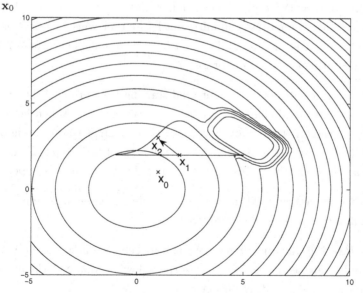

(b) If $\mathbf{x}_1$ is accepted, the center of the Gaussian distribution will be moved to $\mathbf{x}_1$, and the next candidate sample $\mathbf{x}_2$ will be generated in the vicinity of $\mathbf{x}_1$

Fig. 5.11. Illustration of the MCMC sampling algorithm, where a Gaussian distribution is used as the candidate-generating function

improves the sampling efficiency, and this efficiency improvement, however, is accomplished at the cost of losing the sample independence.

Problems

5.1. Consider a Markov chain with the state space $E = \{1, 2, 3\}$ and the following transition matrix:

$$P = \begin{bmatrix} 0.2 \ 0.5 \ 0.3 \\ 0.1 \ 0.1 \ 0.8 \\ 0.5 \ 0.2 \ 0.3 \end{bmatrix} \tag{5.61}$$

(a) What is the stationary distribution of the Markov chain?

(b) Is this chain reversible?

5.2. Let T be the return time to state 1 for the Markov chain in problem 5.1. Calculate $E_1[T]$

5.3. In a Roulette gambling game, assume that each bet of one dollar has a probability of $p = 18/38$ to win one dollar and $1 - p$ to lose one dollar. A gambler decides to continue gambling until he either wins 5 dollars or loses 100 dollars. What is the probability that he wins 5 dollars eventually? What is the expectation of his profit (or loss)?

5.4. A drunkard walks on a straight road starting from origin. When he is at origin, there are equal chances that he steps east or west. When he is away from origin, there is a probability $p > 0.5$ that he steps towards origin, and probability $1 - p$ away from origin. Assume the size of each step is fixed. What is the transition matrix of this process. Is it reducible or not? Is it periodic?

5.5. For the same drunkard in Problem 5.4, after long enough time, what is the probability of seeing the drunkard at origin?

5.6. Let P be the transition matrix of a heterogeneous Markov chain, $x_1, \cdots x_t$ be a sample state sequence. We can use the following Monte Carlo average to estimate the stationary distribution π

$$\hat{\pi}_i = \frac{1}{T} \sum_{t=1}^{T} \delta(x_t, i)$$

Is this an unbiased estimator of π_i? What is the variance of $\hat{\pi}_i$?

5.7. Random samples from exponential and normal distribution. Let X_1 and X_2 be random samples from uniform distribution $[0, 1)$.

(a) Prove that the random variable $Y = -\log X_1$ is an exponential distribution.

(b) Let $Y_1 = \sqrt{-2\log X_1}\cos 2\pi X_2$, $Y_2 = \sqrt{-2\log X_1}\sin 2\pi X_2$. Prove that Y_1 and Y_2 are independent Normal random variables.

5.8. Suppose that we use rejection sampling to get samples from a Gaussian distribution with zero mean and unit variance. We choose $Q(x) = \frac{a}{2}\exp(-a|x|)$ as the instrumental distribution. Find the optimal a that makes the sampling most efficient.

5.9. Importance sampling. One way to calculate the integration $I = \int_{\mathbf{x}\in A} f(\mathbf{x})dx_1\cdots dx_k$ is to use the Monte Carlo method. Let $p(\mathbf{x})$ be a distribution over A. We can draw n independent samples $\mathbf{x}_1\cdots\mathbf{x}_n$ from $p(\mathbf{x})$. Then the Monte Carlo estimation of I is

$$\hat{I} = \frac{1}{N}\sum_{n=1}^{N}\frac{f(\mathbf{x}_i)}{p(\mathbf{x}_i)} \tag{5.62}$$

(a) Show that the expectation of $\hat{I}$ is I.

(b) What is the variance of $\hat{I}$. What kind of $p(\mathbf{x})$ can minimize the variance?

(c) What is the advantages/disadvantages of using the Monte Carlo integration compared to the numerical integration?

5.10. Prove the correctness of the Metropolis algorithm, i.e., the stationary distribution of the constructed Markov chain is the target distribution.

5.11. Suppose the we use the Metropolis algorithm to sample a simple distribution $P(x) = 1/N$ $x \in 1,\cdots, N$. Suppose that we use the following candidate-generating distribution:

$$P(x'|x) = \begin{cases} 1/3 & \text{if } |x' - x| \leq 1 \\ 0 & \text{otherwise} \end{cases} \tag{5.63}$$

(a) For $N = 10$, generate and plot two sample sequences from a chain of 1000 iterations.

(b) For $N = 100$, generate and plot two sample sequences from a chain of 1000 iterations.

5.12. Prove that for an irreducible Markov Chain, all its states possess the same nature: transient, positive recurrent, or null recurrent.

5.13. Prove that an irreducible homogeneous Markov chain is positive current if and only if there exists a stationary distribution. When the stationary distribution exists, it is unique and positive (Theorem 5.6).

5.14. Google's Page Ranking Algorithm. Consider a graph $G = (V, E)$ with a vertex set V and an edge set E, where each vertex $v \in V$ represents a web page, and an edge $(u, v) \in E$ represents a link (or links) between two web pages u and v. Define an $N \times N$ square matrix $\mathbf{A}$ in which each element a_{uv} is the weight of the edge (u, v). If there are $N_u > 0$ links that originate from the web page u, then $a_{uv} = 1/N_u$, otherwise, $a_{uv} = 0$. Let $\mathbf{r}_1 = [r_{11}, r_{12}, \ldots, r_{1N}]$ be the largest eigenvector of $\mathbf{A}$. The page ranking algorithm uses r_{1i} as the page ranking for the i'th web page. Explain the physical meaning of each element r_{1i} of the eigenvector $\mathbf{r}_1$. (Hint: consider the problem from the stationary distribution viewpoint.)

6

Markov Random Fields and Gibbs Sampling

Markov chain theories aim to model sequences of random variables that have certain dependencies among themselves. In this chapter, we present Markov random field theories that extend Markov chains to enable the modeling of local structures/interactions among random variables. Because markov random fields can naturally model signals with both spatial and temporal configurations, they have been widely applied in areas of image processing, computer vision, multimedia computing, etc.

We start this chapter by introducing important concepts and definitions of Markov random fields, followed by describing Gibbs distributions and their equivalence to Markov random fields. We also describe the Gibbs sampling method that is a special version of the Markov chain Monte Carlo method described in the previous chapter. At the end of this chapter, we provide a case study that describes our original work to apply Markov random fields to the video foreground object segmentation task.

6.1 Markov Random Fields

Let S be a finite set representing sites, Λ be another finite set representing values of random variables. A *random field* on S with phases in Λ is a collection of random variables $\mathbf{X} = \{X(s)\}_{s \in S}$ with values in Λ. By convention, the finite sets S and Λ are called the site space and phase space, respectively. Furthermore, we can introduce a space Λ^S called the configuration space, and regard the entire random field as a single random variable taking its values in Λ^S. A configuration $\mathbf{x} \in \Lambda^S$ is a vector, and is denoted as $\mathbf{x} = [x(s), s \in S]$, where $x(s) \in \Lambda$ (recall that in this book, we use bold letters to represent vectors, and regular letters to represent scala values). For a given configuration $\mathbf{x}$ and a given subset $A \subset S$, we define the partial configuration $\mathbf{x}(A)$ as:

$$\mathbf{x}(A) = [x(s),\ s \in A] \ .$$

If we use $S - A$ to represent the complement of A in S, then,

$$\mathbf{x} = [\mathbf{x}(A),\ \mathbf{x}(S - A)] \ .$$

In particular, for any fixed site $s \in S$,

$$\mathbf{x} = [x(s),\ \mathbf{x}(S - s)] \ .$$

Markov random fields (MRF) are a natural extension of markov chains, which aim to model local structures/interactions among random variables. The local structures/interactions are usually defined in terms of an undirected graph $G = (S, E)$ (see Sect. 4.2 for detailed descriptions), where S and E are the site space and the edge set of the random field G, respectively. In general, a neighborhood system N is defined on the site space S, which is a set of neighborhoods $N = \{N_s\}_{s \in S}$ such that for all $s \in S$,

$$s \notin N_s,\ t \in N_s \Rightarrow s \in N_t \ .$$

The subset N_s is called the neighborhood of site s.

With the above preparations, the definition of Markov Random fields is given as follows. The random field $\mathbf{X} = \{X(s)\}_{s \in S}$ is a *Markov random field* with respect to the neighborhood system N if for all sites $s \in S$,

$$P(X(s) = x(s)\,|\,\mathbf{X}(S - s) = \mathbf{x}(S - s)) \ = \ P(X(s) = x(s)\,|\,\mathbf{X}(N_s) = \mathbf{x}(N_s)) \ ,$$
$$(6.1)$$

where $\mathbf{x} \in \Lambda^S$. Define the *local characteristic* of the MRF at site s as:

$$P^{(s)}(\mathbf{x}) \ = \ P(X(s) = x(s)\,|\,\mathbf{X}(N_s) = \mathbf{x}(N_s)) \ . \qquad (6.2)$$

The family $\{P^{(s)}\}_{s \in S}$ is called the *local specification* of the MRF.

In summary, a Markov random field is characterized by the following elements:

1. The site space S.
2. The phase space Λ.
3. The neighborhood system $N = \{N_s\}_{s \in S}$ defined on S.
4. The local specification $\{P^{(s)}\}_{s \in S}$.

Note that any random field will become an MRF if we define a trivial neighborhood system such that the neighborhood of any site s is the whole site space S. However, as will be demonstrated in subsequent sections, interesting Markov random fields are those with relatively small neighborhoods in terms of the models' values and applicabilities.

6.2 Gibbs Distributions

Gibbs distributions were originally introduced by Gibbs in 1902 to model physical interactions between molecules and particles. For this purpose, the notion of *cliques* and *potentials* were developed to embody local configurations and interactions among elements. Given a site space S and a phase space Λ, a Gibbs distribution is described by the following components:

- **Clique:** Any singleton $\{s\}$ is a clique. A subset $C \in S$ with more than one element is a clique if any two distinct sites in C are neighbors. In other words, the subgraph induced by a clique is a complete graph. The set of all cliques is denoted by $\mathcal{C}$.
- **Potential:** A Gibbs potential on Λ^S is a collection $\{V_C\}_{C \in \mathcal{C}}$ of functions $V_C : \Lambda^S \to R$ such that
  (1) $V_C(\mathbf{x}) \equiv 0$ if C is not a clique.
  (2) For all $\mathbf{x}, \mathbf{x}' \in \Lambda^S$ and all $C \in \mathcal{C}$,

$$\mathbf{x}(C) = \mathbf{x}'(C) \;\Rightarrow\; V_C(\mathbf{x}) = V_C(\mathbf{x}') . \tag{6.3}$$

  Note that function $V_C(\mathbf{x})$ depends only on the phases at the sites included in the clique C. Therefore, $V_C(\mathbf{x}(C))$ is a more accurate expression of $V_C(\mathbf{x})$, but we do not use the former notation for typing convenience.
- **Energy function:** The energy function $U : \Lambda^S \to R$ is defined from the potential $\{V_C\}_{C \in \mathcal{C}}$ as follows:

$$U(\mathbf{x}) = \sum_{C \in \mathcal{C}} V_C(\mathbf{x}) . \tag{6.4}$$

Using the above definitions, a Gibbs distribution relative to $\{S, \mathcal{C}\}$ is defined as follows:

$$\pi_T(\mathbf{x}) = \frac{1}{Z_T} e^{-\frac{1}{T} U(\mathbf{x})} \tag{6.5}$$

where $T > 0$ is a constant called *temperature*, and Z_T is the normalizing constant called the *partition function*. A Gibbs distribution $\pi_T(\mathbf{x})$ is a probability measurement on the configuration space Λ^S that takes values in the range of $[0, 1]$. It gives a higher probability to a configuration $\mathbf{x} \in \Lambda^S$ with a lower energy $U(\mathbf{x})$, and vice versa, which is the reflection of physical laws.

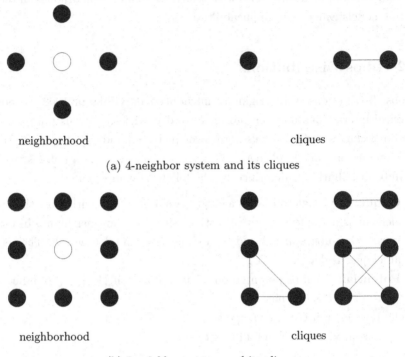

(a) 4-neighbor system and its cliques

(b) 8-neighbor system and its cliques

Fig. 6.1. Two neighborhood systems and their cliques

Figure (6.1) shows two most common neighborhood systems and their corresponding cliques. In the figure, the black dots are the neighbors of the central white dots, and each clique is up to a rotation. Neighborhoods and cliques are defined to capture local interactions among elements in the target system, and a Gibbs potential defined on each clique is used to quantitatively measure the local interaction expressed by the clique.

The following example demonstrates how Gibbs potential and energy function are defined to model a real problem.

Example 6.1. Ising Model

This model was invented by E. Ising in 1925 to help explain ferromagnetic materials. Here, $S = Z_m^2$ (an $m \times m$ integer lattice), $\Lambda = \{+1, -1\}$, and the 4-neighborhood system with the corresponding cliques (see Fig. (6.1)(a)) were used for model construction. The Gibbs potential was defined as

$$V_{\{s\}}(\mathbf{x}) = -\frac{H}{k}x(s) , \tag{6.6}$$

$$V_{\{s,t\}}(\mathbf{x}) = -\frac{J}{k}x(t)x(s) , \tag{6.7}$$

where $\{s\}$, $\{s,t\}$ are the singleton and the 2-element cliques, respectively, k is the Boltzmann constant, H is the external magnetic field, and J is the internal energy of an element magnetic dipole. The energy function corresponding to this potential is

$$U(\mathbf{x}) = -\frac{H}{k}\sum_{s \in S} x(s) - \frac{J}{k}\sum_{\{s,t\}} x(s)x(t) \tag{6.8}$$

where the sums extend over the entire site space S for which the indicated cliques make sense.

It is noteworthy that obtaining explicit formulas for Gibbs distributions is one of the biggest challenges in applying Gibbs models because the partition function Z_T is generally impossible to compute, due to the fact that Z_T needs to sum over all possible configurations $\mathbf{x} \in \Lambda^S$, and the configuration space Λ^S is generally huge for many real problems. However, there are a few exceptions where scientists succeeded in deriving explicit forms of Gibbs distributions, and these successes are mostly made with relatively simple models. The following example provides the simplest one which was solved by Ising in 1925.

Example 6.2. Ising's Toric Model [31]
This model is mostly same as the one in **Example 6.1.** except that the site space $S = \{1, 2, \ldots, N\}$ consists of N points arranged on a circle in this order. The neighbors of site i are $i+1$ and $i-1$, with the convention that site $N+1$ is site 1, and sites N and 1 are neighbors. A configuration $\mathbf{x} \in \Lambda^S$ is denoted as $\mathbf{x} = [x_1, x_2, \ldots, x_N]$. Set $a = \frac{J}{kT}$, and $b = \frac{H}{kT}$, the Gibbs distribution becomes

$$\pi_T(\mathbf{x}) = \frac{1}{Z_T}e^{a\sum_{i=1}^N x_i x_{i+1} + b\sum_{i=1}^N x_i} ,$$

where the partition function is

$$Z_N = \sum_{\mathbf{x} \in \Lambda^S} e^{a\sum_{i=1}^N x_i x_{i+1} + b\sum_{i=1}^N x_i} .$$

Define the quantity

$$R(u, v) = e^{auv + \frac{1}{2}b(u+v)} ,$$

the partition function can be rewritten as,

$$Z_N = \sum_{\mathbf{x} \in \Lambda^S} R(x_1, x_2) R(x_2, x_3) \cdots R(X_N, x_1) \,. \tag{6.9}$$

Defining the transition matrix

$$\mathbf{P} = \begin{pmatrix} R(+1, +1) & R(+1, -1) \\ R(-1, +1) & R(-1, -1) \end{pmatrix} = \begin{pmatrix} e^{a+b} & e^{-a} \\ e^{-a} & e^{a-b} \end{pmatrix} \,,$$

we can rewrite (6.9) as follows

$$Z_N = \sum_{x_1 \in \Lambda} \sum_{x_1, \ldots, x_N \in \Lambda} R(x_1, x_2) R(x_2, x_3) \cdots R(x_n, x_1) = \sum_{x_1 \in \Lambda} \mathbf{P}^N(x_1, x_1) \,,$$

where $\mathbf{P}^N$ is the N-step transition matrix, and $\mathbf{P}^N(x_1, x_1)$ is the (x_1, x_1)'th element of the matrix. Obviously, Z_N is the trace of $\mathbf{P}^N$. In particular, if we denote by λ_+ and λ_- the eigenvalues of $\mathbf{P}$, then

$$Z_N = \lambda_+^N + \lambda_-^N \,.$$

With the above equality, we obtain the explicit formula of the Gibbs distribution as follows

$$\pi_T(\mathbf{x}) = \frac{1}{\lambda_+^N + \lambda_-^N} \, e^{a \sum_{i=1}^N x_i x_{i+1} + b \sum_{i=1}^N x_i} \,.$$

6.3 Gibbs – Markov Equivalence

Although Gibbs distributions and Markov random fields were developed in different contexts, they have been proven to be equivalent. This equivalence is more accurately stated by the following theorem.

Theorem 6.1 (Gibbs – Markov Equivalence). *A Gibbs distribution $\pi_T(\mathbf{x})$ of the following form*

$$\pi_T(\mathbf{x}) = \frac{1}{Z_T} e^{-\frac{1}{T} U(\mathbf{x})} \,,$$

with the energy $U(\mathbf{x})$ derived from a Gibbs potential $\{V_C\}_{C \in \mathcal{C}}$ relative to the neighborhood system N is Markovian relatively to the same neighborhood system. Moreover, its local specification is given by the formula

$$P^{(s)}(\mathbf{x}) = \frac{e^{-\sum_{C \leftarrow s} V_C(\mathbf{x})}}{\sum_{\lambda \in \Lambda} e^{-\sum_{C \leftarrow s} V_C(\lambda, \mathbf{x}(S-s))}} \,, \tag{6.10}$$

where the notion $\sum_{C \leftarrow s}$ means the summation over all the cliques that contain the site s.

Proof: The strategy here is to prove (6.10) satisfies the Markov property (6.1). More precisely, we need to first prove that the right-hand side of (6.10) equals $P(X(s) = x(s) \mid \mathbf{X}(S - s) = \mathbf{x}(S - s))$, and then prove that this quantity further equals $P(X(s) = x(s) \mid \mathbf{X}(N_s) = \mathbf{x}(N_s))$.

By definition of conditional property,

$$
\begin{aligned}
P(X(s) = x(s) \mid \mathbf{X}(S - s) = \mathbf{x}(S - s)) &= \frac{P(X(s) = x(s), \mathbf{X}(S - s) = \mathbf{x}(S - s))}{P(\mathbf{X}(S - s) = \mathbf{x}(S - s))} \\
&= \frac{P(\mathbf{X} = \mathbf{x})}{\sum_{\lambda \in \Lambda} P(\lambda, \mathbf{X}(S - s) = \mathbf{x}(S - s))} \\
&= \frac{\pi(\mathbf{x})}{\sum_{\lambda \in \Lambda} \pi(\lambda, \mathbf{x}(S - s))}
\end{aligned}
\tag{6.11}
$$

where the first and second steps in the above derivations are based on the Bayes's rules. Since

$$
\pi(\mathbf{x}) = \frac{1}{Z} \exp \left\{ - \sum_{C \leftarrow s} V_C(\mathbf{x}) - \sum_{C \not\leftarrow s} V_C(\mathbf{x}) \right\},
\tag{6.12}
$$

$$
\pi(\lambda, \mathbf{x}(S - s)) = \frac{1}{Z} \exp \left\{ - \sum_{C \leftarrow s} V_C(\lambda, \mathbf{x}(S - s)) - \sum_{C \not\leftarrow s} V_C(\lambda, \mathbf{x}(S - s)) \right\},
\tag{6.13}
$$

we can rewrite (6.11) as follows

$$
\begin{aligned}
&P(X(s) = x(s) \mid \mathbf{X}(S - s) = \mathbf{x}(S - s)) \\
&= \frac{\frac{1}{Z} \exp\{-\sum_{C \leftarrow s} V_C(\mathbf{x})\} \exp\{-\sum_{C \not\leftarrow s} V_C(\mathbf{x})\}}{\frac{1}{Z} \sum_{\lambda \in \Lambda} \left\{ \exp\{-\sum_{C \leftarrow s} V_C(\lambda, \mathbf{x}(S - s))\} \exp\{-\sum_{C \not\leftarrow s} V_C(\lambda, \mathbf{x}(S - s))\} \right\}} \\
&= \frac{\exp\{-\sum_{C \leftarrow s} V_C(\mathbf{x})\} \exp\{-\sum_{C \not\leftarrow s} V_C(\mathbf{x})\}}{\exp\{-\sum_{C \not\leftarrow s} V_C(\mathbf{x})\} \sum_{\lambda \in \Lambda} \exp\{-\sum_{C \leftarrow s} V_C(\lambda, \mathbf{x}(S - s))\}} \\
&= \frac{e^{- \sum_{C \leftarrow s} V_C(\mathbf{x})}}{\sum_{\lambda \in \Lambda} e^{- \sum_{C \leftarrow s} V_C(\lambda, \mathbf{x}(S - s))}}
\end{aligned}
\tag{6.14}
$$

In the above derivations, the second equality is based on the fact that if C is a clique and s is not in C, then $V_C(\lambda, \mathbf{x}(S - s)) = V_C(\mathbf{x})$ and therefore is independent of $\lambda \in \Lambda$.

Note that the right-hand side of (6.14) is the same as the right-hand side of (6.10), and it depends on $\mathbf{x}$ only through $x(s)$ and the cliques containing s. Therefore,

$$P^{(s)}(\mathbf{x}) = P(X(s) = x(s) \mid \mathbf{X}(S - s) = \mathbf{x}(S - s))$$
$$= P(X(s) = x(s) \mid \mathbf{X}(N_s) = \mathbf{x}(N_s)) . \tag{6.15}$$

Since the Gibbs distribution satisfies the above Markov property, it is Markovian. (proof-end).

Theorem (6.1) shows that a Gibbs distribution is Markovian. The following theorem further reveals that the converse part is also true. Therefore, the two theorems together conclude that Gibbs distributions and Markov random fields are essentially the same objects, with a provision stated below.

Theorem 6.2. *Let $\pi(\mathbf{x})$ be the probability distribution of a Markov random field with respect to a state space S and a neighborhood system N that satisfies the positivity condition. Then, $\pi(\mathbf{x})$ can be defined as*

$$\pi(\mathbf{x}) = \frac{1}{Z} e^{-U(\mathbf{x})}$$

where $U(\mathbf{x})$ is an energy function derived from a Gibbs potential $\{V_C\}_{C \in \mathcal{C}}$ associated with the same state space S and neighborhood system N.

The proof of the theorem is based on the Mobius formula, and can be found in [37].

Given a Gibbs distribution, the *local energy* at site s of configuration $\mathbf{x}$ is defined as

$$U_s(\mathbf{x}) = \sum_{C \leftarrow s} V_C(\mathbf{x}) . \tag{6.16}$$

With this notation, (6.10) becomes

$$P^{(s)}(\mathbf{x}) = \frac{e^{-U_s(\mathbf{x})}}{\sum_{\lambda \in \Lambda} e^{-U_s(\lambda, \mathbf{x}(S-s))}} . \tag{6.17}$$

Example 6.3. Local Specification of Ising Model
Using (6.10), the local specification of the Ising model becomes

$$P^{(s)}(\mathbf{x}) = \frac{e^{\frac{1}{kT}\{J \sum_{t:|t-s|=1} x(t)+H\}x(s)}}{e^{+\frac{1}{kT}\{J \sum_{t:|t-s|=1} x(t)+H\}} + e^{-\frac{1}{kT}\{J \sum_{t:|t-s|=1} x(t)+H\}}} . \tag{6.18}$$

The local energy at s is

$$U_s(\mathbf{x}) = \frac{1}{k}\left\{ J \sum_{t:|t-s|=1} x(t) + H \right\} x(s) . \tag{6.19}$$

6.4 Gibbs Sampling

As described in Sect. 6.2, one can seldom obtain the explicit formula for a Gibbs distribution because the configuration space Λ^S is often too large to compute the partition function Z_T. Therefore, for many real problems, conducting sampling and simulations of target Gibbs distributions is the only way to obtain solutions. In this section, we present the Gibbs sampling method that is a special version of the Markov chain Monte Carlo simulation.

Consider a random field on S with phases in Λ, and with a probability distribution

$$\pi(\mathbf{x}) = \frac{1}{Z} e^{-U(\mathbf{x})} . \tag{6.20}$$

If we can make $\pi(\mathbf{x})$ as the stationary distribution of an irreducible aperiodic Markov chain, then its distribution at a large time n will be close to $\pi(\mathbf{x})$, and therefore, by analogy to the Markov chain Monte Carlo method, we will obtain a simulation of $\pi(\mathbf{x})$.

To realize the vision discussed above, we introduce a stochastic process $\{\mathbf{X}_n\}_{n\geq 0}$, where

$$\mathbf{X}_n = [X_n(s), s \in S], \quad X_n(s) \in \Lambda .$$

The state at time n of this process is a random field on S with phases in Λ, or equivalently, a random variable with values in the state space Λ^S. For simplicity, we assume that state space is finite. The stochastic process $\{\mathbf{X}_n\}_{n\geq 0}$ is called a *dynamic random field*.

Now the problem becomes how to identify a transition matrix for the above chain to make $\pi(\mathbf{x})$ its stationary distribution. The Gibbs sampler uses a strictly positive probability distribution q_s, $s \in S$, and the transition from $\mathbf{X}_n = \mathbf{x}$ to $\mathbf{X}_{n+1} = \mathbf{y}$ is made according to the following rule.

The new state $\mathbf{y}$ is obtained from the old state $\mathbf{x}$ by changing (or not) the phase at one site only. The site s to be changed at time n is selected independently of the past with probability q_s. When site s is selected, the new configuration $\mathbf{y}$ is constructed from the current configuration $\mathbf{x}$ as follows:

$$\mathbf{y} = [y(s), \mathbf{y}(S - s) = \mathbf{x}(S - s)] ,$$

where $y(s)$ is generated with probability $\pi(y(s) \mid \mathbf{x}(S - s))$. This operation produces the non-zero entries of the transition matrix as follows

$$P(\mathbf{X}_{n+1} = \mathbf{y} \mid \mathbf{X}_n = \mathbf{x}) = q_s \, \pi(y(s) \mid \mathbf{x}(S - s)) ,$$
$$\text{subject to} \quad \mathbf{y}(S - s) = \mathbf{x}(S - s) . \tag{6.21}$$

The corresponding chain is irreducible and aperiodic. To prove that $\pi(\mathbf{x})$ is the stationary distribution of the chain, we use the detailed balance test, which corresponds to proving the following equality

$$\pi(\mathbf{x})P(\mathbf{X}_{n+1} = \mathbf{y} \mid \mathbf{X}_n = \mathbf{x}) = \pi(\mathbf{y})P(\mathbf{X}_{n+1} = \mathbf{x} \mid \mathbf{X}_n = \mathbf{y}),$$

for all $\mathbf{x}, \mathbf{y} \in \Lambda^S$.

Proof: Putting (6.21) into the left-hand side of the above equation,

$$
\begin{aligned}
\pi(\mathbf{x})P(\mathbf{X}_{n+1} = \mathbf{y} \mid \mathbf{X}_n = \mathbf{x}) &= \pi(\mathbf{x})q_s\,\pi(y(s) \mid \mathbf{x}(S - s)) \\
&= \pi(\mathbf{x})q_s \frac{\pi(y(s) \mid \mathbf{x}(S - s))P(\mathbf{x}(S - s))}{P(\mathbf{x}(S - s))} \\
&= \pi(\mathbf{x})q_s \frac{\pi(y(s), \mathbf{x}(S - s))}{P(\mathbf{x}(S - s))} \\
&= \pi(y(s), \mathbf{x}(S - s))q_s \frac{\pi(\mathbf{x})}{P(\mathbf{x}(S - s))} \\
&= \pi(y(s), \mathbf{y}(S - s))q_s \frac{\pi(x(s), \mathbf{x}(S - s))}{P(\mathbf{x}(S - s))} \\
&= \pi(\mathbf{y})q_s \frac{\pi(x(s) \mid \mathbf{x}(S - s))P(\mathbf{x}(S - s))}{P(\mathbf{x}(S - s))} \\
&= \pi(\mathbf{y})q_s\pi(x(s) \mid \mathbf{x}(S - s)) \\
&= \pi(\mathbf{y})q_s\pi(x(s) \mid \mathbf{y}(S - S)) \\
&= \pi(\mathbf{y})P(\mathbf{X}_{n+1} = \mathbf{x} \mid \mathbf{X}_n = \mathbf{y})
\end{aligned}
$$

In the above derivations, equality 3 and 6 are based on the Bayes's rules, and the last equality is based on (6.21). Also, the condition $\mathbf{y}(S - s) = \mathbf{x}(S - s)$ was used repeatedly throughout the derivations. (proof-end).

In the above descriptions, a probability q_s, $s \in S$ was used to choose the site s whose phase is to be changed. In practice, the sites to be updated are not chosen at random, but instead are visited in a well-determined order $s(1), s(2), \ldots, s(N)$ periodically, where N is the total number of sites $s \in S$, and $\{s(i)\}_{1 \le i \le N}$ is an enumeration of all the sites of S, called a *scanning policy*. For image processing tasks, the most common scanning policy is the one that scans pixels of the input image line by line from the upper-left to the bottom-right corner of the image.

Let $\mathbf{X}_k$ be the image before the k'th update. At time k, site $s = k \bmod N$ is updated to produce the new image $\mathbf{X}_{k+1}$. If $\mathbf{X}_n = \mathbf{x}$, then $\mathbf{X}_{n+1} = [y(s), \mathbf{x}(S - s)]$ with probability $\pi(y(s) \mid \mathbf{x}(S - s))$. Obviously, this update scheme uses the probability q_s defined as follows

$$q_s(k) = \begin{cases} 1, & \text{if } s = k \bmod N, \\ 0, & \text{othersise}. \end{cases} \tag{6.22}$$

where $q_s(k)$ is the probability q_s at time k. It can be proven that the Gibbs distribution $\pi(\mathbf{x})$ is the stationary distribution for the irreducible aperiodic Markov chain $\{\mathbf{X}_k\}_{k \geq 0}$ generated above (see Problem 6.7 at the end of the Chapter).

From the above descriptions, one can clearly observe the analogy between Gibbs sampling and the Markov chain Montel Carlo simulation. Indeed, both the algorithms strive to construct an irreducible aperiodic Markov chain, and to make the chain's stationary distribution π equal to the target distribution. In this sense, we say that Gibbs sampling is a special version of the MCMC simulation.

From the implementation's point of view, Gibbs sampling uses the local specification $P^{(s)}$ of the Markov random field to construct the transition matrix $\mathbf{P}$, whereas MCMC needs to first construct a candidate-generating matrix $\mathbf{Q}$, and then makes some twist on it to obtain $\mathbf{P}$. As discussed in Sect. 5.6, to make a fast-converging MCMC, one needs to design a candidate-generating matrix $\mathbf{Q}$ that is close enough to the target transition matrix $\mathbf{P}$, which is a challenging task, especially when one has a limited knowledge about the target distribution. Therefore, for the problems where their local specifications can be defined, Gibbs sampling is a more convenient way to sample/simulate their distributions.

Clearly, Gibbs sampling applies to any multivariate probability distribution

$$P(x(1), \ldots, x(N))$$

on a set N with the phase space Λ. In the literature, there are many research studies that apply Gibbs sampling, and more generally, Monte Carlo Markov chain simulation, outside physics, especially in the areas of image processing, statistics, and bio informatics.

The basic step of Gibbs sampling for a multivariate distribution $P(x(1), \ldots, x(N))$ consists of selecting a coordinate number $i \in [1, N]$ at random, and choosing the new value $y(i)$ of the corresponding coordinate, with probability

$$P(y(i) \mid x(1), \ldots, x(i-1), x(i+1), \ldots, x(N)).$$

It is easy to verify that P is the stationary distribution of the corresponding chain (see Problem 6.8 at the end of the chapter).

In summary, given the state space S, phase space Λ, and the local specification $\pi(x(s) \mid \mathbf{x}(S - s))$, Gibbs sampling generates a sequence of random samples $\{\mathbf{x}_n\}_{n \geq 0}$ that follow the Gibbs distribution $\pi(\mathbf{x})$ with the following steps:

1. Set the initial configuration $\mathbf{x} = \mathbf{0}$, and $n = 0$. Let N_1 be the number of iterations for the operation.
2. Select a site $s \in S$ either with probability q_s, or according to some predefined scanning policy.
3. Change the phase at site s to $y(s) \in \Lambda$ with probability $\pi(y(s) \mid \mathbf{x}(S-s))$.
4. Construct the new configuration

$$\mathbf{y} = [y(s),\ \mathbf{y}(S - s) = \mathbf{x}(S - s)] ,$$

   and output $\mathbf{y}$.
5. Set $\mathbf{x} = \mathbf{y}$, $n = n + 1$. If $n < N_1$, go to Step 2; otherwise, terminate the sampling process.

6.5 Simulated Annealing

Simulated annealing is a generic optimization algorithm that aims to locate a good approximation to the global optimum of a given function in a large search space. It was independently invented by Kirkpatrick, *et al.* in 1983 [38] and by Cerny in 1985 [39].

The method originates from the inspiration of annealing in metallurgy, a technique involving heating and controlled cooling of a metal to increase the size of its crystals and to reduce its defects.

In order to apply the simulated annealing method to a specific problem, one must specify the following model components:

- **State space** S, which consists of each point s of the entire search space.
- **Neighborhood**, which is defined for each state $s \in S$ as a subset $N(s)$ of S. $N(s)$ essentially defines the set of adjacent states that are the candidates for the annealing process to visit next.
- **Transition probability** $P_{ij}(T)$, which defines the probability of transiting from the current state i to a candidate new state j. $P_{ij}(T)$ is generally a function of the energies of the two states i and j, and of a global time-varying parameter T called the temperature: $P_{ij}(T) = P(U(i), U(j), T)$.

- **Annealing schedule**, which defines the schedule to gradually reduce the temperature as the simulation proceeds. Initially, T is set to a high (or infinity) value; it is decreased at each step according to the annealing schedule, and must end with $T = 0$ towards the end of the simulation process.

Let $U : S \to R$ be the function to be minimized. Using the simulated annealing method, the solution seeking process is conducted iteratively as follows: Suppose that at a given stage, a state $i \in S$ is examined. At the next stage, some neighbor state $j \in N(i)$ is chosen according to a rule specific to each algorithm, and the transition probability $P_{ij}(T) = P(U(i), U(j), T)$ is computed. State j is accepted with probability $P_{ij}(T)$; otherwise, the next state is the same state i.

During the above iterative solution seeking process, the temperature T is gradually reduced to zero according to the annealing schedule to control the transition probability. At time n, $T = T_n$, and the transition probability $P_{ij}(T) = P(U(i), U(j), T_n)$.

One essential requirement for the transition probability $P_{ij}(T)$ is that it must be strictly positive for all $i, j \in S$, and all T. This means that the solution seeking process may move to a new state even when it is worse (has a higher energy) than the current one. It is this feature that prevents the method from becoming stuck in a local minimum.

On the other hand, when T goes to zero, the probability $P_{ij}(T) = P(U(i), U(j), T)$ must tend to zero if $U(j) > U(i)$, and to a positive value if $U(j) < U(i)$. With this scheme, for sufficiently small values of T, the algorithm will increasingly favor moves that go "downhill", and avoid those that go "uphill". In particular, when T becomes 0, the procedure will reduce to the greedy algorithm which makes the move if and only if it goes downhill.

The transition probability function $P(U(i), U(j), T)$ is usually chosen so that the probability of accepting a move decreases when the difference $U(j) - U(i)$ increases. That is, small uphill moves are more likely than large ones.

Using the transition probability with the above properties, the transition of state i to state j depends crucially on the temperature T. Roughly speaking, the state evolution is sensitive only to coarser energy variations when T is large, and to finer variations when T is small.

We use the following example to showcase a popular transition probability function for the simulated annealing method.

Example 6.4.

Assume that the current solution (state) at stage n is $i \in S$. At stage $n+1$, a tentative solution $j \in N(i)$ is selected according to some rules. This solution is accepted with probability

$$P_{ij}(T) = e^{-\frac{(U(j)-U(i))^+}{T}}, \tag{6.23}$$

where

$$(x)^+ = \begin{cases} x & \text{if } x \geq 0, \\ 0 & \text{otherwise.} \end{cases}$$

One can verify that the transition probability (6.23) carries all the necessary properties discussed above. First of all, it is strictly positive for all $i, j \in S$. Second, when the difference $U(j) - U(i)$ increases, $P_{ij}(T)$ decreases, meaning that it favors small uphill moves than large ones. Third, when T is large, $P_{ij}(T)$ is sensitive only to large changes in the difference $U(j) - U(i)$, whereas when T goes to zero, slight variations in $U(j) - U(i)$ can cause large changes in $P_{ij}(T)$.

In the following derivations, we reveal what is the stationary distribution of the annealing process, and how the stationary distribution changes when T approaches to zero.

The simulated annealing process using the transition probability (6.23) has the following stationary distribution $\boldsymbol{\pi}(T) = [\pi_i(T)]$

$$\pi_i(T) = \frac{e^{-\frac{U(i)}{T}}}{\sum_{k \in S} e^{-\frac{U(k)}{T}}}. \tag{6.24}$$

To verify this, we compute for all $i \in S$

$$\sum_{i \in S} \pi_i(T) P_{ij}(T) = \frac{\sum_{i \in S} e^{-\frac{U(i)}{T}} \cdot e^{-\frac{(U(j)-U(i))^+}{T}}}{\sum_{k \in S} e^{-\frac{U(k)}{T}}}$$

$$= \frac{e^{-\frac{U(j)}{T}}}{\sum_{k \in S} e^{-\frac{U(k)}{T}}}$$

$$= \pi_j(T).$$

This proves that $\boldsymbol{\pi}^T(T) \mathbf{P}(T) = \boldsymbol{\pi}^T(T)$, which shows that $\boldsymbol{\pi}(T)$ is the stationary distribution for $\mathbf{P}(T)$ (the stationary distribution definition (5.28)).

Note that if we replace $U(i)$ in (6.24) with $\log U(i)$, the stationary distribution $\boldsymbol{\pi}(T)$ of the simulated annealing process becomes

$$\pi_i(T) = \frac{\exp(-\log U(i)^{\frac{1}{T}})}{\sum_{k \in S} \exp(-\log U(k)^{\frac{1}{T}})} = \frac{U(i)^{\frac{1}{T}}}{\sum_{k \in S} U(k)^{\frac{1}{T}}} , \qquad (6.25)$$

which exactly equals the distribution we seek for. Therefore, in real implementations, it is more convenient to use $\log U(i)$ in (6.23) instead of its original form.

Define the set of global minima

$$\mathcal{M} = \{i \in S \mid U(i) \leq U(j), \ \forall j \in S\} ,$$

and let m be the minimum value of the function $U(i)$: $m = \min_{i \in S} U(i)$. By dividing both the numerator and denominator of (6.24) with $e^{\frac{m}{T}}$, we have

$$\pi_i(T) = \frac{e^{-\frac{U(i)-m}{T}}}{\sum_{k \in S} e^{-\frac{U(k)-m}{T}}}$$

$$= \frac{e^{-\frac{U(i)-m}{T}}}{\sum_{k \in \mathcal{M}} e^{-\frac{U(k)-m}{T}} + \sum_{k \notin \mathcal{M}} e^{-\frac{U(k)-m}{T}}}$$

$$= \frac{e^{-\frac{U(i)-m}{T}}}{|\mathcal{M}| + \sum_{k \notin \mathcal{M}} e^{-\frac{U(k)-m}{T}}} , \qquad (6.26)$$

where the third equality in the above derivations uses the fact $U(k) = m$ if $k \in \mathcal{M}$. In (6.26), when T approaches zero, $e^{-\frac{U(k)-m}{T}}$ tends to zero if $U(k) > m$, and to one if $U(k) = m$. Therefore, at the limit $T \to 0$, $\pi_i(T)$ becomes

$$\lim_{T \to 0} \pi_i(T) = \begin{cases} \frac{1}{|\mathcal{M}|} & \text{if } i \in \mathcal{M} , \\ 0 & \text{if } i \notin \mathcal{M} . \end{cases} \qquad (6.27)$$

At the beginning of this section, it is stated that one needs to specify the annealing schedule to set the temperature T to a high value (or infinity) at the start, and gradually reduces the temperature as the simulation proceeds. The purpose of this scheme is to make the solution seeking process to initially wander among a broad region of the search space that may contain good solutions, then drift towards low-energy regions that become narrower and narrower, and finally move downhill according to the steepest descent heuristic.

The result in (6.27) suggests the following annealing schedule: Start the annealing process with $T = a_0$, and wait a sufficiently long time for the process to get close to its stationary regime. Then set $T = a_1 < a_0$, and again wait for the steady state. Repeat this procedure till T approaches zero. At the stage $T \to 0$, one can expect that the state i generated by the annealing process will be in $\mathcal{M}$, the set of global minima, with very high probability.

We use the following example to demonstrate how simulated annealing can be combined with MCMC simulation, and to visualize the effect of temperature reduction on the simulated annealing process.

Example 6.5.
This example is the continuation of **Example 5.5** in Chap. 5. Same as in **Example 5.5**, the target density function $P(\mathbf{X})$ to be simulated is defined by (5.58), and a Gaussian distribution with unit variance is used as the candidate-generating function (the transition probability P_{ij})[1]. Here, we define $P(\mathbf{X})(T)$ as

$$P(\mathbf{X})(T) = P(\mathbf{X})^{\frac{1}{T}} . \tag{6.28}$$

The entire simulation process is the same as described in **Example 5.5** except for that the temperature T is set to a large value at the beginning, and is gradually reduced according to a predefined annealing schedule.

Figure 6.2 (a) and (b) show the trajectories of state transitions in the 2-D space $\mathbf{X} = (X_1, X_2)$ generated by the MCMC simulation at the temperatures $T = 10$, and $T = 1$, respectively. The dotted lines in the figures depict the contour map of the target density function. The swimming-pool shaped contours centered at $(5, 3)$ correspond to the tall heap, while the ellipse shaped contours centered at $(0, 0)$ correspond to the short heap of the target density function (see Fig. 5.9). It can be clearly observed from the contour map that the tall heap resides at energy levels higher than the short heap. It is also obvious that, when temperature T is high, the simulation process wanders among a broad region of the search space, and visits both heaps of the target function. When temperature is low, the state transition trajectory is confined within a narrow, low-energy region that corresponds to the short heap, and the tall heap is no longer visited by the simulation process. Therefore, sampling at high temperatures is the key to the success of sampling the tall heap of the target density function.

Another important aspect of the simulated annealing method is the definition of the neighborhood structure. The neighborhood $N(s)$ of a state s

---

[1] Note that in this example we used the fixed transition probability P_{ij} that is independent of the temperature T.

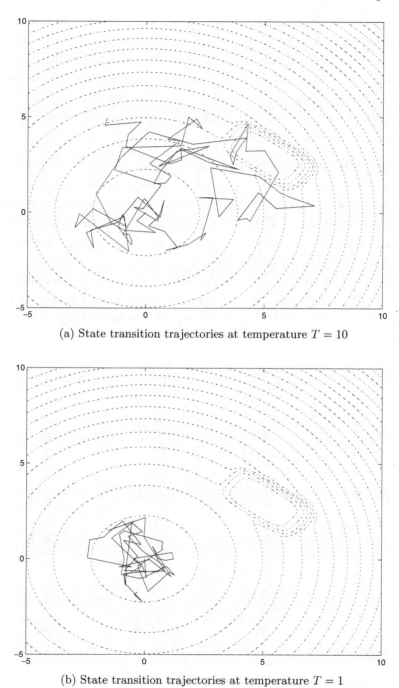

(a) State transition trajectories at temperature $T = 10$

(b) State transition trajectories at temperature $T = 1$

Fig. 6.2. Effect of temperature changes on the simulated annealing process

must consists of the adjacent states that are "good enough" for the annealing process to visit next. The neighborhood definition is particularly critical because it can have a significant impact on the effectiveness of the annealing method. In practice, a rule of thumb is to select such a neighborhood system that neighbors of s are expected to have about the same energy as s.

We use the following example to describe the neighborhood definition for the traveling salesman problem.

Example 6.6. The Traveling Salesman Problem

This problem aims to find the shortest route for a salesman who wants to visit each of K cities exactly once. We define the state space S as the set of $K!$ admissible routes, $U(i)$ as the length of route i. One popular choice for the neighborhood $N(i)$ of route i is the set of all routes j obtained by interchanging a pair of adjacent cities in i.

Let $(\alpha, \alpha + 1)$, and $(\beta - 1, \beta)$ be two pairs of adjacent cities in route i (see Fig. 6.3). The interchange involving cities α and β is conducted by cutting the segments $(\alpha, \alpha + 1)$ and $(\beta - 1, \beta)$, and replacing them by the new segments $(\alpha, \beta - 1)$ and $(\alpha + 1, \beta)$.

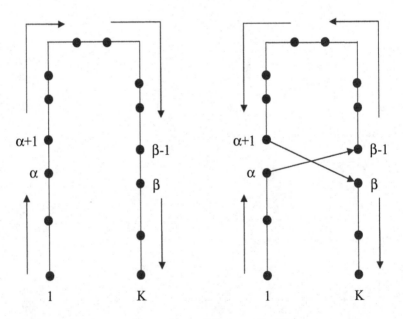

Fig. 6.3. Two neighbor routes of the traveling salesman problem

In such a construction of salesman's routes, there are exactly $K(K-1)+1$ neighbors of a give route. The size of the neighborhood is therefore reasonable in comparison to the size of the entire search space. Note also that the computation of $U(j)$ from the result of $U(i)$ involves only four intercity distances when $j \in N(i)$.

In summary, given the function $U(i)$ to be minimized, the simulated annealing method strives to find the global minimum of $U(i)$ with the following main operations:

1. Define the state space S, the neighborhood $N(s)$ for each state $s \in S$, the probability function $P_{ij}(T) = P(U(i), U(j), T)$ for $i, j \in S$, and the annealing schedule. Let N_1 be the number of iterations for each temperature T, and N_2 be the number of stages for the annealing schedule.
2. Set the initial state $i = i_0$, $n = 0$, $k = 0$, and $T_k = \infty$.
3. Select the next candidate state $j \in N(i)$ according to some predefined rules, and compute the transition probability $P_{ij}(T_k)$.
4. Accept state j with probability $P_{ij}(T_k)$; otherwise, the next state is the same state i.
5. Set $i = j$, $n = n + 1$. If $n < N_1$, go to Step 3; otherwise, go to Step 6.
6. Set $k = k + 1$. If $k < N_2$, reduce T_k according to the annealing schedule, and go to Step 3; otherwise, return state i as the final solution, and terminate the annealing process.

6.6 Case Study: Video Foreground Object Segmentation by MRF

In this case study, we present our original work that applies Markov random field to the video foreground object segmentation task [40]. We first briefly describe the objective of this work, and provide an overview of the entire foreground object segmentation process. Then we provide detailed explanations on the Markov random field model and the Gibbs sampling algorithm that are used to generate dense foreground/background layers from sparse ones. Finally, we present foreground object segmentation results using two real videos that contain both rigid and non-rigid foreground objects.

6.6.1 Objective

Segmentation of foreground objects from background has a lot of applications in object tracking, video compression, human-computer interaction, multimedia content editing and manipulation. Now with the prevalence of broadband Internet, multimedia-enabled personal computers and 3G cellphones, home users can easily establish video connections with friends by which they can see each other's faces and objects of interest. Such developments have opened up new opportunities for various value-added services and applications, and we believe that the foreground object segmentation techniques have a great potential as an enabling tool for accomplishing such tasks as bandwidth reduction, privacy protection, personalized video content editing and hallucination, etc.

In this case study, we present a fully automatic foreground object segmentation method that aims at applications for 3G cellphone and home broadband Internet users. In particular, we are interested in such applications that the user takes video images of his/her face or other objects of interest using a cellphone or a webcam, and wants to send the video clip to another person with the background either eliminated or hallucinated. We assume that the video clip can contain both rigid and non-rigid objects; there always exist motions caused by either moving cameras or moving objects; and the video capturing/transmission device has quite limited computation and storage resources. Indeed, these assumptions account for most of the common usage conditions for this type of applications.

6.6.2 Related Works

To date, most works related to the task of foreground object segmentation can be categorized into the following three categories:

- Motion-based segmentation,
- Multi-cue object segmentation, and
- Alpha matting.

Motion-based segmentation approaches compute optical follows for each pixel, and cluster pixels or color segments into regions of coherent motions. Many approaches solve the problem through an Expectation-Maximization (EM) process to estimate the parametric motion models and the supporting regions [41, 42, 43, 44, 45]. There are also many research studies that group pixels or segments into layers based on the affinity of local measurements [46, 47, 48, 49].

In many cases, motion or color clues alone are not sufficient to distinguish objects because different objects may share similar colors or motions. There have been research efforts that strive to combine spatial and temporal features for improved segmentations [50, 51, 52]. Ke and Kanade [51] described a factorization method to perform rigid layer segmentation in a subspace because all the layers share the same camera motion. Wang and Ji [52] presented a dynamic conditional random field model to combine both intensity and motion cues to achieve segmentations.

On the other hand, video matting is a classic inverse problem in computer vision that involves the extraction of foreground objects and the alpha mattes that describe the opacity of each pixel from image sequences [53, 54, 55, 56, 57, 58, 59]. Apostoloff and Fitzgibbon [56] presented their matting approach for natural scenes assuming the camera was static and the background was known. Wang and Cohen [53] described a unified segmentation and matting approach based on Belief Propagation, which iteratively estimates the opacity value for every pixel in the image using a small sample of foreground and background pixels marked by the user. Li et al. [54] used a 3D graph cut-based segmentation followed by a tracking-based local refinement to obtain a binary segmentation of the video objects, and adopted coherent matting [60] as a prior to produce the alpha matte of the objects.

The methods described above, as well as many others in the literature are generally computationally expensive because (1) they conduct object segmentations on pixel or color blob levels, and (2) they need to compute optical flows for all pixels, which requires a huge amount of computations. Furthermore, many alpha matting approaches are not fully automatic, and often require users to provide the initialization or fine-tuning to the segmentation process.

6.6.3 Method Outline

As described in Sect. 6.6.1, our foreground object segmentation method aims at applications for 3G cellphone and home broadband Internet users, and therefore, it must be able to handle any type of objects, and must be very efficient in computation and storage. We take the following approaches to overcome these challenges.

First, we assume that the input video sequence is composed of two motion layers: foreground and the background, and that the two motion layers follow affine transformations. Although such an assumption will limit our ability to model complex scenes, it is sufficient to model the most common usage patterns for cellphone and home Internet users.

Second, we strive to compute sparse motion layers first, using sparse image features such as edge and corner points extracted from each video frame. This approach will dramatically reduce the computational cost because compared to dense motion layers, it involves much fewer pixels for the costly computation and clustering of optical flows. The joint spatio-temporal linear regression method is developed to compute sparse motion layers of M consecutive frames jointly under the temporal consistency constraint. This method aims to generate more reliable and temporally smoother motion layers for the entire input video sequence.

Third, once the two sparse motion layers have been identified for edge and corner points, we create the corresponding dense motion layers by using the Markov Random Field (MRF) model. The MRF model assigns the rest of the pixels to either of the motion layers by considering both the color attributes and the spatial relations between each pixel and its surrounding edge/corner points. By taking the above approaches together, we strive to accomplish the task of foreground object segmentation with low computation cost and high segmentation accuracy.

In the subsequent section, we will skip the descriptions of the sparse motion layer computation algorithm, and will focus on the creation of dense motion layers using an MRF model. Detailed descriptions of the entire method can be found in [40].

6.6.4 Overview of Sparse Motion Layer Computation

We extract both corner and edge points from each video frame using the Canny edge detector [61], and compute optical flows at the extracted feature points using the Lucas-Kanade method [62]. The set of extracted feature points together with their optical flows form the input to the sparse motion layer computation module.

Let (x_i, y_i) denote a pixel site, and $(\delta x_i, \delta y_i)$ denote the optical flow value at (x_i, y_i). An affine motion model is defined by the following equations:

$$\delta x_i = ax_i + by_i + c \tag{6.29}$$

$$\delta y_i = dx_i + ey_i + f \tag{6.30}$$

where a, b, c, d, e, f are the six parameters defining an Affine transformation. The outcome of the sparse motion layer computation is the two Affine motion models $\mathcal{A}_1 = (a_1, b_1, c_1, d_1, e_1, f_1)$ and $\mathcal{A}_2 = (a_2, b_2, c_2, d_2, e_2, f_2)$, and the two sets of feature points $\mathcal{F}, \mathcal{B}$ that minimize the following Residue Sum of Squares (RSS) function:

$$\mathbf{RSS}(\mathcal{A}_1, \mathcal{A}_2, \mathcal{F}, \mathcal{B}) =$$

$$\sum_{(x_i, y_i) \in \mathcal{F}} \left\| \begin{bmatrix} \delta x_i \\ \delta y_i \end{bmatrix} - \begin{bmatrix} a_1 & b_1 & c_1 \\ d_1 & e_1 & f_1 \end{bmatrix} \cdot \begin{bmatrix} x_i \\ y_i \\ 1 \end{bmatrix} \right\|^2 +$$

$$\sum_{(x_j, y_j) \in \mathcal{B}} \left\| \begin{bmatrix} \delta x_j \\ \delta y_j \end{bmatrix} - \begin{bmatrix} a_2 & b_2 & c_2 \\ d_2 & e_2 & f_2 \end{bmatrix} \cdot \begin{bmatrix} x_j \\ y_j \\ 1 \end{bmatrix} \right\|^2 \tag{6.31}$$

Introducing $\mathbf{x}_i = \begin{bmatrix} x_i \\ y_i \end{bmatrix}$, $\nabla \mathbf{x}_i = \begin{bmatrix} \delta x_i \\ \delta y_i \end{bmatrix}$, and $\mathbf{A}_l = \begin{bmatrix} a_l & b_l & c_l \\ d_l & e_l & f_l \end{bmatrix}$, we can then rewrite (6.31) in a compact form as follows

$$\mathbf{RSS}(\mathcal{A}_1, \mathcal{A}_2, \mathcal{F}, \mathcal{B}) =$$

$$\sum_{\mathbf{x}_i \in \mathcal{F}} \left\| \nabla \mathbf{x}_i - \mathbf{A}_1 \cdot \begin{bmatrix} \mathbf{x}_i \\ 1 \end{bmatrix} \right\|^2 + \sum_{\mathbf{x}_j \in \mathcal{B}} \left\| \nabla \mathbf{x}_j - \mathbf{A}_2 \cdot \begin{bmatrix} \mathbf{x}_j \\ 1 \end{bmatrix} \right\|^2 \tag{6.32}$$

In (6.32), $\nabla \mathbf{x}_i$ is the observed optical flow at pixel site $\mathbf{x}_i$, and $\mathbf{A}_l \cdot \begin{bmatrix} \mathbf{x}_i \\ 1 \end{bmatrix}$ is the optical flow at the same pixel site estimated by the Affine motion model $\mathcal{A}_l$. Minimizing this **RSS** function is equivalent to minimizing the difference between the observed and the estimated optical flows for each $\mathbf{x}_i$. In [40], we developed the joint spatio-temporal linear regression method to efficiently compute sparse motion layers of M consecutive frames jointly under the temporal consistency constraint. Here, we omit the description of the algorithm, and only show the two results generated by the method.

Figure 6.4 show two examples of the sparse motion layer computation. Figure 6.4(a) and (c) show sample frames from two video sequences: one is composed of a static rigid foreground object (a calendar) and arbitrary camera motions, while the other is composed of a moving non-rigid foreground object (a human) and arbitrary camera motions. Figure 6.4(b) and (d) show the sparse motion layers computed from the frames in (a) and (c), respectively. In (c) and (d), each visible point is a feature point extracted from

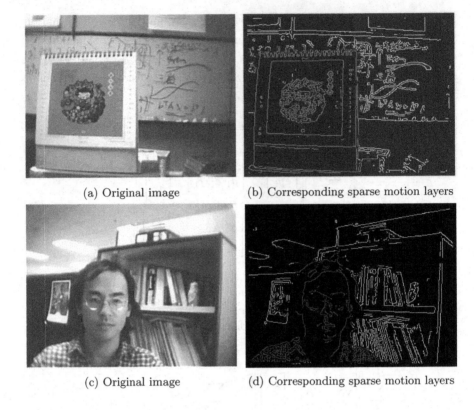

(a) Original image   (b) Corresponding sparse motion layers

(c) Original image   (d) Corresponding sparse motion layers

Fig. 6.4. Examples of sparse motion layer computation

the corresponding frame. Feature points with a high brightness belong to the background motion layer, while feature points with a dark brightness belong to the foreground motion layer. Obviously, the feature points have been appropriately segmented, and the foreground and background layers are correctly separated for these two video frames.

6.6.5 Dense Motion Layer Computation Using MRF

For a video frame $\mathbf{X} = \{\mathbf{x}_i\}$, the sparse motion layer computation generates two Affine motion models $\mathcal{A}_1 = (a_1, b_1, c_1, d_1, e_1, f_1)$, $\mathcal{A}_2 = (a_2, b_2, c_2, d_2, e_2, f_2)$, and a sparse motion layer label $\mathbf{Y}$ in which each element y_i can take one of the three values: 0, 1, 2, which indicate that pixel i in $\mathbf{X}$ is a non-feature point, a foreground feature point, and a background feature point, respectively. Given $\mathbf{X}$, $\mathcal{A} = (\mathcal{A}_1, \mathcal{A}_2)$, and $\mathbf{Y}$, our task here is to generate a dense motion layer label $\mathbf{L}$ to maximize the following *a posteriori* probability

$$\hat{\mathbf{L}} = \arg\max_{\mathbf{L}} P(\mathbf{L}|\mathbf{X}, \mathbf{Y}, \mathcal{A}) \tag{6.33}$$

where elements l_i in $\mathbf{L}$ can be either 1 or 2 to indicate that pixel i belongs to the foreground or the background layer, respectively. This type of probabilistic inference is called the *maximum a posterior* (MAP) estimation method. Before the start of the dense motion layer computation, $\mathbf{L}$ is initialized to $\mathbf{L} = \mathbf{Y}$. This means that all non-feature points i will have their labels equal to zero: $l_i = 0$. The task of the dense motion layer computation is to assign an appropriate label $l_i \in \{1, 2\}$ for all pixels i, including those feature points (labels l_i of those feature points i could be different from their sparse motion layer labels y_i).

To use the Markov random field method to model the above a posterior probability, we define a random field on a site space S, where site $i \in S$ corresponds to pixel i in $\mathbf{X}$, with a phase space $\Lambda = \{1, 2\}$. On the site space S, the 4-neighbor system and the corresponding two types of cliques are adopted: singleton clique $\{i\}$ that is composed of each single site $i \in S$, and 2-element clique $\{i, j\}$ that is composed of $i \in S$ and one of the four neighbors $j \in N(i)$ (see Fig. 6.1(a)). The Gibbs potential is defined as follows

$$V_{\{i\}}(\mathbf{L}|\mathbf{X}, \mathbf{Y}, \mathcal{A}) = \begin{cases} 0, & \text{if } l_i = 0 , \\ \left\| \nabla \mathbf{x}_i - \mathbf{A}_{l_i} \begin{bmatrix} \mathbf{x}_i \\ 1 \end{bmatrix} \right\|^2, & \text{otherwise,} \end{cases} \tag{6.34}$$

$$V_{\{i,j\}}^{(1)}(\mathbf{L}|\mathbf{X}) = \delta(l_i \neq l_j) \exp\left\{ -\|c(i) - c(j)\|^2/\sigma^2 \right\} , \tag{6.35}$$

$$V_{\{i,j\}}^{(2)}(\mathbf{L}|\mathbf{X}, \mathbf{Y}) = \begin{cases} 0, & \text{if } y_i = 0 \, || \, y_j = 0, \\ \delta(l_i \neq l_j)\|\mathbf{d}_{ij} \times \mathbf{d}_i\| \cdot \|\mathbf{d}_{ij} \times \mathbf{d}_j\|, & \text{otherwise,} \end{cases}$$
$$\tag{6.36}$$

where in (6.34), if $l_i = 1$, then $\mathbf{A}_{l_i}$ is the affine transformation corresponding to the foreground, if $l_i = 2$, then $\mathbf{A}_{l_i}$ is the affine transformation corresponding to the background; in (6.35), $c(i)$ is the RGB color values at pixel i, σ is a predefined parameter; in (6.36), $\mathbf{d}_{ij}$ is the unit vector connecting from point i to point j, $\mathbf{d}_i$ is the unit norm vector at edge point i, and $\mathbf{x} \times \mathbf{y}$ is the cross product between vectors $\mathbf{x}$ and $\mathbf{y}$.

With the above potential functions, the corresponding energy function becomes

$$U(\mathbf{L}|\mathbf{X}, \mathbf{Y}, \mathcal{A}) = \alpha \sum_{i \in S} V_{\{i\}}(\mathbf{L}|\mathbf{X}, \mathbf{Y}, \mathcal{A})$$

$$+ \beta \sum_{\{i,j\}} V^{(1)}_{\{i,j\}}(\mathbf{L}|\mathbf{X})$$

$$+ \gamma \sum_{\{i,j\}} V^{(2)}_{\{i,j\}}(\mathbf{L}|\mathbf{X}, \mathbf{Y}), \tag{6.37}$$

where the sums extend over the entire site space S for which the indicated cliques make sense, and α, β, γ are the predefined weight parameters. With the above energy function, the a posterior probability is defined as

$$P(\mathbf{L}|\mathbf{X}, \mathbf{Y}, \mathcal{A}) \propto \frac{1}{Z} \exp\left\{-\frac{1}{T} U(\mathbf{L}|\mathbf{X}, \mathbf{Y}, \mathcal{A})\right\}, \tag{6.38}$$

where Z is the normalizing constant.

In the above potential function definitions, $V_{\{i\}}(\cdot)$ computes for site $i \in S$ the difference between the observed optical flow and the optical flow estimated by Affine motion model $\mathbf{A}_{l_i}$; $V^{(1)}_{\{i,j\}}(\cdot)$ takes a large value if the sites i and j have similar colors $c(i)$, $c(j)$ but different labels l_i, l_j; and $V^{(2)}_{\{i,j\}}(\cdot)$ becomes large if i and j reside on the same edge line but have different labels. Therefore, the labeling $\mathbf{L}$ that maximizes the a posterior probability $P(\mathbf{L}|\mathbf{X}, \mathbf{Y}, \mathcal{A})$, which is equivalent to minimize the energy function $U(\mathbf{L}|\mathbf{X}, \mathbf{Y}, \mathcal{A})$, is the one that

- minimizes the difference between the observed and the Affine estimated optical flows at each site $i \in S$;
- assigns the same label to two sites whose color values are similar;
- assigns the same label to two sites that reside on the same edge line.

6.6.6 Bayesian Inference

Given an observed image $\mathbf{X}$, we want to infer its label (or class) $\mathbf{Y}$ using the MAP estimation method:

$$\hat{\mathbf{Y}} = \arg\max_{\mathbf{Y}} P(\mathbf{Y}|\mathbf{X}).$$

By Bayes' rules, the a posterior probability $P(\mathbf{Y}|\mathbf{X})$ can be computed as follows

$$P(\mathbf{Y}|\mathbf{X}) \propto P(\mathbf{X}|\mathbf{Y})P(\mathbf{Y}), \tag{6.39}$$

where $P(\mathbf{X}|\mathbf{Y})$ is called the likelihood of $\mathbf{X}$ given $\mathbf{Y}$, and $P(\mathbf{Y})$ is called the a prior probability of $\mathbf{Y}$. The principle of Bayesian inference is that, instead of directly computing the a posteriori probability, we compute the likelihood and the a prior probability . The likelihood measures how well the observation $\mathbf{X}$ fits the inference $\mathbf{Y}$, while the a prior probability reflects the designer's prior knowledge on $\mathbf{Y}$. The likelihood measure can be considered as a cost function that aims to minimize the estimation error, while the a prior probability can be considered as a penalty that forces the inference process to reflect the designer's belief.

For the dense motion layer computation described in Sect. 6.6.5, we modeled the a posterior probability $P(\mathbf{L} \mid \mathbf{X}, \mathbf{Y}, \boldsymbol{\mathcal{A}})$ using the energy function defined in (6.37). Indeed, this energy function can be interpreted as a Bayesian inference. The potential function $V_{\{i\}}(\cdot)$ measures how well the labeling $\mathbf{L}$ fits into the Affine motion models $\boldsymbol{\mathcal{A}}$, while $V_{\{i,j\}}^{(1)}(\cdot)$ and $V_{\{i,j\}}^{(2)}(\cdot)$ reflect the designer's prior knowledge on $\mathbf{L}$. Therefore, we can regard $V_{\{i\}}(\cdot)$ as the likelihood measure, and $V_{\{i,j\}}^{(1)}(\cdot)$, $V_{\{i,j\}}^{(2)}(\cdot)$ as the a prior probability of $\mathbf{L}$. Without the a prior probability, the inference process will lead to a labeling that best fits the Affine motion models $\boldsymbol{\mathcal{A}}$. In case that certain parts of the background share the same motion with the foreground object, which is highly probable in many video sequences, this inference may not be able to fully separate the foreground object from the background. When we introduce a non-trivial a prior model into the inference process, it forces a balance between the designer's prior knowledge in the appropriate labeling and the effort of minimizing the model fitting errors. As described at the end of Sect. 6.6.5, $V_{\{i,j\}}^{(1)}(\cdot)$, $V_{\{i,j\}}^{(2)}(\cdot)$ encourage the assignment of the same label to pixels with similar colors, and to pixels residing on the same edge segment, respectively. It is these priors that ensure a correct labeling when the Affine motion models alone are not sufficient to separate the foreground object from the background.

6.6.7 Solution Computation by Gibbs Sampling

The dense motion layer computation strives to generate the labeling $\mathbf{L}$ that maximizes the a posterior probability $P(\mathbf{L} \mid \mathbf{X}, \mathbf{Y}, \boldsymbol{\mathcal{A}})$. However, as this probability is defined by (6.38), for which one can not obtain its explicit formula, Gibbs sampling with simulated annealing is a practical means for finding an approximated solution for this problem.

By Theorem 6.1, the local specification of (6.38) is defined as

$$P^{(i)}(\mathbf{L}|\mathbf{X}, \mathbf{Y}, \boldsymbol{\mathcal{A}}) = \frac{e^{-\Theta_1(i, \mathbf{L}, \mathbf{X}, \mathbf{Y}, \boldsymbol{\mathcal{A}})}}{\sum_{l_i \in \{1,2\}} e^{-\Theta_2(i, l_i, \mathbf{L}, \mathbf{X}, \mathbf{Y}, \boldsymbol{\mathcal{A}})}} , \qquad (6.40)$$

where

$$\Theta_1(i, \mathbf{L}, \mathbf{X}, \mathbf{Y}, \mathcal{A}) = \alpha \ V_{\{i\}}(\mathbf{L} \mid \mathbf{X}, \mathbf{Y}, \mathcal{A})$$
$$+ \beta \sum_{\{i,j\}:j \in N(i)} V_{\{i,j\}}^{(1)}(\mathbf{L} \mid \mathbf{X})$$
$$+ \gamma \sum_{\{i,j\}:j \in N(i)} V_{\{i,j\}}^{(2)}(\mathbf{L} \mid \mathbf{X}, \mathbf{Y}) ,$$

and

$$\Theta_2(i, l_i, \mathbf{L}, \mathbf{X}, \mathbf{Y}, \mathcal{A}) = \alpha \ V_{\{i\}}(l_i, \mathbf{L}(S - i) \mid \mathbf{X}, \mathbf{Y}, \mathcal{A})$$
$$+ \beta \sum_{\{i,j\}:j \in N(i)} V_{\{i,j\}}^{(1)}(l_i, \mathbf{L}(S - i) \mid \mathbf{X})$$
$$+ \gamma \sum_{\{i,j\}:j \in N(i)} V_{\{i,j\}}^{(2)}(l_i, \mathbf{L}(S - i) \mid \mathbf{X}, \mathbf{Y}) .$$

Note that $\mathbf{L}(S - i)$ in the above equalities denotes the labels at all sites $s \in S$ except for site i.

With the above local specification definition, the Gibbs sampling for the dense motion layer computation is implemented as follows:

1. Set the initial configuration $\mathbf{L} = \mathbf{Y}$, $U_{min} = \infty$, $\mathbf{L}_{max} = 0$, and $n = 0$. Let N_1 be the number of iterations for the operation.
2. Select a site $i \in S$ according to the top-down, left-right scanning order.
3. Change the label at site i to $l_i \in \{1, 2\}$ with probability $P^{(i)}(\mathbf{L}|\mathbf{X}, \mathbf{Y}, \mathcal{A})$ defined by (6.40).
4. Construct the new configuration $\mathbf{L} = [l_i, \ \mathbf{L}(S - i)]$, and compute the energy $U(\mathbf{L}|\mathbf{X}, \mathbf{Y}, \mathcal{A})$.
5. If $U_{min} > U(\cdot)$, then set $U_{min} = U(\cdot)$ and $\mathbf{L}_{max} = \mathbf{L}$. Increment n by one. If $n < N_1$, go to Step 2; otherwise, output $\mathbf{L}_{max}$, and terminate the sampling process.

To further avoid the local maxima problem, we construct a pyramid for each video frame $\mathbf{X}$, and conduct the inference at each pyramid layer. The original video frame is at the bottom of the pyramid, and the upper layer is constructed by down-sampling the lower layer of the pyramid. The labeling process starts from the top layer, and the result is used as the initial label configuration of the lower layer. This process is repeated until the bottom layer is reached. Because at the top-layer image, all image details except for prominent features are eliminated, it is more probable that one obtains a good approximation to the globally optimal solution at this layer than other layers. When the labeling process goes down to lower layers of the pyramid, more image details become available, and the labeling process is able to refine the labeling result obtained at the coarser levels. At the bottom layer, a fine-tuned labeling that is close to the global optimum will be obtained with a high probability.

6.6.8 Experimental Results

We tested our foreground object segmentation method using real videos taken under different lighting and camera motions. In this subsection we show two examples captured by a low-cost Creative webcam. The frame resolution is 640 by 480, and the frame rate is 6 fps. The quality of the webcam is close to many cellphone video cameras. We allow the webcam to move during video shootings and do not require that either the foreground or the background is known or static. We obtain the weights for the potential functions through experiments, and set $\alpha = 2$, $\beta = 3$, and $\gamma = 2$ in our implementation.

The first sequence was taken from a rigid scene with a moving camera. The scene is composed of a desktop calendar as the foreground object and a flat background. Figure 6.5(a) shows the 1'st, 6'th, 11'th, 16'th and 21'st frames of the sequence. Due to the low quality of the webcam, shape distortions can be clearly observed from these images. Figure 6.5(b) presents the foreground layer extracted by our method. From these images, it is clear that except for mis-classifications of some pixels along the boundary of the calendar, the entire foreground object has been correctly extracted in its entirety throughout the whole sequence.

The second sequence was taken from a person moving and talking in front of a camera while holding the camera himself. The camera was shaking randomly with the person's movement. Most features on the face were undergoing non-rigid motions. There are areas of in the background with colors that are almost identical to the human's hair. Moreover, the human's hair has a very irregular shape, with some portions sticking out a lot (the top and right ear portions). Despite these difficulties, it is clear from Figure 6.6 that our foreground object segmentation method was able to extract the human and his hair with relatively high accuracy. Again, there exist few mis-classifications along the boundary of the human hair.

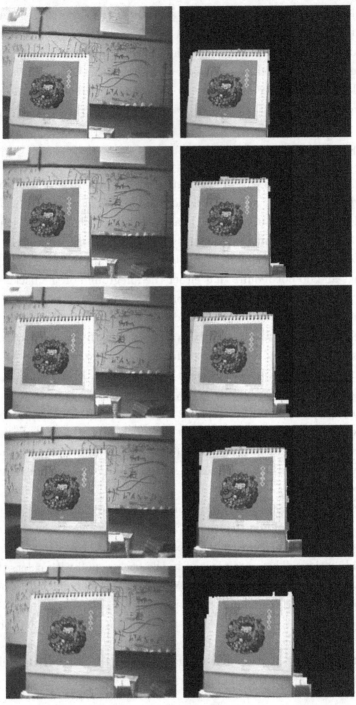

(a) Original video frames   (b) Extracted foreground images

Fig. 6.5. Foreground object segmentation result for the calendar video sequence

(a) Original video frames   (b) Extracted foreground images

Fig. 6.6. Foreground object segmentation result for the human video sequence

Problems

6.1. For Gibbs distribution $\pi(\mathbf{x}) = \frac{1}{Z} \exp(-\frac{1}{T} U(\mathbf{x}))$. Define $\langle f \rangle = \sum_{\mathbf{x}} \pi(\mathbf{x}) f(\mathbf{x})$. Show that

$$\langle U \rangle = T^2 \frac{\partial \log Z}{\partial T} \tag{6.41}$$

6.2. Consider the following energy function for $\mathbf{x} \in R^n$

$$E(\mathbf{x}) = \sum_{ij} w_{ij} x_i x_j$$

Under what condition this energy function defines a proper probability distribution?

6.3. Consider a probability distribution over binary-valued random variables X and Y: $P(X = 0, Y = 0) = P(x = 1, Y = 1) = a$, $P(X = 0, Y = 1) = P(X = 1, Y = 0) = 0.5 - a$. Suppose that we use the Gibbs sampling which uniformly randomly chooses X or Y to update.

(a) Calculate the transition matrix of the implied Markov chain.

(b) Use some software such as MATLAB to plot a graph of a vs. the absolute value of the second eigenvalue of the transition matrix.

6.4. Consider a data set that is composed of two clusters. The cluster membership $c \in \{1, 2\}$ of each data vector $\mathbf{x} \in R^2$ follows a binomial distribution $p(c) \sim Binomial(\pi, 1 - \pi)$, where

$$p(\pi) \sim Beta(0.5, 0.5) \tag{6.42}$$
$$p(\mu_i) \sim N(0, I) \tag{6.43}$$
$$p(\mathbf{x}|c = i, \mu_i) \sim N(\mu_i, I) \tag{6.44}$$

The data set D consists of 4 points $\mathbf{x}_1 = (-1, 0)$, $\mathbf{x}_2 = (-1, -1)$, $\mathbf{x}_3 = (1, 0)$, and $\mathbf{x}_4 = (2, 0)$. Use Gibbs sampling to estimate the probability of $P(c_i = c_j)$ for $i \neq j$

6.5. Let $\{X_t\}_{0 \leq t \leq T}$ be a random sequence defined by

$$X_{t+1} = aX_t + \epsilon_t$$

where $X_0, \epsilon_0, \cdots \epsilon_{T-1}$ are independent Gaussian random variables with zero mean and unit variance.

(a) Show that this model can be represented by a Markov random field. Identify its neighborhood system.

(b) What is the potential function for this MRF?

6.6. Consider a Gibbs sampler for a two dimensional Gaussian distribution $P(X, Y)$ with zero mean. Suppose we sample X and Y alternatively. Let X_t be the t-th sample from the Markov chain. Show that

$$X_{t+1} = \rho^2 X_t + \sigma_x \sqrt{1 - \rho^4} \epsilon_t$$

where $\rho = \frac{Cov(X,Y)}{\sqrt{Var(X)Var(Y)}}$ is the correlation coefficient, $\sigma_x^2 = Var(X)$ and ϵ_t is a Gaussian random variable with zero mean and unit variance.

6.7. Prove the correctness of Gibbs sampling when the sites to be updated are chosen according to a predetermined order.

6.8. Gibbs sampling can be appled to any multivariate probability distribution

$$P(x(1), \ldots, x(N))$$

on a set N with the phase space Λ. The basic step of Gibbs sampling for a multivariate distribution $P(x(1), \ldots, x(N))$ consists of selecting a coordinate number $i \in [1, N]$ at random, and then choosing the new value $y(i)$ of the corresponding coordinate, with probability

$$P(y(i) \mid x(1), \ldots, x(i-1), x(i+1), \ldots, x(N)) .$$

Prove that P is the stationary distribution of the corresponding chain.

6.9. In **Example 6.6** of the traveling salesman problem, a neighborhood system of the state space is defined. Prove any two states is connected, i.e., for any two states s and t, there always exists a sequence of states $s_1 \cdots s_n$ such that $s_1 \in N(s)$, $s_n \in N(t)$, and $s_k \in N(s_{k+1})$

7

Hidden Markov Models

In Chap. 5, we described Markov chains in which each state corresponds to an observable physical event/object. However, this model is too restrictive to be applicable to many problems of interest. In this chapter, we present hidden Markov models that extend Markov chains by adding more model freedoms while avoiding a substantial complication to the basic structure of Markov chains. Hidden Markov models achieve this additional model freedoms by letting the states of the chain generate observable data and hiding the state sequence itself from the observer.

We start the chapter with a sample problem that can not be fully modeled by Markov chains. Through this example, we demonstrate why more model freedoms are needed, and how Markov chains are extended by Hidden Markov Models (HMM). Following the introduction, we present three basic problems for HMMs and describe their respective solutions. We also introduce the Expectation-Maximization (EM) algorithm and use it to prove the Baum-Welch algorithm. The EM algorithm is a very powerful, general method that is applicable to many training-based model estimation problems, while the Baum-Welch algorithm is a special version of the EM algorithm that is particularly useful for estimating maximum likelihood parameters for HMMs. At the end of the chapter, we provide a case study to apply HMMs for the task of baseball highlight detections from TV broadcasted videos.

7.1 Markov Chains vs. Hidden Markov Models

Consider a sequence of ball drawing experiments with the following scenario. A room is partitioned into two parts with an opaque curtain. At one side of the curtain, person A conducts the ball drawing experiments, while at the other side of the curtain, person B records the outcomes of the experiments. The experiments are conducted with a total of N boxes, each of which contains a large number of balls of M different colors. The ball drawing process starts with an initial box. From the box, person A draws a ball at random, and tells person B the color of the ball. Except for the ball's color, person B will not be informed of any other information. After the observation, the ball is returned to the box from which it was drawn. Next, person A selects a new box according to the random selection process associated with the current box, and performs the operations of randomly drawing a ball, telling person B the color of the ball, and returning the ball to the box. In such a manner, a sequence of hidden ball drawing experiments are performed, yielding a sequence of ball color observations. Here the problems are:

1. Can we compute the probability of observing a specific sequence of observations?
2. Given a specific sequence of observations, can we compute the most likely sequence of boxes from which the balls are drawn?
3. Given many observation sequences, can we compute the probabilities of transiting between pairs of boxes, as well as the probabilities of observing specific ball colors for each of the boxes?

It is obvious that there are two stochastic processes associated with the ball drawing experiments: a process of randomly drawing balls from the selected boxes and observing their colors, which is an observable process, and a process of randomly selecting boxes to draw balls, which is a hidden process, from person B's point of view. It is also obvious that a Markov chain is insufficient to model this problem. Given a Markov chain, each state of the chain must correspond to an observable physical event/object, which is the color of a ball in the above example. Therefore, using a Markov chain, we can only model the observable process of ball drawings and color observations, and will completely drop off the hidden process of box selections. Consequently, with a Markov chain, solutions to problems 2 and 3 listed above are completely out of the question, while a solution to problem 1 is also doubtful due to the insufficient modeling of the problem by the Markov chain.

The above ball drawing experiments explain the reason why we want to extend Markov chains to allow more model freedoms. HMMs achieve this goal by letting each state of the chain generate observable data with a probability distribution while hiding the state sequence from the observer. Using an HMM,

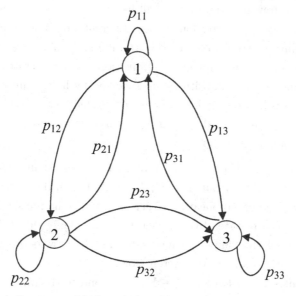

(a) A three-state Markov chain with complete interconnections

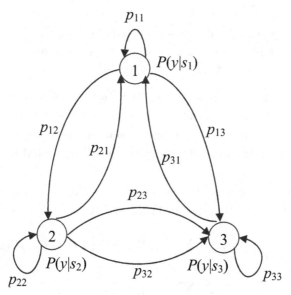

(b) The corresponding three-state hidden Markov model

Fig. 7.1. Markov chain vs. hidden Markov model. With the Markov chain model, each state corresponds to a ball color, whereas with the hidden Markov model, each state corresponds to a box, and is characterized by the conditional probability distribution $P(y|s)$ over the ball colors y given the state s

the above ball drawing experiments will be modeled as shown in Fig. 7.1. In this figure, each state corresponds to a different box, and is characterized by a probability distribution over the M different ball colors. The random box selection process is modeled as transitions between states. In analogy to Markov chains, state transitions are specified by links connecting pairs of states, with each link possessing a transition probability.

In summary, a hidden Markov model is uniquely determined by the following five model components:

1. A state space S. The state space of an HMM is usually countable, and its elements can be denoted by $i, j, k, \cdots$. Although the states are hidden, for many practical applications, there is often some physical implication attached to each state of the model. For example, in the HMM modeling the above ball drawing experiments, each state corresponds to a different box containing balls of M different colors.
2. An output set Y. Elements $y_i \in Y$ correspond to the physical outputs of the system being modeled. In the ball drawing experiments, the outputs are the colors of the balls drawn from the selected boxes.
3. A state transition matrix $\mathbf{P} = \{p_{ij}\}$, where $p_{ij} = P(j|i)$, $i, j \in S$.
4. An output probability distribution matrix $\mathbf{Q} = \{q_{sy}\}$, where $q_{sy} = P(y|s)$ is the probability of generating output y at state s, and $y \in Y$, $s \in S$.
5. An initial state distribution $\boldsymbol{\pi} = \{\pi_i\}$, where $i \in S$.

Comparing the above model elements with those of Markov chains (Sect. 5.1), one observes that elements 1, 3, 5 are common for both the models, while elements 2, 4 are the extensions to Markov chain models. Indeed, they are the elements that model the physical outputs generated by each state of the HMM.

Given the above model elements, the probability of observing an output sequence $y_1, y_2, \ldots, y_n$ from the HMM is given by

$$P(y_1, y_2, \ldots, y_n) = \sum_{s_1, \ldots, s_n} \pi_{s_1} P(y_1|s_1) \prod_{i=2}^{n} P(s_i|s_{i-1}) P(y_i|s_i)$$

$$= \sum_{s_1, \ldots, s_n} \pi_{s_1} q_{s_1 y_1} \prod_{i=2}^{n} p_{s_{i-1} s_i} q_{s_i y_i} , \tag{7.1}$$

where $s_1, \ldots, s_n$ denotes one possible state transition sequence generating the specified output sequence, and s_1 is the initial state of the HMM. Given a particular state transition sequence $s_1, s_2, \ldots, s_n$, the output sequence $y_1, y_2, \ldots, y_n$ is generated as follows.

1. Set $i = 1$.
2. If $i = 1$, select the initial state s_1 according to the initial state distribution π.
3. If $i > 1$, transit to the next state s_i according to the state transition probability distribution $P(s_i|s_{i-1})$.
4. Generate y_i according to the output probability distribution $P(y_i|s_i)$.
5. Set $i = i + 1$. Go to Step 3 if $i < n$; otherwise terminate the procedure.

Clearly, the above procedure can be regarded as a model to explain how a specific output sequence $y_1, y_2, \ldots, y_n$ can be generated by the system being modeled. The probability of observing $y_1, y_2, \ldots, y_n$ from the system can be computed by enumerating all possible state transition sequences $s_1, s_2, \ldots, s_n$, and summing the probabilities that $s_1, s_2, \ldots, s_n$ generates $y_1, y_2, \ldots, y_n$. Because of this property, HMMs are categorized as a typical generative model for statistical inferences.

7.2 Three Basic Problems for HMMs

In Sect. 7.1, we enumerated three problems using the example of ball drawing experiments. These three problems are the most basic problems for HMMs, and other problems concerning HMMs can be decomposed into one of them in general. In this section, we formalize these three basic problems, and describe their typical applications in real-world problems.

As described in Sect. 7.1, an HMM can be uniquely determined by the five model components: state space S, output set Y, state transition matrix $\mathbf{P}$, output probability distribution matrix $\mathbf{Q}$, and initial state distribution π. Among these five model components, S and Y correspond to the physical structure, while $\mathbf{P}$, $\mathbf{Q}$, and π are the statistical parameters of an HMM. It turns out that there exist no good ways to estimate both the structure and the parameters for an HMM automatically. The best we can do is to use our knowledge of the problem and our intuition to design the HMM structure, and to estimate the parameters for the HMM of the given structure. In the following part of this chapter, we use the compact notation $\lambda = (\mathbf{P}, \mathbf{Q}, \pi)$ to denote the complete parameter set of an HMM.

We formalize the three basic problems as follows:

Problem 1: Given the model λ and the observation sequence $\mathbf{y} = y_1, y_2, \cdots, y_n$, how do we efficiently compute $P(\mathbf{y}|\lambda)$, the probability of the observation sequence given the model?

Problem 2: Given the model λ and the observation sequence $\mathbf{y} = y_1, y_2, \cdots, y_n$, how do we efficiently compute the most probable state sequence $\mathbf{s}^* = s_1, s_2, \cdots, s_n$ that generates the observation sequence $\mathbf{y}$, $\mathbf{s}^* = \arg\max_\mathbf{s} P(\mathbf{s} \,|\, \mathbf{y}, \lambda)$.

Problem 3: Given many observation sequences $\mathbf{y}_i$, how do we find the optimal model parameter set λ that maximizes $P(\mathbf{y}_i | \lambda)$ for all $\mathbf{y}_i$.

In the above list, Problem 1 is the evaluation problem that aims to compute the likelihood of generating the observed output sequence by the given model. The likelihood computation is extremely useful for statistical inferences. Consider the case where HMMs are used to detect events of interest from baseball game videos (such as home runs, outfield flies, infield hit, etc). One common way of conducting such event detections is to train an individual HMM for each type of events. For a new video clip, its event can be inferred by computing the likelihood of the video clip using all the HMMs, and choosing the event whose corresponding HMM gives the highest likelihood measure. Therefore, the solution to Problem 1 lays the foundation for HMM-based statistical inferences.

Problem 2 is the one that strives to identify the hidden part of the given model, i.e., to find the most probable state sequence generating the observed output sequence. The solution to Problem 2 plays essential roles for speech recognition problems. For the task of speech recognition, HMMs are generally constructed in such a way that vocal utterances correspond to the observations, and words correspond to the hidden states. Therefore, to recognize the words spoken by the given utterance sequence, one needs to identify the most probable state sequence generating that utterance sequence.

Problem 3 is the one that concerns the training of HMMs. During the HMM training process, a large amount of observation sequences are provided as training data, and the model parameters are adjusted to best fit the provided training data. HMM training is crucial for appropriate applications of HMMs. It allows us to create the models that maximize the likelihood of the provided training data, and these models are generally the ones that best describe the real systems/phenomena to be modeled.

7.3 Solution to Likelihood Computation

Given an observation sequence $\mathbf{y} = y_1, y_2, \cdots, y_n$, we wish to compute the probability of observing the sequence $P(\mathbf{y}|\lambda)$, given the model λ.

The most straightforward way of computing this is to use the formula (7.1). In other words, we obtain $P(\mathbf{y}|\boldsymbol{\lambda})$ by computing the probability $P(y_1, y_2, \ldots, y_n \mid s_1, s_2, \ldots, s_n)$ that $s_1, s_2, \ldots, s_n$ generates $y_1, y_2, \ldots, y_n$, and summing it over all possible state transition sequences $s_1, s_2, \ldots, s_n$. However, a simple math reveals that this straightforward procedure has the complexity of $O(2n \cdot |S|^n)$ ($|S|$ is the number of states in the state space S), which is computationally prohibitive even for small values of $|S|$ and n. For example, for $|S| = 5$, $n = 100$, it requires the order of $2 \cdot 100 \cdot 5^{100} \approx 10^{72}$ computations!

There exists a more efficient procedure to compute the probability $P(\mathbf{y}|\boldsymbol{\lambda})$, called the *forward-backward* algorithm. The forward part of this algorithm defines the forward variable $\alpha_t(i)$ as follows

$$\alpha_t(i) = P(y_1, y_2, \ldots, y_t, s_t = i) , \tag{7.2}$$

where $s_t = i$ means that the stochastic process visits state i at time t. This is the joint probability of observing the partial observation sequence $y_1, y_2, \ldots, y_t$, and state i at time t. The forward variable $\alpha_t(i)$ can be computed recursively as follows:

(1) Initialization:

$$\alpha_1(i) = \pi_i q_{iy_1}, \quad 1 \leq i \leq |S|. \tag{7.3}$$

(2) Recursion:

$$\alpha_t(j) = \left[\sum_{i=1}^{|S|} \alpha_{t-1}(i) p_{ij} \right] q_{jy_t}, \quad 2 \leq t \leq n, \ 1 \leq j \leq |S|. \tag{7.4}$$

By definition (7.2), the probability $P(y_1, y_2, \ldots, y_n|\boldsymbol{\lambda})$ then becomes

$$P(y_1, y_2, \ldots, y_n|\boldsymbol{\lambda}) = \sum_{i=1}^{|S|} \alpha_n(i). \tag{7.5}$$

The computation complexity for calculating $\alpha_t(j)$, $1 \leq t \leq n$, $1 \leq j \leq |S|$, is $O(n \cdot |S|^2)$, compared to $O(2n \cdot |S|^n)$ for the straightforward procedure. For $|S| = 5$, $n = 100$, we need about 3000 computations for the forward algorithm, versus 10^{72} computations, a saving of about 69 orders of magnitude.

The reason behind such a huge discrepancy between the two algorithms is that the straightforward procedure computes the probability $P(y_1, y_2, \ldots, y_n \mid s_1, s_2, \ldots, s_n)$ for each possible state sequence $\mathbf{s} = s_1, s_2, \ldots, s_n$ with a huge amount of repeated calculations. Consider the following two specific state sequences: $\mathbf{s} = s_1, s_2, \ldots, s_{n-1}, i$, and $\mathbf{s}' = s_1, s_2, \ldots, s_{n-1}, j$, where all the states except for the last one are the same. The naive straightforward algorithm computes the probabilities $P(\mathbf{y}|\mathbf{s}, \boldsymbol{\lambda})$, and $P(\mathbf{y}|\mathbf{s}', \boldsymbol{\lambda})$ as follows

$$P(\mathbf{y}|\mathbf{s}, \boldsymbol{\lambda}) = \pi_{s_1} q_{s_1 y_1} p_{s_1 s_2} q_{s_2 y_2} \cdots p_{s_{n-2} s_{n-1}} q_{s_{n-1} y_{n-1}} p_{s_{n-1} i} q_{i y_n},$$

$$P(\mathbf{y}|\mathbf{s}', \boldsymbol{\lambda}) = \pi_{s_1} q_{s_1 y_1} p_{s_1 s_2} q_{s_2 y_2} \cdots p_{s_{n-2} s_{n-1}} q_{s_{n-1} y_{n-1}} p_{s_{n-1} j} q_{j y_n}.$$

Clearly, all the factors except for the last two are the same in the right-hand side of the above two equalities, and most computation efforts have been wasted on repeating the same multiplications in computing the probabilities for the two very similar state sequences. The forward algorithm accomplishes the dramatic computational saving by taking the advantage of the trellis structure of HMMs to eliminate the repeated computations of the same factors (see Fig. 7.2). The key is that since there are only $|S|$ states, all the possible state sequences will re-merge into these $|S|$ states at each stage, no matter how long the observation sequence. Therefore, instead of enumerating all the possible state sequences by traversing through one state sequence after another (horizontal enumeration), we can enumerate them by traversing through all the possible states $s_t = j$, $1 \le j \le |S|$, at each time slot t in the trellis (vertical enumeration). This traversing order can be mathematically expressed as follows

$$
\begin{aligned}
P(\mathbf{y}|\boldsymbol{\lambda}) &= \sum_{s_1, s_2, \ldots, s_n} \pi_{s_1} q_{s_1 y_1} p_{s_1 s_2} q_{s_2 y_2} \cdots p_{s_{n-1} s_n} q_{s_n y_n} \\
&= \sum_{s_n} \cdots \sum_{s_2} \sum_{s_1} (\pi_{s_1} q_{s_1 y_1}) p_{s_1 s_2} q_{s_2 y_2} \cdots p_{s_{n-1} s_n} q_{s_n y_n} \\
&= \sum_{s_n} \cdots \sum_{s_2} \left(\sum_{s_1} \alpha_1(s_1) p_{s_1 s_2} \right) q_{s_2 y_2} \cdots p_{s_{n-1} s_n} q_{s_n y_n} \\
&= \sum_{s_n} \cdots \sum_{s_3} \left(\sum_{s_2} \alpha_2(s_2) p_{s_2 s_3} \right) \cdots p_{s_{n-1} s_n} q_{s_n y_n} \\
&\quad \cdots \cdots \\
&= \sum_{s_n} \left(\sum_{s_{n-1}} \alpha_{n-1}(s_{n-1}) p_{s_{n-1} s_n} \right) q_{s_n y_n} \\
&= \sum_{s_n} \alpha_n(s_n). \quad\quad\quad (7.6)
\end{aligned}
$$

From the above computations, one can observe that the forward variables $\alpha_t(s_t)$ are shared by many terms. The strategy here is to pre-compute these

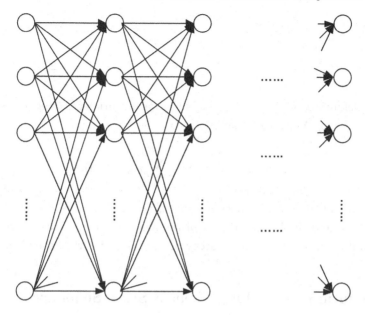

Fig. 7.2. The trellis structure within the HMM computation

forward variables, and re-use them whenever they are needed. At each step t, $1 \leq t \leq n$, it only calculates values of $\alpha_t(s_t)$, $1 \leq s_t \leq |S|$, where each calculation involves only $|S|$ pre-computed values of $\alpha_{t-1}(s_{t-1})$. Indeed, by changing the order of enumerations from horizontal to vertical and pre-computing the forward variables, the forward algorithm completely eliminates the repeated multiplications of the same factors.

Generally, we only need the forward part of the forward-backward algorithm to compute the likelihood of an observation sequence. In the following part of this section, we will introduce the backward part of the algorithm as well since it will be used to help solve Problem 3.

In a similar manner, the backward part of the algorithm defines the backward variable $\beta_t(i)$ as follows

$$\beta_t(i) = P(y_{t+1}, y_{t+2}, \ldots, y_n \mid s_t = i), \tag{7.7}$$

which is the probability of the partial observation sequence from y_{t+1} to the end, given state $s_t = i$ at time t. Again, we can compute $\beta_t(i)$ recursively as follows:

(1) Initialization:

$$\beta_n(i) = 1, \quad 1 \leq i \leq n. \tag{7.8}$$

(2) Recursion:

$$\beta_t(i) = \sum_{j=1}^{|S|} p_{ij} q_{jy_{t+1}} \beta_{t+1}(j), \quad t = n-1, n-2, \ldots, 1, \quad 1 \le i \le |S|. \quad (7.9)$$

From definition (7.7), using the backward variables, the probability $P(y_1, y_2, \ldots, y_n | \boldsymbol{\lambda})$ can be computed as

$$P(y_1, y_2, \ldots, y_n | \boldsymbol{\lambda}) = \sum_{i=1}^{|S|} \pi_i q_{iy_1} \beta_1(i). \quad (7.10)$$

Again, the complexity of computing $\beta_t(i)$, $1 \le t \le n$, $1 \le i \le |S|$ is $O(n \cdot |S|^2)$, and the backward part of the algorithm eliminates the repeated computations using the same strategy of the forward part of the algorithm.

7.4 Solution to Finding Likeliest State Sequence

Given an observation sequence $\mathbf{y} = y_1, y_2, \ldots, y_n$, we wish to find the most likely state sequence $\mathbf{s}^* = s_1^*, s_2^*, \ldots, s_n^*$ that generates it, i.e., $\mathbf{s}^* = \arg\max_{\mathbf{s}} P(\mathbf{s} | \mathbf{y})$. Note that

$$P(s_1, s_2, \ldots, s_n | y_1, y_2, \ldots, y_n) = \frac{P(s_1, s_2, \ldots, s_n, y_1, y_2, \ldots, y_n)}{P(y_1, y_2, \ldots, y_n)}, \quad (7.11)$$

thus maximizing $P(\mathbf{s} | \mathbf{y})$ is equivalent to maximizing the numerator of the right-hand side of the above equation.

Observe that because the underlying state process is Markovian, according to the generalized Markov property (5.12) defined in Chap. 5, for all t,

$$P(s_1, \ldots, s_t, s_{t+1}, \ldots, s_n, y_1, \ldots, y_t, y_{t+1}, \ldots, y_n)$$
$$= P(s_1, \ldots, s_t, y_1, \ldots, y_t) P(s_{t+1}, \ldots, s_n, y_{t+1}, \ldots, y_n | s_1, \ldots, s_t, y_1, \ldots, y_t)$$
$$= P(s_1, \ldots, s_t, y_1, \ldots, y_t) P(s_{t+1}, \ldots, s_n, y_{t+1}, \ldots, y_n | s_t). \quad (7.12)$$

Therefore,

$$\max_{s_1, s_2, \ldots, s_n} P(s_1, \ldots, s_t, s_{t+1}, \ldots, s_n, y_1, \ldots, y_t, y_{t+1}, \ldots, y_n)$$
$$= \max_{s_t, s_{t+1}, \ldots, s_n} [P(s_{t+1}, \ldots, s_n, y_{t+1}, \ldots, y_n | s_t)$$
$$\times \max_{s_1, s_2, \ldots, s_{t-1}} P(s_1, \ldots, s_{t-1}, s_t, y_1, \ldots, y_t)] \quad (7.13)$$

Defining

$$\gamma_t(i) = \max_{s_1, s_2, \ldots, s_{t-1}} P(s_1, \ldots, s_{t-1}, s_t = i, y_1, \ldots, y_t) \qquad (7.14)$$

and substituting it into (7.13), we have

$$\max_{s_1, s_2, \ldots, s_n} P(s_1, \ldots, s_t, s_{t+1}, \ldots, s_n, y_1, \ldots, y_t, y_{t+1}, \ldots, y_n)$$

$$= \max_i \left\{ \max_{s_{t+1}, \ldots, s_n} [P(s_{t+1}, \ldots, s_n, y_{t+1}, \ldots, y_n \mid s_t = i) \gamma_t(i)] \right\}. \qquad (7.15)$$

What this equation tells us is that, we can find the most likely state sequence $s_1, \ldots, s_{t-1}, s_t, s_{t+1}, \ldots, s_n$ with the following three steps:

(1) For each state $s_t = i$ at time t, $i \in S$, find the most likely sub-sequence $s_1(i), \ldots, s_{t-1}(i)$ leading into $s_t = i$. This corresponds to the computation of $\gamma_t(i)$.

(2) Find the most likely sequence $s_{t+1}(i), \ldots, s_n(i)$ leading out of $s_t = i$. This corresponds to the computation of $\max_{(s_{t+1}, \ldots, s_n)} P(s_{t+1}, \ldots, s_n, y_{t+1}, \ldots, y_n \mid s_t = i)$.

(3) Find the state s_t that maximizes the probability of the complete state sequence. This corresponds to the computation of the outer-most maximum $\max_i \{ \cdot \}$ of (7.15).

Again, the quantity $\gamma_t(i)$ can be computed recursively as follows:

$$\gamma_{t+1}(j) = \left(\max_i \gamma_t(i) p_{ij} \right) q_{j y_{t+1}}. \qquad (7.16)$$

Note that from definition (7.14),

$$\max_{s_1, \ldots, s_n} P(s_1, \ldots, s_n, y_1, \ldots, y_n) = \max_i \gamma_n(i). \qquad (7.17)$$

Therefore, instead of computing the most likely state sequence using the above procedure, it will be more efficient to compute it by recursively computing the quantities $\gamma_t(i)$.

Equation (7.16) leads directly to the *Viterbi algorithm* that finds the maximizing state sequence for the given observation sequence. In the algorithm, we use 2-D array $A(t, j)$ to keep track of the arguments that maximize (7.16) for each t and j. The complete procedure can be stated as follows:

(1) Initialization:

$$\gamma_1(i) = \pi_i q_{i y_1}, \quad A(1, i) = 0, \quad 1 \le i \le |S|. \qquad (7.18)$$

(2) Recursion:

$$\gamma_t(j) = \left(\max_i \gamma_{t-1}(i)p_{ij}\right) q_{jy_t}, \tag{7.19}$$

$$A(t, j) = \arg\max_i \left[\gamma_{t-1}(i)p_{ij}\right], \tag{7.20}$$

$$\text{for } 2 \le t \le n, \ 1 \le j \le |S|.$$

(3)Termination:

$$\max_{\mathbf{s}} P(\mathbf{s}, \mathbf{y}) = \max_i \gamma_n(i), \tag{7.21}$$

$$\mathbf{s}^* = \arg\max_i \gamma_n(i). \tag{7.22}$$

(4) Path backtracking:

$$s_t^* = A(t+1, s_{t+1}^*), \quad t = n-1, n-2, \dots, 1. \tag{7.23}$$

It is noteworthy that the Viterbi algorithm is one of the famous dynamic programming methods. It has wide applications in data alignment, data encoding and decoding, string matching and search, etc.

7.5 Solution to HMM Training

In the proceeding two sections, we presented the solutions for computing the likelihood of an observation sequence $P(\mathbf{y}|\boldsymbol{\lambda})$, and for finding the most likely state sequence that generates the observation sequence $\mathbf{s}^* = \arg\max_{\mathbf{s}} P(\mathbf{s}|\mathbf{y})$. These two solutions all assume that the HMM model parameters $\boldsymbol{\lambda} = (\mathbf{P}, \mathbf{Q}, \boldsymbol{\pi})$ are given, and rely on these parameters intensively throughout the computations. In this section, we provide the solution for estimating the maximum likelihood model parameters for the HMM using the observation sequences (training data) generated by it, $\boldsymbol{\lambda}^* = \arg\max_{\boldsymbol{\lambda}} P(\mathbf{y}_i|\boldsymbol{\lambda})$. In the literature, the process of estimating the optimal parameters for a statistical inference model based on a set of training data observed from the system to be modeled is called the training process. As pointed out at the beginning of Sect. 7.2, for HMM training, there is no good resolution for estimating both the HMM structure and the parameters automatically. The best we can do is to manually design the HMM structure using our knowledge about the problem, and to automatically estimate the parameter values for the model of the given structure.

The HMM training algorithm uses both the forward and backward variables $\alpha_t(i)$, $\beta_t(i)$, as well as the following notation

$$\xi_t(i,j) = P(s_t = i, s_{t+1} = j \mid y_1, y_2, \ldots, y_n), \tag{7.24}$$

which is the probability of being in state i at time t, and state j at time $t+1$. From the definitions of the forward and backward variables, it is clear that we can write $\xi_t(i,j)$ in the form

$$\xi_t(i,j) = \frac{\alpha_t(i) p_{ij} q_{jy_{t+1}} \beta_{t+1}(j)}{\sum_{i=1}^{|S|} \sum_{j=1}^{|S|} \alpha_t(i) p_{ij} q_{jy_{t+1}} \beta_{t+1}(j)}. \tag{7.25}$$

Define the variable $c_t(i)$ as

$$c_t(i) = P(s_t = i \mid y_1, y_2, \ldots, y_n), \tag{7.26}$$

i.e. the probability of being in state i at time t, we have

$$c_t(i) = \sum_{j=1}^{|S|} \xi_t(i,j). \tag{7.27}$$

If we sum $c_t(i)$ over the time index t, we get a quantity that can be interpreted as the expected number of times state i is visited, or equivalently, the expected number of transitions made from state i (if we exclude the time instant $t = n$ from the summation). Similarly, the summation of $\xi_t(i,j)$ over t (from $t = 1$ to $t = n - 1$) can be interpreted as the expected number of transitions from state i to state j. That is

$$\sum_{t=1}^{n-1} c_t(i) = \text{expected no. of transitions from state } i, \tag{7.28}$$

$$\sum_{t=1}^{n-1} \xi_t(i,j) = \text{expected no. of transitions from state } i \text{ to state } j. \tag{7.29}$$

Using the above formulas, we can estimate the model parameters of an HMM as follows

$$\overline{\pi}_i = c_1(i), \tag{7.30}$$

$$\overline{p}_{ij} = \frac{\sum_{t=1}^{n-1} \xi_t(i,j)}{\sum_{t=1}^{n-1} c_t(i)}, \tag{7.31}$$

$$\overline{q}_{jy_k} = \frac{\sum_{t=1}^{n} c_t(j) \delta(y_t = y_k)}{\sum_{t=1}^{n} c_t(j)}, \tag{7.32}$$

where $\delta(y_t = y_k)$ is the delta function that equals one if the observation at time t is $y_t = y_k$, and equals zero otherwise.

The above estimation procedure seems to have a fatal flaw: Equations (7.30), (7.31), and (7.32) use the values of the quantities $\xi_t(i,j)$ and $c_t(i)$, which in turn are computed using the values of the model parameters $\boldsymbol{\lambda} = (\boldsymbol{\pi}, \mathbf{P}, \mathbf{Q})$. Fortunately, there is a good way out: We put the above algorithm into a loop, start with a guess at $\overline{\pi}_i$, $\overline{p}_{ij}$, and $\overline{q}_{iy_k}$ to compute $\xi_t(i,j)$ and $c_t(i)$, obtain better estimates of $\overline{\pi}_i$, $\overline{p}_{ij}$, and $\overline{q}_{iy_k}$ by plugging $\xi_t(i,j)$ and $c_t(i)$ into (7.30), (7.31), and (7.32), ..., and run the algorithm repeatedly until the model parameters converge.

The above procedure leads directly to the Baum-Welch method which is a special version of the EM algorithm (the mathematical proof of the method will be provided in the following section). The summary of the Baum-Welch method is described as follows:

1. Initialization: Make a guess at $\overline{\pi}_i$, $\overline{p}_{ij}$, and $\overline{q}_{iy_k}$ for all $1 \leq i \leq |S|$. Denote $\overline{\boldsymbol{\lambda}} = (\overline{\mathbf{P}}, \overline{\mathbf{Q}}, \overline{\boldsymbol{\pi}})$.
2. Forward-backward pass: Use the model parameters $\overline{\boldsymbol{\lambda}}$ to compute $\alpha_t(i)$ and $\beta_t(j)$ for all $1 \leq i \leq |S|$, $1 \leq t \leq n$, using (7.3), (7.4), and (7.8), (7.9), respectively.
3. Parameter estimation: Use the forward and backward variables $\alpha_t(i)$ and $\beta_t(j)$ to estimate better model parameters $\overline{\boldsymbol{\lambda}} = (\overline{\mathbf{P}}, \overline{\mathbf{Q}}, \overline{\boldsymbol{\pi}})$ by (7.30), (7.31), and (7.32).
4. Repeat Step 2 and 3 until the model parameters $\overline{\boldsymbol{\lambda}} = (\overline{\mathbf{P}}, \overline{\mathbf{Q}}, \overline{\boldsymbol{\pi}})$ converge.

7.6 Expectation-Maximization Algorithm and its Variances

In this section, we will derive the Expectation-Maximization (EM) algorithm and use it to verify the mathematical correctness of the Baum-Welch algorithm. Baum-Welch algorithm can be considered as a special version of the EM algorithm, and is particularly useful for estimating maximum likelihood parameters for HMMs. It is noteworthy that the applicability of the EM algorithm is, of course, not restricted to the training of HMMs, it is applicable to most training-based model estimation problems.

7.6.1 Expectation-Maximization Algorithm

The derivation of the EM algorithm is mainly based on a special case of Jensen's inequality given by the following theorem.

Theorem 7.1 (Jensen's Inequality). *If $P(X)$ and $Q(X)$ are two discrete probability distributions, then*

$$\sum_x P(x) \log P(x) \geq \sum_x P(x) \log Q(x) , \tag{7.33}$$

with equality if and only if $P(X) = Q(X)$ for all x.

We will now develop the main theorem. Let Y, X be two random variables that denote observable and hidden data, respectively. X is usually an auxiliary variable governed by the parameter set $\boldsymbol{\theta}$ that generates Y. Let $P_{\boldsymbol{\theta}}(Y)$, $P_{\boldsymbol{\theta}'}(Y)$ be the probability distributions of Y under the model parameter sets $\boldsymbol{\theta}$ and $\boldsymbol{\theta}'$, respectively. Because $P_{\boldsymbol{\theta}'}(X|Y)$ is a probability distribution that satisfies

$$\sum_x P_{\boldsymbol{\theta}'}(x|y) = 1 ,$$

and we can multiply a quantity by one without changing its value, we can perform the mathematical derivations as follows:

$$
\begin{aligned}
&\log P_{\boldsymbol{\theta}}(y) - \log P_{\boldsymbol{\theta}'}(y) \\
&= \sum_x P_{\boldsymbol{\theta}'}(x|y) \log P_{\boldsymbol{\theta}}(y) - \sum_x P_{\boldsymbol{\theta}'}(x|y) \log P_{\boldsymbol{\theta}'}(y) \\
&= \sum_x P_{\boldsymbol{\theta}'}(x|y) \log P_{\boldsymbol{\theta}}(y) \frac{P_{\boldsymbol{\theta}}(x,y)}{P_{\boldsymbol{\theta}}(x,y)} - \sum_x P_{\boldsymbol{\theta}'}(x|y) \log P_{\boldsymbol{\theta}'}(y) \frac{P_{\boldsymbol{\theta}'}(x,y)}{P_{\boldsymbol{\theta}'}(x,y)} \\
&= \sum_x P_{\boldsymbol{\theta}'}(x|y) \log \frac{P_{\boldsymbol{\theta}}(x,y)}{P_{\boldsymbol{\theta}}(x|y)} - \sum_x P_{\boldsymbol{\theta}'}(x|y) \log \frac{P_{\boldsymbol{\theta}'}(x,y)}{P_{\boldsymbol{\theta}'}(x|y)} \\
&= \sum_x P_{\boldsymbol{\theta}'}(x|y) \log P_{\boldsymbol{\theta}}(x,y) - \sum_x P_{\boldsymbol{\theta}'}(x|y) \log P_{\boldsymbol{\theta}'}(x,y) \\
&\quad + \sum_x P_{\boldsymbol{\theta}'}(x|y) \log P_{\boldsymbol{\theta}'}(x|y) - \sum_x P_{\boldsymbol{\theta}'}(x|y) \log P_{\boldsymbol{\theta}}(x|y) \\
&= \sum_x P_{\boldsymbol{\theta}'}(x|y) \log P_{\boldsymbol{\theta}}(x,y) - \sum_x P_{\boldsymbol{\theta}'}(x|y) \log P_{\boldsymbol{\theta}'}(x,y) + \Omega \\
&\geq \sum_x P_{\boldsymbol{\theta}'}(x|y) \log P_{\boldsymbol{\theta}}(x,y) - \sum_x P_{\boldsymbol{\theta}'}(x|y) \log P_{\boldsymbol{\theta}'}(x,y) , \tag{7.34}
\end{aligned}
$$

where following from Theorem 7.1,

$$\Omega = \sum_x P_{\boldsymbol{\theta}'}(x|y) \log P_{\boldsymbol{\theta}'}(x|y) - \sum_x P_{\boldsymbol{\theta}'}(x|y) \log P_{\boldsymbol{\theta}}(x|y) \geq 0 .$$

The above derivations have revealed that if the last quantity is positive, so is the first. Therefore, we have proven the following theorem.

Theorem 7.2. *Let θ be the parameter set of the underlying statistical model, Y and X be two random variables that denote observable and hidden data, respectively, which are both governed by the parameter set θ. If*

$$\sum_x P_{\theta'}(x|y) \log P_{\theta}(x, y) > \sum_x P_{\theta'}(x|y) \log P_{\theta'}(x, y) , \qquad (7.35)$$

then

$$P_{\theta}(Y) > P_{\theta'}(Y) . \qquad (7.36)$$

Theorem 7.2 provides the mathematical foundation for the EM algorithm. It says that if we start with the parameter set θ' and find a new parameter set θ for which the inequality (7.35) holds, then the observed data y will be better modeled by θ than θ'

To take the best advantage of this hill-climbing theorem, typical implementations of the EM algorithm generally strive to find the parameter set θ that maximizes the left-hand side of (7.35). As a result, the standard EM algorithm usually starts with some initial values of the parameter set θ', and repeats the following two alternative steps until the value of $P_{\theta'}(Y)$ stops climbing.

(1) **Expectation**: Take the expectation of the random variable $\log P_{\theta}(X, Y)$ with respect to the old distribution $P_{\theta'}(X|Y)$.
(2) **Maximization**: Maximize the expectation as a function of the argument θ.

The above procedure explains the reason for the name *Expectation-Maximization*. The key to the success in applying the EM algorithm is a judicious choice of the auxiliary variable X that will allow us to maximize the expectation of the left-hand side of (7.35). Such a choice is possible for HMMs.

7.6.2 Baum-Welch Algorithm

We will now use Theorem 7.2 to derive the Baum-Welch algorithm. Denote sequences of observations by $\mathbf{y} = y_1, y_2, \ldots, y_n$, and sequences of states by $\mathbf{s} = s_1, s_2, \ldots, s_n$. The parameter set $\boldsymbol{\lambda} = (\boldsymbol{\pi}, \mathbf{P}, \mathbf{Q})$ consists of the totality of the parameters that uniquely defines the HMM in question.

The derivation starts with the definition of the function

$$\phi(\lambda) = \sum_{\mathbf{s}} P_{\lambda'}(\mathbf{s}|\mathbf{y}) \log P_{\lambda}(\mathbf{s}, \mathbf{y}) , \qquad (7.37)$$

which corresponds to the expectation step of the EM algorithm. We want to find the maximum of the function with respect to λ, which corresponds to the maximization step of the EM algorithm. Here, we will only show the maximization of $\phi(\lambda)$ with respect to $\mathbf{P} = \{p_{ij}\}$, and will leave the rest of derivations as a problem (Problem 7.9) at the end of this chapter.

The maximization of $\phi(\lambda)$ with respect to $\mathbf{P} = \{p_{ij}\}$ can be accomplished by differentiating $\phi(\lambda)$ with respect to p_{ij}, $1 \le i, j \le |S|$, and equating the result to zero. However, because p_{ij}'s are the state transition probabilities that satisfy

$$\sum_{j} p_{ij} = 1 ,$$

the maximization has to be conducted subject to the above stochastic constraint. Therefore, the parameter estimation problem becomes a constrained optimization of $\phi(\lambda)$, and the Lagrange multiplier technique can be used to find the solution. The Lagrange multiplier technique involves the definition of the Lagrangian function using the Lagrangian multiplier μ_i

$$L(\lambda) = \phi(\lambda) - \mu_i \sum_{j} p_{ij} , \qquad (7.38)$$

and the differentiation of $L(\lambda)$ with respect to p_{ij}

$$\frac{\partial}{\partial p_{ij}} L(\lambda) = \frac{\partial}{\partial p_{ij}} \left[\phi(\lambda) - \mu_i \sum_{j} p_{ij} \right]$$

$$= \sum_{\mathbf{s}} P_{\lambda'}(\mathbf{s}|\mathbf{y}) \frac{\frac{\partial}{\partial p_{ij}} P_{\lambda}(\mathbf{s}, \mathbf{y})}{P_{\lambda}(\mathbf{s}, \mathbf{y})} - \mu_i . \qquad (7.39)$$

Since $P_{\lambda}(\mathbf{s}, \mathbf{y})$ can be written as

$$P_{\lambda}(\mathbf{s}, \mathbf{y}) = \pi_{s_1} q_{s_1 y_1} p_{s_1 s_2} q_{s_2 y_2} p_{s_2 s_3} \cdots p_{s_{n-1} s_n} q_{s_n y_n} , \qquad (7.40)$$

if we define $c_{ij}(\mathbf{s})$ as the number of times the transition p_{ij} takes place in the state sequence $\mathbf{s}$, then there will exist the factor $p_{ij}^{c_{ij}(\mathbf{s})}$ in the right-hand side of the above equality. Therefore,

$$\frac{\frac{\partial}{\partial p_{ij}} P_{\lambda}(\mathbf{s}, \mathbf{y})}{P_{\lambda}(\mathbf{s}, \mathbf{y})} = \frac{c_{ij}(\mathbf{s})}{p_{ij}} . \qquad (7.41)$$

Equating (7.39) to zero yields

$$\sum_{\mathbf{s}} P_{\boldsymbol{\lambda}'}(\mathbf{s}|\mathbf{y})\frac{c_{ij}(\mathbf{s})}{p_{ij}} = \mu_i \,, \tag{7.42}$$

or equivalently,

$$p_{ij} = \frac{1}{\mu_i P_{\boldsymbol{\lambda}'}(\mathbf{y})}\sum_{\mathbf{s}} P_{\boldsymbol{\lambda}'}(\mathbf{s},\mathbf{y})c_{ij}(\mathbf{s}) = \frac{1}{K_i}\sum_{\mathbf{s}} P_{\boldsymbol{\lambda}'}(\mathbf{s},\mathbf{y})c_{ij}(\mathbf{s}) \,, \tag{7.43}$$

where K_i is a normalizing constant that ensures the stochastic constraint $\sum_j p_{ij} = 1$. Using the delta function $\delta(\cdot)$, we can re-write $c_{ij}(\mathbf{s})$ as

$$c_{ij}(\mathbf{s}) = \sum_{t=1}^{n-1} \delta((s_t, s_{t+1}) = (i,j)) \,, \tag{7.44}$$

where (s_t, s_{t+1}) denotes the transition from state s_t to state s_{t+1}. Using the above definition, equality (7.43) becomes

$$
\begin{aligned}
p_{ij} &= \frac{1}{K_i}\sum_{t=1}^{n-1}\sum_{\mathbf{s}} P_{\boldsymbol{\lambda}'}(\mathbf{s},\mathbf{y})\delta((s_t, s_{t+1}) = (i,j)) \\
&= \frac{1}{K_i}\sum_{t=1}^{n-1} P_{\boldsymbol{\lambda}'}(y_1, \dots, y_t, s_t = i)p'_{ij}q'_{jy_{t+1}}P_{\boldsymbol{\lambda}'}(y_{t+2}, \dots, y_n \mid s_{t+1} = j) \\
&= \frac{1}{K_i}\sum_{t=1}^{n-1} \alpha_t(i)p'_{ij}q'_{jy_{t+1}}\beta_{t+1}(j) \\
&= \frac{\sum_{t=1}^{n-1}\xi_t(i,j)}{\sum_{t=1}^{n-1}c_t(i)} \,, \tag{7.45}
\end{aligned}
$$

where $\alpha_t(i)$, $\beta_t(j)$ are the forward, backward variables defined by (7.2), (7.7), and $\xi_t(i,j)$, $c_t(i)$ are the quantities defined by (7.25), (7.26), respectively.

Clearly, the maximization of $\phi(\boldsymbol{\lambda})$ with respect to $\mathbf{P}$ (subject to the constraint $\sum_j p_{ij} = 1$) has resulted in the transition probability p_{ij} that is exactly the same as the quantity (7.31). In other words, the Baum-Welch algorithm described in Sect. 7.5 computes the next values of the entire parameter set using the EM algorithm at each iteration of the procedure. According to Theorem 7.2, the new values $\boldsymbol{\lambda}$ of the parameter set models the observed data Y better than the old values $\boldsymbol{\lambda}'$: $P_{\boldsymbol{\lambda}}(Y) > P_{\boldsymbol{\lambda}'}(Y)$. Therefore, we have proven the correctness of the Baum-Welch algorithm based on Theorem 7.2.

7.7 Case Study: Baseball Highlight Detection Using HMMs

In this case study, we present our original work that applies hidden Markov models to extract highlights from TV broadcasted baseball game videos [63]. We first briefly describe the objective of this work, followed by an overview of the entire baseball highlight detection system. Then we provide detailed explanations on the two major components of the system: camera shot classification and highlight detection based on hidden Markov models. Finally, we present experimental evaluations using baseball videos, and reveal performance results of the described system.

7.7.1 Objective

There are certain types of sport game videos, such as baseball, soccer, American football, etc, where eye-catching events usually account for a very small percentage of a video. Living in a fast-paced information society with busy daily lives, people are in increasing needs for technologies that will enable them to watch only the highlights, or the portions of a video program that are of particular interest to them. The ability to access highlights and skip the less interesting portions of a video will become even more valuable for video access using mobile terminal devices because these devices have limited memory and battery capacities, and are subject to expensive telecommunication charges.

This work strives to automatically detect highlights from TV broadcasted baseball game videos. We use HMMs to explore the specific spatial and temporal structures of highlights in baseball game videos, which leads to improved performances. Compared to previous works in the literature, our system can detect more specific and higher level events, such as home runs or good catch plays. It is worth noting that although our system is tuned for baseball games, the statistical framework can be applied to other broadcast sports game videos which have their own specific spatial and temporal structures.

7.7.2 Overview

Baseball videos have well-defined structures and domain rules. A baseball game usually contains nine innings, and each inning consists of a top half and a bottom half. Each half contains many plays, and each play starts with a ball pitching by a pitcher. Among all the valid baseball plays, those plays which either bring changes to the out-count, or contribute directly or indirectly to the overall score are the candidates of baseball highlights which are of interest to most baseball fans. In this work, we are interested in four types of highlights: *home run, hit, catch,* and *in-diamond play.* Hit and catch refer to good plays by the offense and defense team, respectively. In-diamond play refers to a highlight when the ball never goes outside the diamond area. The result can be in favor of either team. Actually it is often difficult to visually decide the outcome of an in-diamond play especially when they are close calls, therefore we put them all in one category.

As with any successful vision systems, specific domain knowledge is exploited for developing our baseball highlight detection system. Typically, the broadcast of a baseball game is made by a fixed number of cameras at fixed locations around the field, and each camera has a certain assignment for broadcasting the game. For example, a pitching view is usually taken by a camera located behind the pitcher, an outfield fly is usually shot by a camera behind home base, and an in-diamond play is usually tracked by cameras either at the left or right side of the baseball diamond field. This baseball game broadcasting technique results in a few unique types of camera shots[1] that constitute most part of a baseball video. Each category of highlights typically consists of a similar transitional pattern of these unique camera shots. For example, a typical home run highlight usually consists of four or more shots, which starts from a pitcher's view, followed by a panning outfield and audience view in which the video camera follows the flying ball, and ends with a global or closeup view of the player running to home base. The limited number of unique view types and similar patterns of view transitions for each type of highlights have certainly made the tasks of detecting and classifying baseball highlights feasible and tractable.

Based on the above observations, we develop our baseball highlight detection system using the following approach. First, we identify seven important types of camera shots, which constitute most baseball highlights of interest. The seven types of camera shots are: (1) pitch view, (2) catch overview, (3) pitcher closeup view, (4) running overview, (5) running closeup view, (6) audience view, and (7) touch-base closeup view (see Fig. 7.3 for examples). Given an input video, we segment it into individual camera shots, and classify each

---

[1] A shot is defined as a video segment taken by the same camera with continuous camera motion.

shot into one of the above seven types. Although camera shots of the same view type differ from game to game, they strongly exhibit common statistical properties of certain measurements due to the fact that they are likely to be taken by the broadcasting cameras mounted at similar locations, covering similar portions of the field, and used by the camera-man for similar purposes. In Sect. 7.7.3, we will present a method for camera shot classifications using Naive Bayes classifier. The output of this method is a set of probabilities each of which indicates the likelihood of the input shot belonging to a particular view class.

Second, we take the camera shot classification probabilities as the input, and use an HMM to model each type of highlights. As stated earlier, most highlights are composed of the seven types of camera shots, and the same type of highlights usually have a similar transition pattern of these view types. Since the contexts of the same type of highlights may vary to certain extent, we use HMMs to model common statistical patterns as well as variations of the highlights. In Sect. 7.7.5, we will explain how to apply HMMs to the tasks of baseball highlight detections and classifications.

In summary, our baseball highlight detection system consists of the following main operations:

1. Camera shot segmentation: Segment a digitized baseball game video into camera shots.
2. View type classification: For each camera shot, compute the probabilities of the shot being each of the seven view types.
3. Highlight detection: Take the sequence of the view classification probabilities as the input, compute the probability of each type of highlights using the corresponding HMM, assign the sequence to the highlight type whose corresponding HMM gives the highest probability that exceeds a predefined threshold.

7.7.3 Camera Shot Classification

In Sect. 7.7.2, we defined seven types of camera shots that constitute most part of a baseball video. Typical images from these types of camera shots are shown in Figure 7.3. We notice that camera shots of the same type often have similar distributions of color, texture, and camera motion, while camera shots of different types usually differ in those distributions. For example, the color distribution of a catch overview is very different from that of a running

(1) Pitch view

(2) Catch overview

(3) Pitcher closeup view

(4) Running overview

(5) Running closeup view

(6) Audience view

(7) Touch-base closeup view

Fig. 7.3. Seven important types of camera shots which constitute most baseball highlights of interest

overview because cameras cover different portions of the baseball field. The camera motion distribution of a catch closeup view is very different from that of a running closeup view since the camera movement is relatively slow in the former and very fast in the later. Therefore we expect that with a proper statistical model it is feasible to extract the common statistical properties among the same type of camera shots and use those statistics to discriminate among different types of shots.

In addition, we have the following considerations for the camera shot classifier.

1. The classification should be based on features that can be computed efficiently and reliably. This consideration is to ensure timely processing and robustness of the system, and it excludes those features which involve difficult image processing tasks, such as identification of players or the stadium.

2. We use the same feature set across all the view types, therefore the method is readily extendible to new types of camera shots if added.

We first present the classifier and then describe the features we use in more details.

Given a set of features $\mathbf{y} = \{M_k \,|\, k = 1, \ldots, n\}$, extracted from a camera shot, we are interested in computing the probability of the shot being the view type s_i, $1 \le i \le 7$. This probability $P(s_i \,|\, \mathbf{y})$ can be computed using the Bayes' rule

$$P(s_i \,|\, \mathbf{y}) = \frac{P(\mathbf{y} \,|\, s_i) P(s_i)}{P(\mathbf{y})} . \tag{7.46}$$

Assuming all the features are independent of each other, (7.46) can be simplified as follows:

$$P(s_i \,|\, \mathbf{y}) = \frac{P(s_i) \prod_{k=1}^{n} P(M_k \,|\, s_i)}{\sum_{i=1}^{7} (P(s_i) \prod_{k=1}^{n} P(M_k \,|\, s_i))} . \tag{7.47}$$

The priori probability of each view type $P(s_i)$ can be estimated from the training data. The estimation of $P(M_k \,|\, s_i)$ for each feature M_k requires more considerations because a camera shot is composed of multiple video frames (say, N), and we will have multiple measurements of M_k from the shot, $M_k = m_k^j$, $j = 1, \ldots, N$. Therefore, a more accurate expression of $P(M_k \,|\, s_i)$ can be written as $P(M_k = m_k^j, j = 1, \ldots, N \,|\, s_i)$. In the next subsection, we will introduce two ways of computing the probability $P(M_k = m_k^j, j = 1, \ldots, N \,|\, s_i)$.

7.7.4 Feature Extraction

The features we currently use are the field descriptor, edge descriptor, grass amount, sand amount, camera motion and player height. These features are extracted from a given camera shot as follows.

Field descriptor: We divide each video frame into 3×3 blocks and label each block as either *field* if the grass or sand color is detected from it, or *non-field* otherwise. Field descriptor describes the shape of the field if the field is in the video frame.

Edge descriptor: The video frame is divided into 3×3 blocks, analogous to computing the field descriptor. Each block is labeled as either *edge* if certain amount of edge pixels are detected or *non-edge* otherwise. Edge descriptor describes the pattern of highly textured regions, such as regions of the audience and players.

Grass and sand: The amount of grass and sand colors detected in the frame by color matching.

Camera motion: The camera motion is represented by the motion parameters estimated from adjacent pair of video frames. The parameters include pan, tilt and zoom of the camera.

Player height: In each video frame, vertical edges are first detected and are grouped into boxes. Given a video segment, those boxes which are consistently detected are assumed to be players. The height of each box is measured as the height of a player in the frame.

Given a camera shot, we compute all the features M_k for each frame, therefore for each feature M_k we have a set of measurements denoted as m_k^j, $j = 1, \ldots, N$, where N is the number of frames in the camera shot. There are several possible ways to compute the probability $P(M_k = m_k^j, j = 1, \ldots, N \mid s_i)$:

(1) Assume M_k is independent from frame to frame, then

$$P(M_k = m_k^j, j = 1, \ldots, N \mid s_i) = \prod_{j=1}^{N} P(M_k = m_k^j \mid s_i) , \qquad (7.48)$$

where $P(M_k = m_k^j \mid s_i)$ can be easily computed from the histogram $H_{M_k}^{(s_i)}$ representing $P(M_k \mid s_i)$. More precisely, for each pair of feature M_k and view type s_i, a histogram $H_{M_k}^{(s_i)}$ is learned from training data during the training stage. Using $H_{M_k}^{(s_i)}$, $P(M_k = m_k^j \mid s_i)$ is obtained by finding the histogram bin that contains m_k^j, and calculating the ratio of this bin to the entire histogram.

(2) Alternatively we can construct a histogram $H_{M_k}^{(s)}$ with $m_k^j, j = 1, \ldots, N$, for the entire shot s, and then compute the distance between $H_{M_k}^{(s)}$ and $H_{M_k}^{(s_i)}$. The probability $P(M_k = m_k^j, j = 1, \ldots, N \mid s_i)$ can then be defined by this distance. In our implementation, this distance is computed using the standard histogram intersection metric.

Both methods appear to be theoretically reasonable, but our experiments show the method (2) works better in practice.

7.7.5 Highlight Detection

We accomplish the task of highlight detection and classification by applying HMMs to model the context of camera shots. To apply HMMs, we need to define the following model components:

1. State space S: which corresponds to the seven view types defined in Sect. 7.7.2.
2. Observation set $Y = \{\mathbf{y}_l\}$: which is the feature set we compute for each camera shot.
3. Observation probability set $\mathbf{Q} = \{P(\mathbf{y}_l|s_i)\}$: In Sect. 7.7.4, we already explained how to compute the probability $P(M_k = m_k^j, j = 1, \ldots, N \mid s_i)$. The probability $P(\mathbf{y}_l|s_i)$ for a particular camera shot can be computed as

$$P(\mathbf{y}_l|s_i) = \prod_{k=1}^{n} P(M_k = m_k^j, j = 1, \ldots, N \mid s_i) ,$$

where n is the number of feature types extracted from each camera shot.
4. State transition probability $\mathbf{P} = \{p_{ij}\}$: given the class of highlights, the transition probability between view types $p_{ij} = P(s_j \mid s_i)$ can be learned from training data.
5. Initial state distribution $\boldsymbol{\pi}$: given the class of highlights, the initial distribution can also be learned from training data.

For each class of highlights, we construct an HMM whose structure reflects the view transition pattern of that class. All it takes is to learn the transition probabilities and initial state distribution, and the HMM training algorithm described in Sect. 7.5 is used to learning these model parameters. Figure 2 shows the four HMMs corresponding to the four classes of highlights we currently work on.

The following is the algorithm for detecting highlights composed of L camera shots:

1. For each camera shot i, extract all the features M_k, $k = 1, \ldots, n$, from the shot i.
2. Compute the observation probability $P(\mathbf{y}_i \mid s_j)$, for each camera shot i and each view type s_j.
3. For each HMM $\boldsymbol{\lambda}_k$ representing highlight category k, compute the probability of observing the given observation sequence: $\zeta_k = P(\mathbf{y}_1, \ldots, \mathbf{y}_L \mid \boldsymbol{\lambda}_k)$. The probability ζ_k can be computed with the standard forward-backward algorithm described in Sect. 7.3.
4. If $\zeta = \max\{\zeta_i\}$ exceeds certain threshold, then camera shot i is assigned to the highlight category $h = \arg\max_i\{\zeta_i\}$.

7.7.6 Experimental Evaluation

We tested our baseball highlight detection system using six digitized baseball game videos with a total of 18 hours. These games were recorded from TV broadcasting, and consist of different teams, and stadiums. We manually labeled all six videos, and used half of them as training and the other has as testing data.

We use the precision and recall as the evaluation metrics. These two metrics are defined as follows:

$$\text{precision} = \frac{\text{No. of correctly labeled videos in the category}}{\text{total No. of videos labeled as the category}} \quad (7.49)$$

$$\text{recall} = \frac{\text{No. of correctly labeled videos in the category}}{\text{total No. of videos in the category}} \quad (7.50)$$

Table 7.1 shows the experimental result for camera shot classifications. The classification rate of running closeup view and touch base closeup view are relatively low. The reason mainly lies in the large view variation for those shots, which in turn cause the distributions of the features we used less peaked. In other words, the features are less discriminative for those types of camera shots. More features are needed to improve the performance. For shots with less variations, our system works satisfactorily.

Table 7.2 shows the recalls and precisions for detecting the four categories of highlights. The results are reasonable, especially we are able to detect five home runs out of the total six. The highlight category of in-diamond play has the lowest recall and precision values compared to other categories, because

Table 7.1. Experimental result for camera shot classifications

View Type	Precision	Recall
Pitch View	0.90	0.89
Catch Overview	0.81	0.76
Running Overview	0.83	0.81
Audience View	0.75	0.71
Running Closeup	0.65	0.51
Touch Base Closeup	0.44	0.53

this category has the most complex temporal structures and the largest variations in view transition patterns. Through these evaluation results, we have demonstrated that HMM-based classifiers are capable of detecting complex baseball highlights.

Table 7.2. Experimental result for highlight classifications

Highlight Type	Precision	Recall
Home Run	0.83	0.71
Catch	0.75	0.68
Hit	0.83	0.66
In-diamond Play	0.67	0.40

Problems

7.1. Consider a HMM model with two states, s_1, s_2, and two outputs, o_1, o_2. The state transition probability table is

	s_1	s_2
s_1	0.8	0.2
s_2	0.3	0.7

The output probability table is

	s_1	s_2
o_1	0.9	0.1
o_2	0.1	0.9

Calculate the probability of observing outputs o_1 and o_2, respectively, if the model has been running for long enough time.

7.2. Same HMM model as problem 7.1. Assume that, after the model has been running for long enough time, we observed output o_1

(a) What is the probability that the model is at state s_1?

(b) What is the probability that the model is at state s_1 at the previous time step.

7.3. For any probability distribution $P(x, y)$ and $Q(x, y)$, prove the following inequality

$$\log P(y) \geq \sum_x Q(x|y) \log P(x, y) - \sum_x Q(x|y) \log Q(x|y).$$

Give the condition when the equality holds.

7.4. This chapter derives the HMM training algorithm based on the EM algorithm. An alternative way is to use gradient-based algorithms such as conjugate gradient method to directly maximize the log-likelihood

$$L(\boldsymbol{\lambda}) = \sum_i \log P(y_1^{(i)}, y_2^{(i)}, \ldots, y_n^{(i)} \mid \boldsymbol{\lambda}),$$

where $y_1^{(i)}, y_2^{(i)}, \ldots, y_n^{(i)}$ is the i'th observed sequence of the HMM. Derive the equations for calculating the gradients of the log-likelihood $L(\boldsymbol{\lambda})$ with respect to the parameters $\boldsymbol{\lambda}$ of HMM. Here the initial state distribution π_i, transition probabilities p_{ij} and output probabilities q_{sy} are parameterized as

$$\pi_i = \frac{\exp(\gamma_i)}{\sum_i \exp(\gamma_i)} \tag{7.51}$$

$$p_{ij} = \frac{\exp(\alpha_{ij})}{\sum_j \exp(\alpha_{ij})} \tag{7.52}$$

$$q_{sy} = \frac{\exp(\beta_{sy})}{\sum_y \exp(\beta_{sy})} \tag{7.53}$$

7.5. Consider the following probabilistic cluster model for data vector $\mathbf{x} \in R^d$ and its cluster membership $c \in \{1, \cdots, K\}$.

$$p(\mu_i) \sim N(0, I) \tag{7.54}$$

$$p(\pi_1, \cdots, \pi_K) \sim Dirichlet(\alpha_1, \cdots, \alpha_K) \tag{7.55}$$

$$p(c) \sim Multinomial(\pi_1, \pi_2, \cdots, \pi_K) \tag{7.56}$$

$$p(\mathbf{x}|c = i, \mu_i) \sim N(\mu_i, I) \tag{7.57}$$

Given a set of data samples $D = \{\mathbf{x}_1, \cdots, \mathbf{x}_N\}$, derive the EM algorithm for finding the maximum a posterior estimation of π_i and μ_i.

7.6. In the HMM described in this chapter, the output is discrete variable. Consider the case where output y is a multidimensional continuous variable with a Gaussian distribution whose mean and variance are determined by the current state s

$$P(y|s) \sim N(\mu_s, \Sigma_s) \tag{7.58}$$

Derive the equations for estimating μ_s and Σ_s

7.7. In the HMM described in this chapter, observations are generated for all time steps. If we only observe the outputs $y_{t_1}, \cdots, y_{t_k}$ at the time steps $t_1, \cdots, t_k$. Modify the forward algorithm to calculate $P(\mathbf{y}|\lambda)$

7.8. Consider the following dynamic model for $\{Y_t\}_{0 \leq t \leq T}$

$$X_t = aX_{t-1} + u_t,$$
$$Y_t = bX_t + v_t,$$

where $X_0 \sim N(0,1)$, $u_t \sim N(0,q)$, $v_t \sim N(0,r)$, and $\{X_0, u_1 \cdots u_T, v_1, \cdots, v_T\}$ are mutually independent.

(a) Show that this is a hidden Markove model. Identify the initial distribution, transition distribution and output distribution.

(b) Suppose both X and Y are one dimensional. Derive a closed form formula for $P(X_t|Y_1, \cdots, Y_t)$ using the forward-backward algorithm.

7.9. For proving the Baum-Welch algorithm in Sect. 7.6.2, we computed the maximum of the function $\phi(\boldsymbol{\lambda})$ defined by (7.37) with respect to $\mathbf{P} = \{p_{ij}\}$. Compute the maximum of $\phi(\boldsymbol{\lambda})$ with respect to $\boldsymbol{\pi} = \{\pi_i\}$ and $\mathbf{Q} = \{q_{sy}\}$.

8

Inference and Learning for General Graphical Models

In previous chapters, we described several probabilistic models that capture certain structures of the given data. In this chapter, we will see that these models are all under a general umbrella called probabilistic graphical models.

8.1 Introduction

A graphical model can be understood as a probability distribution of a set of random variables that factorizes according to the structure of a given graph. Formally speaking, let $G = (V, E)$ be a graph of a set of vertices V and edges E. Each vertex $v \in V$ is associated with a random variable x_v. Depending on wether G is directed on not, we have directed graphical model or undirected graphical model.

Directed graphical models: Also known as Bayesian networks. G must be a directed acyclic graph (DAG). For each node $v \in V$, there is a set $\pi(v)$ of all the parent nodes of v. Then the probability distribution is factorized as

$$P(\mathbf{x}) = \sum_{v \in G} P(x_v | \mathbf{x}_{\pi(v)}).$$

Figure 8.1 is a simple example of directed graphical model. In this example, we have

$$P(B, E, A, C) = P(B)P(E)P(A|B, E)P(C|A) \tag{8.1}$$

The hidden Markov model we studied in Chap. 7 also belongs to the class of directed graphical models.

Undirected graphical models: The undirected graphical model is another name of Markov random field. The probability distribution is factorized as a set of functions $\psi_C(\mathbf{x}_C)$ defined over each clique C of the graph G:

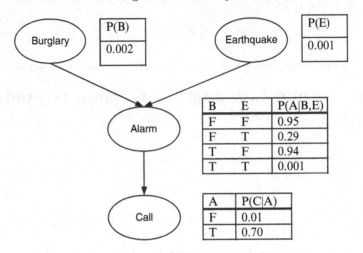

Fig. 8.1. A simple directed graphical model. Your home has a burglary alarm. The probability of the alarm being activated is directly affected by the burglary and earthquake sensors. In the event of the alarm being activated, the neighbor will notify you by phone, and of course there are some chances that your neighbor makes mistakes

$$P(\mathbf{x}) = \frac{1}{Z} \prod_C \psi_C(\mathbf{x}_C)$$

In order to present the algorithms for directed and undirected graphical models in a unified framework, we will introduce factor graphs first [64].

Definition 8.1. *A factor graph is a bipartite graph that expresses the structure of the factorization of a function g of a set of variables* $\{x_1, \cdots, x_n\}$. *A factor graph has one variable node for each variable* x_i, *and one factor node for each local function* f_j, *and an edge-connecting variable node* x_i *to factor node* f_j *if and only if* x_i *is an argument of* f_j. *Let* $\mathbf{x}_j$ *be the set of variable nodes connecting to the factor node* f_j, *then g is*

$$g(x_1, \cdots, x_n) = \prod_j f_j(\mathbf{x}_j)$$

If g is a positive function, a probability distribution of $\mathbf{x}$ can be obtained from the normalized version of g

$$P(\mathbf{x}) = \frac{1}{Z} g(\mathbf{x}) = \frac{1}{Z} \prod_{j=1}^{J} f_j(\mathbf{x}_j) \tag{8.2}$$

where the normalization constant Z is defined by

$$Z = \sum_{\mathbf{x}} g(\mathbf{x}) \tag{8.3}$$

Both the directed and undirected graphical model can be easily represented using factor graphs. For directed graphical model, each conditional distribution function $P(x_v|x_{\pi(v)})$ corresponds to one factor node f_v and the arguments of f_v are x_v and $\mathbf{x}_{\pi(v)}$. For example, Fig. 8.2 is the equivalent factor graph of the directed graphical model in Fig. 8.1, where $f_1(x_1) = P(B = x_1)$, $f_2(x_2) = P(E = x_2)$, $f_3(x_1, x_2, x_3) = P(A = x_3|B = x_1, E = x_2)$, and $f_4(x_3, x_4) = P(C = x_4|A = x_3)$.

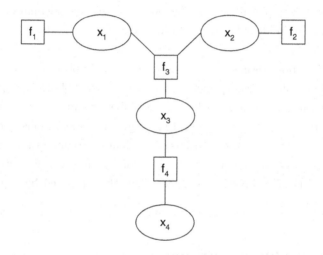

Fig. 8.2. The factor graph corresponding to Fig. 8.1

To convert an undirected graphical model UG to factor graph, each node in UG is mapped to one variable node in the factor graph, each clique function ψ_C is mapped to a factor node f_C and there is an edge connecting x_i and f_C if and only if x_i is in clique C in UG.

The marginal function g_A for a subset $\mathbf{x}_A = \{x_i|i \in A\}$ of variables is defined as

$$g_A(\mathbf{x}_A) = \sum_{\{x_i|i \notin A\}} g(\mathbf{x}) \tag{8.4}$$

Here we note that for continuous variable, the sum is understood as integration and we will use sum instead of integration through out the derivations in this chapter.

Two major tasks in the application of graphical models are: (1) inference, and (2) learning. In the inference task, the parameters of the model are known, and the goal is to find out certain property of a set of variables $\mathbf{x}_A$ given the observation of another set $\mathbf{x}_A$ of variables. Typically, this requires the calculation of the conditional probability $P(\mathbf{x}_A|\mathbf{x}_B)$. It is clear that

$$P(\mathbf{x}_A|\mathbf{x}_B) = \frac{g_{A\cup B}(\mathbf{x}_A, \mathbf{x}_B)}{g_B(\mathbf{x}_B)} \tag{8.5}$$

For the learning task, a data set $D = \{\mathbf{x}_{A_1}^{(1)}, \cdots \mathbf{x}_{A_n}^{(n)}\}$ of observed samples are given. The task is to estimate the parameters θ of the model so that the likelihood $P_\theta(D)$ is maximized. We note that from the Bayesian point of view, learning is a special case of inference because the model parameter θ and data are jointly modelled and the task of learning is to infer the conditional distribution $P(\theta|D)$.

From the above discussion we know that it is important to compute the marginal functions. But in general, this is an untractable task. Suppose that there are n variables, each of which has k different values. Then to calculate the sum in (8.4), we need to enumerate all different combinations of $x_1, \cdots, x_n$. The number of different combinations is k^n. Hence the computation cost grows exponentially with the total number of variables. However, for certain factor graphs, the marginal functions can be efficiently computed by exploring the structure of the graph.

8.2 Sum-product algorithm

In this section, we will focus on tree-structured factor graphs, i.e., there is no cycles in the graph. The whole idea is very similar to the forward-backward algorithm presented for the hidden Markov model. In fact, the sum-product algorithm is a generalization of the forward-backward algorithm for tree-structured graphical models.

The idea is the divide and conquer of dynamic programming. We first use Fig. 8.3 to illustrate the idea. Consider the following decomposition of $g_i(x_i)$,

$$g_i(x_i) = \sum_{x_j, x_k, x_l, x_m} f_u(x_j) f_v(x_k) f_r(x_j, x_k, x_i) f_s(x_i, x_l) f_t(x_i, x_m) \tag{8.6}$$

$$= \sum_{x_j, x_k} f_u(x_j) f_v(x_k) f_r(x_j, x_k, x_i) \sum_{x_l} f_s(x_i, x_l) \sum_{x_m} f_t(x_i, x_m). \tag{8.7}$$

With this decomposition, the big sum involving summing over the four variables in (8.6) is avoided. Instead, we only need to calculate several smaller sums that involve less variables in (8.7). We can compare the computation cost of (8.6) and (8.7). In (8.6), there are $|X|^4$ different combinations of x_j, x_k, x_l, x_m and we need to calculate the sum for each different x_i, so the cost is $O(|X|^5)$. In (8.7), the cost is $O(|X|^3)$, which is a huge save from $O(|X|^5)$. This difference is even dramatic when there are more variables in the model.

We define the set of variables $\mathbf{x}_r$ that rth factor depends on, by $\mathcal{N}(r)$. For the example in Fig. 8.2, $\mathcal{N}(1) = \{1,3\}$, $\mathcal{N}(2) = \{2,3\}$, $\mathcal{N}(3) = \{3,4\}$, and $\mathcal{N}(4) = \{4\}$. Similarly, $\mathcal{M}(i)$ is defined as the set of factors in which variable i participates. In Fig. 8.2, $\mathcal{M}(1) = \{1,3\}$, $\mathcal{M}(2) = \{2,3\}$, $\mathcal{M}(3) = \{3,4\}$, $\mathcal{M}(4) = \{4\}$. Since the graph is a tree, for any two connected nodes r and i, we can define a subtree $T_{i \to r}$ to be the subgraph that can be reached from r by paths that do not pass through i. We also denotes $\mathbf{x} \backslash i$ as the set of variables in $\mathbf{x}$ with variable x_i excluded.

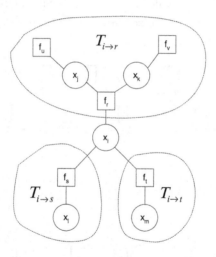

Fig. 8.3. Divide and conquer

Consider the calculation of $g_i(x_i)$ in a factor graph in Fig. 8.3. By definition,

$$g_i(x_i) = \sum_{\mathbf{x} \backslash i} g(\mathbf{x}) = \sum_{\mathbf{x} \backslash i} \prod_{j=1}^{J} f_j(\mathbf{x}_j). \qquad (8.8)$$

The critical observation here is that x_i separates the tree into three parts $T_{i \to r}$, $T_{i \to s}$ and $T_{i \to t}$, where we can calculate the sums independently within each part. This is formally described by the following equation:

$$g_i(x_i) = \sum_{\mathbf{x} \setminus i} \prod_{r \in \mathcal{M}(i)} \prod_{f_s \in T_{i \to r}} f_s(\mathbf{x}_s) \tag{8.9}$$

$$= \prod_{r \in \mathcal{M}(i)} \sum_{\{x_j \in T_{i \to r}\}} \prod_{f_s \in T_{i \to r}} f_s(\mathbf{x}_s). \tag{8.10}$$

We define $m_{r \to i}$ to be

$$m_{r \to i}(x_i) = \sum_{\{x_j \in T_{i \to r}\}} \prod_{f_s \in T_{i \to r}} f_s(\mathbf{x}_s). \tag{8.11}$$

Hence

$$g_i(x_i) = \prod_{r \in \mathcal{M}(i)} m_{r \to i}(x_i). \tag{8.12}$$

Now let us see how to calculate $m_{r \to i}(x_i)$. Similar to the calculation of $g_i(x_i)$, $m_{r \to i}(x_i)$ can be factorized into several parts by observing that f_r separates $T_{i \to r}$ into two parts $T_{r \to j}$ and $T_{r \to k}$:

$$m_{r \to i}(x_i) = \sum_{\{x_j \in T_{i \to r}\}} f(\mathbf{x}_r) \prod_{j \in \mathcal{N}(r) \setminus i} \prod_{f_s \in T_{r \to j}} f_s(\mathbf{x}_s) \tag{8.13}$$

$$= \sum_{\mathbf{x}_r \setminus i} f(\mathbf{x}_r) \prod_{j \in \mathcal{N}(r) \setminus i} \sum_{\{x_k \in T_{r \to j} \setminus x_j\}} \prod_{f_s \in T_{r \to j}} f_s(\mathbf{x}_s). \tag{8.14}$$

We define $M_{j \to r}$ to be

$$M_{j \to r}(x_j) = \sum_{\{x_k \in T_{r \to j} \setminus x_j\}} \prod_{f_s \in T_{r \to j}} f_s(\mathbf{x}_s). \tag{8.15}$$

Then

$$m_{r \to i}(x_i) = \sum_{\mathbf{x}_r \setminus i} f(\mathbf{x}_r) \prod_{j \in \mathcal{N}(r) \setminus i} M_{j \to r}(x_j). \tag{8.16}$$

$M_{i \to r}(x_i)$ can also be decomposed using $m_{s \to i}(x_i)$

$$M_{i \to r}(x_i) = \sum_{\{x_j \in T_{r \to i} \setminus x_i\}} \prod_{s \in \mathcal{M}(i) \setminus r} \prod_{f_u \in T_{i \to s}} f_u(\mathbf{x}_u) \tag{8.17}$$

$$= \prod_{s \in \mathcal{M}(i) \setminus r} \sum_{\{x_j \in T_{i \to s}\}} \prod_{f_u \in T_{i \to s}} f_u(\mathbf{x}_u) \tag{8.18}$$

$$= \prod_{s \in \mathcal{M}(i) \setminus r} m_{s \to i}(x_i). \tag{8.19}$$

Thus the desired result can be obtained by passing two types of messages along the edges of the graph: messages $m_{r\to i}$ from factors to variables, and messages $M_{i\to r}$ from variables to factors. The calculation of these two types of messages are summarized as the following two equations:

From factor to variable:

$$m_{r\to i}(x_i) = \sum_{\mathbf{x}_r\setminus i} f(\mathbf{x}_r) \prod_{j\in\mathcal{N}(r)\setminus i} M_{j\to r}(x_j), \qquad (8.20)$$

From variable to factor:

$$M_{i\to r}(x_i) = \prod_{s\in\mathcal{M}(i)\setminus r} m_{s\to i}(x_i). \qquad (8.21)$$

In the following, we give a step-by-step detailed example for calculating the messages for the graphical model in Fig. 8.3

Step 1

$$m_{u\to j}(x_j) = f_u(x_j),$$
$$m_{v\to k}(x_k) = f_v(x_k),$$
$$M_{l\to s}(x_l) = 1,$$
$$M_{m\to t}(x_m) = 1.$$

Step 2

$$M_{j\to r}(x_j) = m_{u\to j}(x_j),$$
$$M_{k\to r}(x_k) = m_{v\to k}(x_k),$$
$$m_{s\to i}(x_i) = \sum_{x_l} f_s(x_i, x_l) M_{l\to s}(x_l),$$
$$m_{t\to i}(x_i) = \sum_{x_m} f_t(x_i, x_m) M_{m\to t}(x_m).$$

Step 3

$$m_{r\to i}(x_i) = \sum_{x_j, x_k} f_r(x_i, x_j, x_k) M_{j\to r}(x_j) M_{k\to r}(x_k),$$
$$M_{i\to r}(x_i) = m_{s\to i}(x_i) m_{t\to i}(x_i).$$

Step 4

$$m_{r\to j}(x_j) = \sum_{x_i, x_k} f_r(x_i, x_j, x_k) M_{k\to r}(x_k) M_{i\to r}(x_i),$$
$$m_{r\to k}(x_k) = \sum_{x_i, x_j} f_r(x_i, x_j, x_k) M_{j\to r}(x_j) M_{i\to r}(x_i),$$
$$M_{i\to s}(x_i) = m_{r\to i}(x_i) m_{t\to i}(x_i),$$

$$M_{i \to t}(x_i) = m_{r \to i}(x_i) m_{s \to i}(x_i) \,.$$

Step 5

$$M_{j \to u}(x_j) = m_{r \to j}(x_j) \,,$$

$$M_{k \to v}(x_k) = m_{r \to k}(x_k) \,,$$

$$m_{s \to l}(x_l) = \sum_{x_i} f(x_i, x_l) M_{i \to s}(x_i) \,,$$

$$m_{t \to m}(x_m) = \sum_{x_i} f(x_i, x_m) M_{i \to t}(x_i) \,.$$

Now all the messages have been obtained and we can read out result:

$$g_j(x_j) = m_{u \to j}(x_j) m_{r \to j}(x_j) \,,$$

$$g_k(x_k) = m_{v \to k}(x_k) m_{r \to k}(x_k) \,,$$

$$g_i(x_i) = m_{r \to i}(x_i) m_{s \to i}(x_i) m_{t \to i}(x_i) \,,$$

$$g_l(x_l) = m_{s \to l}(x_l) \,,$$

$$g_m(x_m) = m_{t \to m}(x_m) \,.$$

Message passing with normalization: For probabilistic graphical models, we may only need the normalized marginal functions $\frac{g_i(x_i)}{\sum_{x_i} g_i(x_i)}$. In this case, we can modify message passing rule (8.21) to calculate normalized messages as:

$$M_{i \to r}(x_i) = \alpha_{ir} \prod_{s \in \mathcal{M}(i) \backslash r} m_{s \to i}(x_i) \,, \tag{8.22}$$

where α_{ir} is the quantity such that $\sum_{x_i} M_{i \to r}(x_i) = 1$. The use of normalized messages has two advantages: first, it prevents overflow or underflow during computation; second, the message itself now can be interpreted as probabilities.

Given the message update rule (8.20) and (8.21), we also need to decide which message to update first, which second. Fortunately, for a graph with tree structure, the update sequence can be easily determined with the following message passing method.

Message passing method 1: For all the leaf variable nodes i, set $M_{i \to r}(x_i) = 1$. For all the leaf factor nodes r, set $m_{r \to i}(x_i) = f_r(x_i)$. Then a message is created according to (8.20) and (8.21) only if all the messages on which it depends are present.

Message passing method 2: Initialize all messages from variables to 1. Then alternate between message update rule (8.20) and (8.20). After a number of iterations equals the diameter of the graph, the algorithm will converge to the correct result.

It is clear that the message passing method 2 requires much more computation cost than method 1. The reason is that, if the graph is not a tree, then method 1 cannot be applied, because some messages may never be updated due to the fact that some of the messages it depends on will never be available. However, we can always apply method 2 to any graph, though it may not converge to the exact result.

When the graph is not a tree, it is possible to convert it into a model without loop. For example, the factor graph in Fig. 8.4(a) can be converted to the factor graph model in 8.4(b), where $f(x_1, x_2, x_3) = f_2(x_1, x_2)f_3(x_1, x_3)f_4(x_2, x_3)$.

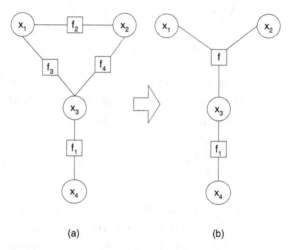

(a)   (b)

Fig. 8.4. (a) A factor graph with loop. (b) An equivalent factor graph without loop

There is a general strategy called junction tree algorithm [65, 66] that can convert a graphical model with loops to an equivalent tree-structured graphical model. However, this algorithm is of little use when the original graph structure is complex. For general graphs, after the conversion, the number of variables involved in one factor is in the same order of the total number of variables in the graph. Hence the computation cost at each step in the sum-product algorithm will increase exponentially with the size of the graph.

8.3 Max-product algorithm

The sum-product algorithm efficiently solves the problem of marginalization. Another common task for graphical model is to find the most probable configuration $\mathbf{x}^*$ that maximizes the probability $P(\mathbf{x}^* | \mathbf{x}_A)$ given some observation $\mathbf{x}_A$. We define $g_A^*(\mathbf{x}_A)$ as:

$$g_A^*(\mathbf{x}_A) = \max_{\{x_i | i \notin A\}} g(\mathbf{x}). \tag{8.23}$$

The definition of $g*_A$ looks very similar to that of the marginal function g_A in (8.4). The only difference is the replacement of the $\sum$ operator with the max operator. Both of these two operators have the following properties of an operation $\bigvee$:

$$\bigvee_{x_1} \bigvee_{x_2} f(x_1, x_2) = \bigvee_{x_2} \bigvee_{x_1} f(x_1, x_2), \tag{8.24}$$

$$\bigvee_{x} a f(x) = a \bigvee_{x} f(x). \tag{8.25}$$

The first property allows us to simply use $\bigvee_{x_1, x_2}$ to represent $\bigvee_{x_1} \bigvee_{x_2}$. The second property is called the distributive law. Following is an example that shows how these two properties can be used to simplify calculation:

$$\bigvee_{x_1} \bigvee_{x_2} (f_1(x_1) f_2(x_2)) = \bigvee_{x_1} \left(f_1(x_1) \bigvee_{x_2} f_2(x_2) \right) = \left(\bigvee_{x_1} (f_1(x_1)) \right) \left(\bigvee_{x_2} f_2(x_2) \right). \tag{8.26}$$

A close examination of the sum-product algorithm reveals that only the above two properties of $\sum$ are necessary for the derivation of the algorithm. Hence if we replace the $\sum$ operator with the max operator, same procedure can be used to calculate $g_A^*(x_A)$:

From factors to variables:

$$m_{r \to i}^*(x_i) = \max_{\mathbf{x}_r \setminus i} f(\mathbf{x}_r) \prod_{j \in \mathcal{N}(r) \setminus i} M_{j \to r}^*(x_j). \tag{8.27}$$

From variables to factors:

$$M_{i \to r}^*(x_i) = \prod_{s \in \mathcal{M}(i) \setminus r} m_{s \to i}^*(x_i). \tag{8.28}$$

And $g_i^*(x_i)$ can be obtained using the following equation:

$$g_i^*(x_i) = \prod_{r \in \mathcal{M}(i)} m_{r \to i}^*(x_i). \tag{8.29}$$

The new algorithm is called max-product algorithm. In practice, the product is often carried out as sum in the logarithm domain, hence the algorithm is also called max-sum algorithm. Comparing to the Viterbi algorithm in Chap. 7, we can see that the max-product algorithm is the generalization of the Viterbi algorithm for tree-structured graphical models.

8.4 Approximate inference

The sum-product algorithm in section 8.2 is based on the assumption that the graph has a tree structure. But in many real applications, the graphical structure can not be simply described using a tree. It is a known fact that the exact inference for graphical models with arbitrary structures is an NP complete problem. Even for the tree structured models, the integration (note that sum is interpreted as integration for continuous variables) may be too complex to be calculated in closed form. So we have to use approximate methods in order to get a desired result within a reasonable amount of time. There are many approximate methods. We will briefly discuss several of them in this section.

The first method for approximate inference is to use Monte Carlo methods. As long as we can generate a set of independent random samples $\{\mathbf{x}^{(1)}, \cdots, \mathbf{x}^{(N)}\}$ from a given graphical model, then the inference can be done by calculating the average value of certain function over those samples. For example, $P(x_i = c)$ can be evaluated by

$$P(x_i = c) \approx \frac{1}{N} \sum_{n=1}^{N} \delta_c(\mathbf{x}^{(n)}), \qquad (8.30)$$

where function $\delta_c(\mathbf{x})$ is equal to 1 if the i-th variable of $\mathbf{x}$ is equal to c, and is equal to 0 otherwise. In order to generate a random sample from the graphical model, we can use Gibbs sampling. Using the notation in section 8.2, we can see that x_i is conditionally independent of other variables given the values of the variables in the set $\mathcal{L}(i) = \bigcup_{r \in \mathcal{M}(i)} \mathcal{N}(r) \backslash i$. Hence one Gibbs sampling step can be achieved by sampling from following distribution:

$$P(x_i | \mathbf{x} \backslash i) \propto \prod_{r \in \mathcal{M}(i)} f_r(\mathbf{x}_r). \qquad (8.31)$$

The second approximation method is based on variational methods. Variational methods in this context refer to the methods for approximating a complex distribution $P(\mathbf{x})$ by a simpler one $Q_\theta(\mathbf{x})$ which is parameterized by adjustable parameters θ. The parameter θ is adjusted so that Q_θ is the best approximation to P in some sense. We will use the mean field approximation to illustrate this idea. In the mean field approximation, we use a fully factored distribution $Q_\theta(\mathbf{x}) = \prod Q_i(x_i; \theta_i)$ to approximate P. The quality of the approximation is measured using the KL divergence between Q and P:

$$KL(Q\|P) = \sum_{\mathbf{x}} Q_\theta(\mathbf{x}) \log \frac{Q_\theta(\mathbf{x})}{P(\mathbf{x})}. \tag{8.32}$$

Consider a distribution for binary valued vector $\mathbf{x}$:

$$P(\mathbf{x}) = \frac{1}{Z} \exp(-\phi(\mathbf{x})), \tag{8.33}$$

the KL-divergence between Q and P is:

$$KL(Q\|P) = \sum_{\mathbf{x}} Q_\theta(\mathbf{x}) \log \frac{Q_\theta(\mathbf{x})}{\exp(-\phi(\mathbf{x}))/Z} \tag{8.34}$$

$$= \sum_{\mathbf{x}} Q_\theta(\mathbf{x})\phi(\mathbf{x}) + \sum_{\mathbf{x}} Q_\theta(\mathbf{x}) \log Q_\theta(\mathbf{x}) + \log Z \tag{8.35}$$

$$= E_Q(\phi(\mathbf{x})) - H_Q + \log Z, \tag{8.36}$$

where $E_Q(\phi(\mathbf{x}))$ is the average of energy function under distribution Q and H_Q is the entropy of distribution Q.

Consider a distribution for binary valued vector $\mathbf{x} \in \{-1, 1\}^d$ where the energy function is

$$\phi(\mathbf{x}) = -\frac{1}{2}\mathbf{x}^T W \mathbf{x} - \mathbf{x}^T \mathbf{b}. \tag{8.37}$$

Since each Q_i is a distribution for a binary variable x_i, we only need one parameter θ_i to define Q_i. $Q_i(1; \theta_i) = \frac{1+\theta_i}{2}$ and $Q_i(-1; \theta_i) = \frac{1-\theta_i}{2}$. Hence

$$Q_i(x_i; \theta_i) = \frac{1 + x_i\theta_i}{2}. \tag{8.38}$$

So the entire approximation distribution Q_θ is:

$$Q_\theta(\mathbf{x}) = \prod_i \frac{1 + x_i\theta_i}{2}. \tag{8.39}$$

$E_Q(\phi(\mathbf{x}))$ and H_Q in (8.36) can be calculated as:

$$E_Q(\phi(\mathbf{x})) = -\frac{1}{2} \sum_{ij} \sum_{x_i, x_j} W_{ij} x_i x_j Q_i(x_i; \theta_i) Q_j(x_j; \theta_j) \tag{8.40}$$

$$-\sum_{i}\sum_{x_i} x_i b_i Q_i(x_i; \theta_i) \tag{8.41}$$

$$= -\frac{1}{2}\sum_{ij} W_{ij}\theta_i\theta_j - \sum_i b_i\theta_i, \tag{8.42}$$

$$H_Q = -\sum_{i}\sum_{x_i} \frac{1+x_i\theta_i}{2} \log \frac{1+x_i\theta_i}{2} \tag{8.43}$$

$$= -\sum_i \left(\frac{1+\theta_i}{2} \log \frac{1+\theta_i}{2} + \frac{1-\theta_i}{2} \log \frac{1-\theta_i}{2} \right). \tag{8.44}$$

Taking the derivative of $KL(Q||P)$ with respect to θ, we obtain the fixed point condition for the optimal θ:

$$\frac{1}{2} \log \frac{1+\theta_i}{1-\theta_i} = \sum_j W_{ij}\theta_j + b_i\theta_i. \tag{8.45}$$

The third approximation method is to apply the sum-product algorithm. Although sum-product algorithm is derived for tree structured graphical models, one of the most surprising use of the sum-product algorithm is to apply it to graphical models with loops. To apply sum-product algorithm to graph with loops, we use the normalized messages as in (8.22) and message passing method 2. Once the messages converge (if they do) after some iterations, we can use the messages to calculate the desired probabilities as we do for tree-structured models. Although sounding a quite heuristic approach, this way of using the sum-product algorithm is really supported by theory. In fact, the converged messages are the solution to a particular variation approximation called Bethe/Kickuchi to the original distribution [67].

8.5 Learning

Suppose that the model has parameter θ and we have a training data set $\mathbf{D} = \{D_1, \cdots, D_N\}$, where each case D_n consists of an assignment of values to some subset of variables in the graphical model, the learning task concerns about making a prediction of an unknown quantity $\mathbf{x}$. In full Bayesian learning, the prediction of $\mathbf{x}$ is given by the following equation

$$P(\mathbf{x}|\mathbf{D}) = \int_\theta P(\mathbf{x}|\theta)P(\theta|\mathbf{D}). $$

Thus the learning requires the computation of $P(\theta|\mathbf{D})$. In most practical problems, it is too difficult to calculate $P(\theta|\mathbf{D})$, and the maximum a posteriori

(MAP) solution $\theta_{MAP} = \arg\max_\theta P(\theta|D)$ is used instead of the full posterior distribution. The prediction based on the MAP solution is $P(\mathbf{x}|\theta_{MAP})$. By Bayes rule

$$P(\theta|D) \propto P(\mathbf{D}|\theta)P(\theta),$$

where $P(\theta)$ is the prior distribution of θ. Hence

$$\theta_{MAP} = \arg\max_\theta P(\theta|D) = \arg\max_\theta P(\mathbf{D}|\theta)P(\theta).$$

For many models, it is still not possible to obtain the closed form solution for the MAP solution. Hence learning using general purpose nonlinear optimization methods is most widely applied to different models. For many nonlinear optimization methods, gradient is required, so we will spend some efforts to study how to calculate the gradient of the log-likelihood with respect to the parameters

$$L = \log P(\mathbf{D}|\theta)P(\theta) = \log P(\theta) + \sum_n \log P(D_n|\theta).$$

The gradient $\frac{\partial L}{\partial \theta}$:

$$\frac{\partial L}{\partial \theta} = \frac{\partial \log P(\theta)}{\partial \theta} + \sum_n \frac{\partial \log P(D_n|\theta)}{\partial \theta}.$$

Suppose that for the training case D_n, $\mathbf{x}_A$ are the observed variables and $\mathbf{x}_{\bar{A}}$ are the unobserved variables, then

$$\begin{aligned}
&\frac{\partial \log P(D_n|\theta)}{\partial \theta} \\
&= \frac{\partial \log P(\mathbf{x}_A)}{\partial \theta} = \frac{\partial}{\partial \theta} \log\left(\frac{g_A(\mathbf{x}_A)}{Z}\right) \\
&= \frac{\partial}{\partial \theta}(\log g_A(\mathbf{x}_A)) - \frac{\partial \log Z}{\partial \theta}.
\end{aligned}$$

The first term in the last equality of the above equation is:

$$\begin{aligned}
&\frac{\partial}{\partial \theta}(\log g_A(\mathbf{x}_A)) \\
&= \frac{\partial}{\partial \theta}(\log \sum_{\mathbf{x}_{\bar{A}}} g(\mathbf{x})) \\
&= \frac{1}{g_A(\mathbf{x}_A)}\frac{\partial}{\partial \theta}(\sum_{\mathbf{x}_{\bar{A}}} g(\mathbf{x}))
\end{aligned}$$

$$= \frac{1}{g_A(\mathbf{x}_A)} \sum_{\mathbf{x}_{\bar{A}}} g(\mathbf{x}) \frac{\partial \log g(\mathbf{x})}{\partial \theta}$$

$$= \sum_{\mathbf{x}_{\bar{A}}} P(\mathbf{x}|\mathbf{x}_A) \frac{\partial \log g(\mathbf{x})}{\partial \theta}$$

$$= \sum_{i} \sum_{\mathbf{x}_{\bar{A}}} P(\mathbf{x}|\mathbf{x}_A) \frac{\partial \log g_i(\mathbf{x}_i)}{\partial \theta}$$

$$= \sum_{i} \sum_{\mathbf{x}_i \backslash A} P(\mathbf{x}_i|\mathbf{x}_A) \frac{\partial \log g_i(\mathbf{x}_i)}{\partial \theta}.$$

The second term, for directed graphical models, since $Z = 1$, $\frac{\partial \log Z}{\partial \theta} = 0$. For undirected graphical models:

$$\frac{\partial \log Z}{\partial \theta} = \frac{1}{Z} \frac{\partial Z}{\partial \theta}$$

$$= \frac{1}{Z} \frac{\partial}{\partial \theta} \sum_{\mathbf{x}} g(\mathbf{x})$$

$$= \frac{1}{Z} \sum_{\mathbf{x}} g(\mathbf{x}) \frac{\partial \log g(\mathbf{x})}{\partial \theta}$$

$$= \sum_{\mathbf{x}} P(\mathbf{x}) \frac{\partial \log g(\mathbf{x})}{\partial \theta}$$

$$= \sum_{\mathbf{x}} P(\mathbf{x}) \sum_{i} \frac{\partial \log g(\mathbf{x}_i)}{\partial \theta}$$

$$= \sum_{i} \sum_{\mathbf{x}_i} P(\mathbf{x}_i) \frac{\partial \log g(\mathbf{x}_i)}{\partial \theta}.$$

Hence for directed graphical models

$$\frac{\partial \log P(\mathbf{x}_A)}{\partial \theta} = E\left(\frac{\partial \log g(\mathbf{x})}{\partial \theta} | \mathbf{x}_A\right).$$

For undirected graphical models

$$\frac{\partial \log P(\mathbf{x}_A)}{\partial \theta} = E\left(\frac{\partial \log g(\mathbf{x})}{\partial \theta} | \mathbf{x}_A\right) - E\left(\frac{\partial \log g(\mathbf{x})}{\partial \theta}\right). \tag{8.46}$$

Let us have a close look at the gradient. The first term is the expectation of $\frac{\partial \log g(\mathbf{x})}{\partial \theta}$ conditioned on the observed variables $\mathbf{x}_A$. The second term is the expectation of $\frac{\partial \log g(\mathbf{x})}{\partial \theta}$ without any condition.

There are several methods to calculate these expectations. The first method requires the computation of $P(\mathbf{x}_i|\mathbf{x}_A)$ and $P(\mathbf{x}_i)$. As shown in the previous sections, these values can be efficiently calculated if the graphical model is tree-structured. Otherwise, approximate methods such as those described in section 8.4 need to be applied to calculate them. The second method is based on the Monte Carlo estimation of the expectation. The key is to generate random samples from the distributions $P(\mathbf{x}|\mathbf{x}_A)$ and $P(\mathbf{x})$. The MCMC sampling methods in previous chapters can be used to generate these samples.

Once we are able to obtain the gradient, we can apply existing optimization algorithms to find the best solution. Stochastic gradient descent, conjugate gradient, and quasi-Newton method are some of the most popular optimization algorithms used for this problem. Sometimes the gradient is so simple, we can also find the solution analytically.

Example: Directed graphical models with completely observed data. Suppose that the parameter for each factor g_i is θ_i and the prior distribution for θ_i is $P(\theta_i)$. Then,

$$\frac{\partial \log P(\mathbf{x}|\theta)}{\partial \theta_i} = \frac{\partial \log g_i(\mathbf{x}_i)}{\partial \theta_i}.$$

The maximum a posteriori solution can be simply found by solving the following equations for θ_i

$$\frac{\partial \log P(\theta_i)}{\partial \theta_i} + \sum_n \frac{\partial \log g_i(\mathbf{x}_i^{(n)})}{\partial \theta_i} = 0.$$

Example: Conditional a random field with a chain structure. Conditional random field (CRF) of $\mathbf{y}$ given $\mathbf{x}$ is a probabilistic model that uses a Markov random field, whose parameters depend on $\mathbf{x}$, to model the conditional distribution $P(\mathbf{y}|\mathbf{x})$. CRF takes the following form:

$$P(\mathbf{y}|\mathbf{x}) = \frac{1}{Z(\mathbf{x})} \exp\left(\sum_i \phi_i(\mathbf{y}_i, \mathbf{x})\right). \qquad (8.47)$$

Figure 8.5 shows a conditional random field model with chain structure. In this model, there are two types of potential functions: $f_\lambda(y_i, y_{i+1}, i, \mathbf{x})$ for the edges between adjacent y's, and $g_\mu(y_i, i, \mathbf{x})$ for the single y's, where λ and μ are the parameters. The training data for CRF is a set $\{\mathbf{x}^{(t)}, \mathbf{y}^{(t)}\}$ of paired $\mathbf{x}$ and $\mathbf{y}$. For this model, using (8.46), we get the gradient for λ and μ as

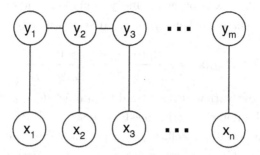

Fig. 8.5. A chain-structured conditional random field model

$$\frac{\partial \log P(\mathbf{y}|\mathbf{x})}{\partial \lambda} = \sum_i \frac{\partial f_\lambda(y_i, y_{i+1}, i, \mathbf{x})}{\partial \lambda} - \sum_i \sum_{y_i, y_{i+1}} P(y_i, y_{i+1}|\mathbf{x}) \frac{\partial f_\lambda(y_i, y_{i+1}, i, \mathbf{x})}{\partial \lambda},$$

$$\tag{8.48}$$

$$\frac{\partial \log P(\mathbf{y}|\mathbf{x})}{\partial \lambda} = \sum_i \frac{\partial g_\mu(y_i, i, \mathbf{x})}{\partial \mu} - \sum_i \sum_{y_i} P(y_i|\mathbf{x}) \frac{\partial g_\mu(y_i, i, \mathbf{x})}{\partial \mu}. \tag{8.49}$$

The conditional marginal probability $P(y_i|\mathbf{x})$ and $P(y_i, y_{i+1}|\mathbf{x})$ can be calculated efficiently using the sum-product algorithm described in Sect. 8.2 because of the simple chain structure.

Example: Restricted Boltzmann machines. A restricted Boltzmann machine is an MRF with bipartite graph structure (Fig. (8.6)).

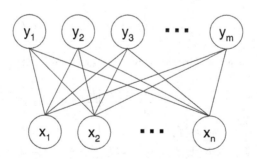

Fig. 8.6. Restricted Boltzmann machine

The energy function is:

$$E = -\sum_{ij} x_i w_{ij} y_j - \sum_i a_i x_i - \sum_j b_j y_j = -\mathbf{x}^T \mathbf{W} \mathbf{y} - \mathbf{a}^T \mathbf{x} - \mathbf{b}^T \mathbf{y}. \tag{8.50}$$

In the training data, $\mathbf{x}$ is observed and $\mathbf{y}$ is hidden. The first term in (8.46) can be easily calculated because $y_1 \cdots y_m$ are conditionally independent given $\mathbf{x}$:

$$P(y_j|\mathbf{x}) = \frac{\exp(y_j(b_j + \sum_i x_i W_{ij}))}{\sum_y \exp(y(b_j + \sum_i x_i W_{ij}))}.$$

However, exact evaluation of the second term in (8.46) is prohibitive because the exponential number of terms need to be summed. Because both $P(\mathbf{y}|\mathbf{x})$ and $P(\mathbf{x}|\mathbf{y})$ can be sampled efficiently, a practical way to evaluation the expectation is to use Gibbs sampling to calculate the expectation in the second term.

Problems

8.1. Draw a directed graphical model corresponding to the cluster model for 3 data points in problem 7.5

8.2. For the model in Fig. 8.1

(a) Calculate the probability of a burglary event given that you received a call.

(b) Suppose that in addition to receiving a call, you also found out that there was an earthquake. Calculate the probability of a burglary event.

8.3. (a) Draw the factor graph for the following function

$$g(x_1, x_2, x_3, x_4, x_5, x_6) = f_1(x_1, x_2)f_2(x_2, x_3)f_3(x_3, x_4, x_5)f_4(x_5, x_6)f_5(x_6) \tag{8.51}$$

(b) The values of the functions $f_1 \cdots f_5$ are listed in the following tables.

x_1	x_2	f_1
0	0	2
0	1	1
1	0	1
1	1	3

x_2	x_3	f_2
0	0	2
0	1	1
1	0	1
1	1	2

x_3	x_4	x_5	f_3
0	0	0	2
0	0	1	1
0	1	0	1
0	1	1	2
1	0	0	1
1	0	1	2
1	1	0	2
1	1	1	1

x_5	x_6	f_4
0	0	1
0	1	2
1	0	2
1	1	3

x_6	f_4
0	3
1	2

Use the sum-product algorithm to calculate the marginal function $g(x_2)$.

8.4. Use the max-product algorithm to find the maximal values of g in Problem 8.3 and the corresponding values of $x_1, \cdots, x_6$.

8.5. Describe how to calculate more complex marginal functions such as $Z_{1,2}(x_1, x_2)$ using the messages computed by the sum-product algorithm. Focusing the cases where x_1 and x_2 are connected to a common factor node.

8.6. Consider a Gaussian Markov random field with energy function

$$E(\mathbf{x}) = \frac{1}{2} \sum_{i,j} x_i A_{ij} x_j + \sum_i x_i b_i, \tag{8.52}$$

where $\mathbf{x}$ is a continuous state variable and $\mathbf{A}$ is a positive definite matrix. If the none zero elements of $\mathbf{A}$ correspond to a tree, the sum-product algorithm can be used to evaluate the marginal distribution of each variable. Derive the message passing equations for this model.

8.7. Consider an undirected graphical model

$$p(\mathbf{x}) = \frac{1}{Z} \prod_{t=1}^{T} f(x_{t-1}, x_t), \tag{8.53}$$

where $x_t \in \{1, \cdots, M\}$. Show that this model can be converted to a directed graphical model

$$p(\mathbf{x}) = p_0(x_0) \prod_{t=1}^{T} p(x_t | x_{t-1}). \tag{8.54}$$

Derive the formulas to calculate $p_0(x_0)$ and $p(x_t | x_{t-1})$.

8.8. Consider a distribution $P(x = i, y = i) = p_i$ and $P(x = i, y = j) = 0$ for $i \neq j$. Suppose that we use a factorized distribution $Q(x, y) = Q_x(x) Q_y(y)$ to approximate P.

(a) For the approximation criterion $KL(P||Q)$, find the best Q.
(b) For the approximation criterion $KL(Q||P)$, find the best Q.

8.9. For the cluster model 7.5, use the mean field method described in Sect. 8.4 to find the posterior distribution $P(\mu_i|D)$ and $P(\pi_1, \cdots, \pi_K|D)$. Compare with the solution found by the EM algorithm. (Hint: use distribution of the form $Q_\pi(\pi) \prod_{k=1}^{K} Q_{\mu_k}(\mu_k) \prod_{n=1}^{N} Q_{c_n}(c_n)$ to approximate $P(\pi, \mu, c|D)$).

Part III

Discriminative Graphical Models

9

Maximum Entropy Model and Conditional Random Field

In Part II of this book, we described typical generative graphical models that attempt to model the probability $P(x|k)$ of generating the observation x given the class k. Generative models have been traditionally popular for data classification tasks because modeling $P(x|k)$ is often easier than modeling $P(k|x)$, and there exist well-established, easy-to-implement algorithms such as the EM and the Baum-Welch algorithms (see Chap. 7) to efficiently estimate the model through a learning process. The ease of use, and the theoretical beauty of generative models, however, do come with a cost. Many complex events, such as baseball highlights described in the case study in Chap. 7, need to be represented by a vector **x** of many features that depend on each other. To make the model estimation process tractable, generative models commonly assume conditional independence among all the features comprising the feature vector **x**. Because this assumption is for the sake of mathematical convenience rather than the reflection of a reality, generative models often have limited performance accuracies for classifying complex data sets.

In Part III, we will present discriminative models that are particularly powerful and effective for modeling multimedia data. Discriminative models strive to learn $P(k|x)$ directly from a training set without the attempt to model the observation x. They typically make very few assumptions about the data and the features, and in a sense, let the data speak for themselves. Recent research studies have shown that discriminative models outperform generative models in many applications such as natural language processing, web page classifications, baseball highlight detections, etc.

In this chapter, we will describe a statistical model that conforms to the maximum entropy principle (we will call it the maximum entropy model, or

ME model in short) [68, 69]. Through mathematical derivations, we will show that the maximum entropy model is a kind of exponential model, and is a close sibling of the Gibbs distribution described in Chap. 6. An essential difference between the two models is that the former is a discriminative model, while the latter is a generative model. Through a model complexity analysis, we will show why discriminative models are generally superior to generative models in terms of data modeling power. We will also describe the Conditional Random Field (CRF), one of the latest discriminative models in the literature, and prove that CRF is equivalent to the maximum entropy model. At the end of this chapter, we will provide a case study where the ME model is applied to baseball highlight detections, and is compared with the HMM model described in Chap. 7.

9.1 Overview of Maximum Entropy Model

The principle of the maximum entropy model is simple: model all that is known and assume nothing about what is unknown. In other words, given a collection of facts, the maximum entropy method chooses a model which is consistent with all the facts, but otherwise is as uniform as possible.

The maximum entropy principle can be illustrated using a simple example. Assume that we wish to construct a baseball highlight detector able to detect the following five types of highlights from TV broadcasted baseball videos: *home run (HR)*, *infield hit (IH)*, *infield out (IO)*, *outfield hit (OH)*, and *outfield out (OO)*. Our baseball highlight detector assigns to each video scene[1] s having the feature vector $\mathbf{x}$ a probability $P(y|\mathbf{x})$ that s contains highlight y, where $y \in \{HR, IH, IO, OH, OO, OT\}$, and OT represents any other events. For developing the model $P(Y|X)$[2], we collect a large sample of baseball videos to learn what features/facts are useful for highlight detections. Suppose that one statistic we have discovered from the sample is that the above five types of highlights constitute 80% of all baseball events after a batter hits the ball (the remaining 20% goes to the OT category). With this information in hand, we can impose the first constraint on our model $P(Y|X)$:

---

[1] Here a video scene is defined as one or more video shots which contains a complete baseball event.

[2] Remind that in this book, we use uppercase letters to represent random variables, and use lowercase letters to denote observed values of random variables

$$P(HR|BT) + P(IH|BT) + P(IO|BT) + P(OH|BT) + P(OO|BT) = 0.8 ,$$
$$(9.1)$$

where BT denotes the observation (the feature) that a batter hits the ball.

There are an infinite number of models $P(Y|X)$ that satisfy the above constraint. One such model is $P(HR|BT) = 0.8$. In other words, the model always predicts a home run event after observing a batting of the ball. Another model that obeys the above constraint predicts HR and OO with the probabilities of 0.5 and 0.3 respectively, that is, $P(HR|BT) = 0.5$, $P(OO|BT) = 0.3$. However, both of these models are not correct because they do not agree with our common sense about baseball games. The key problem with these two models is that they assume more than we actually know about the statistics of the training sample. All we know at this moment is that the five types of highlights listed above make up a total of 80% of all baseball events after a batter hits the ball. Clearly, the above two models are making rather bold assumptions that can not be justified by the knowledge we have right now.

Based on the above discussions, the most appealing model will be the one that allocates the total probability evenly among the five types of highlights:

$$P(HR|BT) = 0.16, \quad P(IH|BT) = 0.16, \quad P(IO|BT) = 0.16,$$
$$P(OH|BT) = 0.16, \quad P(OO|BT) = 0.16 .$$

This is the most uniform model subject to our knowledge, and is the one that is advocated and searched for by the maximum entropy method.

To make our model more accurate in detecting the five types of baseball highlights, we want to collect more statistics of baseball games. Suppose that, through a further examination of our sample, we have discovered a second statistic that the highlights IO and OO occur 70% of the time after a batter hits the ball. We can apply this knowledge to update our model by requiring that $P(Y|X)$ satisfy the following constraint as well:

$$P(IO|BT) + P(OO|BT) = 0.7 . \qquad (9.2)$$

Again, there are many models $P(Y|X)$ that obey both of the constraints (9.1) and (9.2). In the absence of any other knowledge, the maximum entropy method prefers the model $P(Y|X)$ that allocates its probability as evenly as possible, subject to the constraints:

$$P(IO|BT) = 0.35, \quad P(OO|BT) = 0.35, \quad P(HR|BT) = 1/30,$$
$$P(IH|BT) = 1/30, \quad P(OH|BT) = 1/30 .$$

We can once again inspect the sample data to discover new statistics, and look for the model $P(Y|X)$ that is consistent with all the constraints, and is as uniform as possible otherwise. As we add more constraints to the model, the task of finding the model that satisfies the maximum entropy principle becomes more and more difficult. In the next section, we will formalize what we have described above using mathematical terms, and will present the maximum entropy method that aims to systematically construct the model that satisfies the maximum entropy principle under a set of constraints.

9.2 Maximum Entropy Framework

To construct a statistical model $P(Y|X)$ that satisfies the maximum entropy principle in a systematic way, we need to first solve the following three problems. First, how do we mathematically express those facts/statistics we have discovered from data samples? Second, how do we construct the model that is consistent with all the facts, and is as uniform as possible otherwise (we call such a model the maximum entropy model)? Third, for many real world problems, it is unlikely that we will obtain an analytic solution for constructing a maximum entropy model. So what is the efficient numeric method for constructing such a model? In this section, we will present the solutions to these three problems.

9.2.1 Feature Function

The maximum entropy method solves the first problem by introducing the *feature functions*, often binary-valued, and by computing the expected values of the feature functions with respect to the empirical distributions obtained from the training sample. For example, we can use the following feature function to express the fact that the video scene corresponds to a home run event if the ball flying over the fence is observed

$$f(X, Y) = \begin{cases} 1 & \text{if } Y = HR \text{ and } X = \text{ball flying over the fence,} \\ 0 & \text{otherwise.} \end{cases} \tag{9.3}$$

Using this feature function, the statistic that a home run event occurs 50% of the time if the ball flying over the fence has been observed can be expressed as the expected value of f with respect to the empirical distribution $\tilde{P}(X, Y)$

$$\tilde{P}(f) = \sum_{\mathbf{x},y} \tilde{P}(\mathbf{x}, y) f(\mathbf{x}, y) = 0.5 , \qquad (9.4)$$

where $\tilde{P}(\mathbf{x}, y)$ can be obtained by counting the number of times that $(\mathbf{x}, y)$ occurs in the training sample. This way, we can express any statistic of a training sample as the expected value $\tilde{P}(f)$ of an appropriately defined feature function $f(X, Y)$ that represents an important fact/event of the sample.

9.2.2 Maximum Entropy Model Construction

The maximum entropy method constructs the maximum entropy model $P_{me}(Y|X)$ by solving an optimization problem under a set of constraints. Here, the constraints serve to enforce the compliance of the model $P_{me}(Y|X)$ with the statistics of the training sample. As described in Sect. 9.2.1, we define a feature function $f(X, Y)$ (often binary-valued) for each important fact/feature of the training sample. The expected value of f with respect to the model $P_{me}(Y|X)$ is defined as

$$P_{me}(f) = \sum_{\mathbf{x},y} \tilde{P}(\mathbf{x}) P_{me}(y|\mathbf{x}) f(\mathbf{x}, y) , \qquad (9.5)$$

where $\tilde{P}(\mathbf{x})$ is the empirical distribution of $\mathbf{x}$ in the training sample. The maximum entropy method demands that the expected value of f with respect to the model $P_{me}(Y|X)$ equal the expected value of f with respect to the empirical distribution $\tilde{P}(X, Y)$ (i.e. the statistic of the training sample):

$$P_{me}(f) = \tilde{P}(f) . \qquad (9.6)$$

We call (9.6) a *constraint equation* or simply a *constraint*. By restricting attention to those models $P_{me}(Y|X)$ for which (9.6) holds, we are eliminating from consideration those models that do not comply with the statistics of the training sample.

Suppose that we have defined n feature functions $f_i(X, Y)$, which determine the statistics we want our model $P_{me}(Y|X)$ to comply with. Then, the set $\mathcal{P}$ of models that are the candidates of the maximum entropy model can be defined as

$$\mathcal{P} = \{ P(Y|X) \mid P(f_i) = \tilde{P}(f_i),\ i = 1, 2, \ldots, n \} \qquad (9.7)$$

Now we have a means of representing statistics of a training sample (namely $\tilde{P}(f)$), and also a means of requiring that our model comply with these statistics (namely $P_{me}(f) = \tilde{P}(f)$). The next problem is: How do we enforce the uniformity of a model subject to the constraints, as requested by the maximum entropy principle?

A mathematical measure of the uniformity of a conditional distribution $P(Y|X)$ is provided by the conditional entropy

$$H(P) = -\sum_{x,y} \tilde{P}(x) P(y|x) \log P(y|x) . \tag{9.8}$$

Using the conditional entropy and the notations we have developed above, we can mathematically define the model $P_{me}(Y|X)$ that satisfies the maximum entropy principle as follows

$$P_{me} = \arg\max_{P \in \mathcal{P}} H(P) . \tag{9.9}$$

This definition is nothing but a mathematical statement of the maximum entropy principle: Be consistent with all the facts (which is expressed by $P \in \mathcal{P}$), but otherwise as uniform as possible (which is expressed by the maximization of $H(P)$).

Finding the solution to (9.9) is a typical constrained optimization problem, which can be generally solved using the Lagrange multiplier technique [26]. We outline the application of the Lagrange multiplier method to problem (9.9) as follows.

The Lagrange multiplier method first defines a Lagrangian function using a set of Lagrangian multipliers λ_i, one for each constraint

$$L(P, \lambda) = H(P) + \sum_{i=1}^{n} \lambda_i (P(f_i) - \tilde{P}(f_i)) . \tag{9.10}$$

Next, fixing λ, we compute the unconstrained maximum of the Lagrangian function $L(P, \lambda)$ over all $P \in \mathcal{P}$. This can be accomplished by differentiating $L(P, \lambda)$ with respect to P, and then setting the differential to zero:

$$\frac{\partial L(P, \lambda)}{\partial P} = -\tilde{P}(x) \log P(y|x) - \tilde{P}(x) P(y|x) \frac{1}{P(y|x)} + \sum_{i=1}^{n} \lambda_i \tilde{P}(x) f_i(x, y)$$

$$= -\tilde{P}(x) \log P(y|x) - \tilde{P}(x) + \sum_{i=1}^{n} \lambda_i \tilde{P}(x) f_i(x, y)$$

$$= 0 . \tag{9.11}$$

Therefore, the P that maximizes the Lagrangian function $L(P, \lambda)$ (denoted as P_λ) becomes

$$P_\lambda(y|\mathbf{x}) = \frac{1}{Z_\lambda(\mathbf{x})} \exp\left(-1 + \sum_{i=1}^{n} \lambda_i f_i(\mathbf{x}, y)\right)$$

$$= \frac{1}{Z_\lambda(\mathbf{x})} \exp\left(\sum_{i=1}^{n} \lambda_i f_i(\mathbf{x}, y)\right), \tag{9.12}$$

where $Z_\lambda(\mathbf{x})$ is a normalizing constant that ensures $\sum_y P_\lambda(y|\mathbf{x}) = 1$ for all $\mathbf{x}$:

$$Z_\lambda(\mathbf{x}) = \sum_y \exp\left(\sum_{i=1}^{n} \lambda_i f_i(\mathbf{x}, y)\right). \tag{9.13}$$

Note that we obtain the second equality of (9.12) by dividing both the numerator and the denominator by $\exp(-1)$.

Let $\Theta(\mathbf{x}, y) = \sum_{i=1}^{n} \lambda_i f_i(\mathbf{x}, y)$. With P_λ, the value of the Lagrangian function $L(P, \lambda)$ becomes

$$
\begin{aligned}
L(P_\lambda, \lambda) &= H(P_\lambda) + \sum_i \lambda_i (P_\lambda(f_i) - \tilde{P}(f_i)) \\
&= -\sum_{\mathbf{x},y} \tilde{P}(\mathbf{x}) \frac{1}{Z_\lambda(\mathbf{x})} \exp(\Theta(\mathbf{x}, y)) \log \frac{1}{Z_\lambda(\mathbf{x})} \exp(\Theta(\mathbf{x}, y)) \\
&\quad + \sum_i \lambda_i \left(\sum_{\mathbf{x},y} \tilde{P}(\mathbf{x}) \frac{1}{Z_\lambda(\mathbf{x})} \exp(\Theta(\mathbf{x}, y)) f_i(\mathbf{x}, y) - \tilde{P}(f_i) \right) \\
&= -\sum_{\mathbf{x},y} \tilde{P}(\mathbf{x}) \frac{1}{Z_\lambda(\mathbf{x})} \exp(\Theta(\mathbf{x}, y)) \left[\log \exp(\Theta(\mathbf{x}, y)) - \log Z_\lambda(\mathbf{x}) \right] \\
&\quad + \left(\sum_{\mathbf{x},y} \tilde{P}(\mathbf{x}) \frac{1}{Z_\lambda(\mathbf{x})} \exp(\Theta(\mathbf{x}, y)) \sum_i \lambda_i f_i(\mathbf{x}, y) - \sum_i \lambda_i \tilde{P}(f_i) \right) \\
&= -\sum_{\mathbf{x},y} \tilde{P}(\mathbf{x}) \frac{1}{Z_\lambda(\mathbf{x})} \exp(\Theta(\mathbf{x}, y)) \Theta(\mathbf{x}, y) \\
&\quad + \sum_{\mathbf{x}} \tilde{P}(\mathbf{x}) \frac{1}{Z_\lambda(\mathbf{x})} \log Z_\lambda(\mathbf{x}) \sum_y \exp(\Theta(\mathbf{x}, y)) \\
&\quad + \left(\sum_{\mathbf{x},y} \tilde{P}(\mathbf{x}) \frac{1}{Z_\lambda(\mathbf{x})} \exp(\Theta(\mathbf{x}, y)) \Theta(\mathbf{x}, y) - \sum_i \lambda_i \tilde{P}(f_i) \right) \\
&= \sum_{\mathbf{x}} \tilde{P}(\mathbf{x}) \log Z_\lambda(\mathbf{x}) - \sum_i \lambda_i \tilde{P}(f_i). \tag{9.14}
\end{aligned}
$$

The function $L(P_\lambda, \lambda)$ is called the *dual function*. The Lagrangian multiplier method finds the final optimal solution by computing the λ_{min} that minimizes the dual function $L(P_\lambda, \lambda)$

$$\lambda_{min} = \arg \min_{\lambda} L(P_\lambda, \lambda). \tag{9.15}$$

The problem of optimizing (9.15) is called the dual optimization problem, whereas optimizing (9.9) is called the primal optimization problem. The Kuhn-Tucker theorem asserts that under certain conditions, the primal and the dual problems are equivalent to each other, and the solution to one problem is also the solution to the other one [26]. Applying this theorem to our problem here, we can assert that if λ_{min} is the solution to the dual problem, then $P_{\lambda_{min}}$ is the solution to the primal problem; that is $P_{me} = P_{\lambda_{min}}$.

Based on the above mathematical derivations using the Lagrangian multiplier method, we can summarize the maximum entropy model as follows: The maximum entropy model subject to the constraints $\mathcal{P}$ has the parametric form

$$P_\lambda(y|\mathbf{x}) = \frac{1}{Z_\lambda(\mathbf{x})} \exp\left(\sum_{i=1}^n \lambda_i f_i(\mathbf{x}, y)\right),$$

and the optimal parameter values λ_{min} can be determined by minimizing the dual function

$$L(P_\lambda, \lambda) = \sum_{\mathbf{x}} \tilde{P}(\mathbf{x}) \log Z_\lambda(\mathbf{x}) - \sum_i \lambda_i \tilde{P}(f_i).$$

9.2.3 Parameter Computation

For all but the most simple problem, we can not analytically compute the λ_{min} that minimizes the dual function $L(P_\lambda, \lambda)$, and must resort to numerical methods to find the solution. There are a variety of numerical methods that can be used to compute λ_{min}. Since the first order derivative of $L(P_\lambda, \lambda)$ with respect to λ can be easily computed as follows (see Problem 9.9 at the end of this chapter)

$$\frac{\partial L(P_\lambda, \lambda)}{\partial \lambda_i} = P_\lambda(f_i) - \tilde{P}(f_i), \tag{9.16}$$

we can use the gradient descent method to incrementally minimize $L(P_\lambda, \lambda)$ through a hill descent process. More specifically, the gradient descent method starts at an initial guess λ_0, and then successively generates vectors $\lambda_1, \lambda_2, \ldots$ using the following equation

$$\lambda_{k+1} = \lambda_k - \alpha \nabla L(P_{\lambda_k}, \lambda_k), \tag{9.17}$$

where α is called the stepsize for the gradient descent, and must be a positive but sufficiently small constant. It can be mathematically proven that the successively generated vectors $\lambda_1, \lambda_2, \ldots$ monotonically decrease the value of $L(P_\lambda, \lambda)$:

$$L(P_{\lambda_{k+1}}, \lambda_{k+1}) > L(P_{\lambda_k}, \lambda_k), \quad k = 0, 1, 2, \ldots \qquad (9.18)$$

Therefore, λ_{min} will be reached with a sufficiently large number of iterations. One thing to be noticed is that there is no guarantee that the gradient descent method will generate a globally optimal solution λ_{min}, and that we could well end up with one of many local minimum solutions.

A variation of the above gradient descent method is the coordinate-wise descent method, which incrementally improves the solution by updating one dimension λ_i of λ at each iteration using the following equations

$$\lambda_i^{(k+1)} = \lambda_i^{(k)} - \alpha(P_{\lambda^{(k)}}(f_i) - \tilde{P}(f_i)), \qquad (9.19)$$
$$\lambda^{(k+1)} \leftarrow \{\lambda_1^{(k)}, \ldots, \lambda_i^{(k+1)}, \ldots, \lambda_n^{(k)}\}, \qquad (9.20)$$

and cycling through all the dimensions of λ in sequence. When applied to the maximum entropy problem, this technique yields the popular Brown Algorithm [70].

An optimization method specially tailored to the maximum entropy problem is the iterative scaling algorithm developed by Darroch and Ratcliff [71]. The algorithm is applicable whenever the feature functions satisfy the condition of $f_i(\mathbf{x}, y) \geq 0$ for all i, $\mathbf{x}$, and y. This is, of course, true for the binary-valued feature functions we introduced in Sect. 9.2.1. The general procedure of the algorithm can be described as follows:

1. Start with $\lambda_i = 0$, where $i = 1, 2, \ldots, n$.
2. Set $i = 1$.
3. Compute the increment $\Delta\lambda_i$ that solves the following equation

$$\sum_{\mathbf{x},y} \tilde{P}(\mathbf{x})P(y|\mathbf{x})f_i(\mathbf{x}, y) \exp\left(\Delta\lambda_i f^\#(\mathbf{x}, y)\right) = \tilde{P}(f_i), \qquad (9.21)$$

   where $f^\#(\mathbf{x}, y) = \sum_{i=1}^n f_i(\mathbf{x}, y)$.
4. Update λ_i by $\lambda_i \leftarrow \lambda_i + \Delta\lambda_i$.
5. If $i < n$, set $i = i + 1$, goto Step 3; otherwise, if not all λ_i have converged, goto Step 2; otherwise, terminate the operation.

The proof of the monotonicity and convergence of the iterative scaling algorithm can be found in [69], It is noteworthy that although this algorithm is specially tailored to the maximum entropy problem, its performance is not superior to other general purpose optimization algorithms. Our past experiences have shown that the gradient ascent and the conjugate gradient methods are at least as good as, or even better than the iterative scaling algorithm in terms of the computational simplicity and convergence speed.

9.3 Comparison to Generative Models

In Sect. 9.2.2 we have shown that the maximum entropy model subject to the constraints $\mathcal{P}$ takes the parametric form of

$$P_\lambda(Y|X) = \frac{1}{Z_\lambda(X)} \exp\left(\sum_{i=1}^{n} \lambda_i f_i(X, Y)\right).$$

Obviously, this is an exponential model, and is a close sibling of the Gibbs distribution described in Chap. 6. Nonetheless, there are some essential differences between the maximum entropy and the Gibbs distribution models. First of all, maximum entropy model uses only feature functions (often binary-valued) to construct the exponent, while Gibbs distribution uses functions of more varieties to define the exponent. Second, Gibbs distribution attempts to model the joint probability of the observed variable X and the hidden variable Y using the equation

$$\pi_T(X, Y) = \frac{1}{Z_T(X, Y)} \exp\left(-\frac{1}{T} U(X, Y)\right).$$

Because $\pi_T(X, Y)$ intends to explain not only the hidden variable Y but also the observed variable X, it is a generative model. By contrast, maximum entropy model takes the observed variable X as the given input, and restricts its efforts to modeling the hidden variable Y only (i.e. the conditional probability $P(Y|X)$). Therefore, by definition it is a discriminative model.

Discriminative models offer several advantages over generative models. First, because discriminative models do not model observed variables, savings on modeling efforts are significant, which often lead to reduced requirements for training data in order to accomplish the same level of modeling accuracies. Second, which is related to the first one, generative models often incur excessive modeling complexity because of the need for modeling both the observed and hidden variables. The excessive modeling complexity often leads to either an untractable learning problem, or a requirement of unpractical amount of training data. To reduce the model complexity, generative models commonly assume conditional independence among all the features comprising the observed variable X. This conditional independence assumption enables us to approximate the joint probability $P(X, Y)$ as follows

$$\begin{aligned} P(X, Y) &= P(X|Y)P(Y) \\ &= P(X_1, X_2, \ldots, X_m|Y)P(Y) \\ &= P(X_1|Y)P(X_2|Y) \cdots P(X_m|Y)P(Y) \,, \end{aligned} \qquad (9.22)$$

where X_i denotes the i'th dimension of the variable X. Although the feature independence assumption dramatically reduces the modeling complexity for generative models, it does come with a cost. Because this assumption is for the sake of model tractability rather than the reflection of a reality, it undermines generative models' ability to model interacting features or long-range dependencies of the observations. As a consequence, generative models often have limited performance accuracies for modeling complex data sets/events where feature interactions play important roles in characterizing the problem.

Discriminative models, on the other hand, typically make very few assumptions about the data and the features. The conditional probability $P(Y|X)$ of the hidden variable Y can depend on arbitrary, non-independent features of the observation variable X without forcing the model to account for the distribution of those dependencies. The chosen features may represent attributes of the same observation at different levels of granularity (for example, pixel-level features and object-level features of an image), or may aggregate properties of not only the current observation, but also past and future observations.

The third advantage of discriminative models, which is the most important one, originates from the difference in the loss functions the two types of approaches strive to optimize. Given a training set $\mathbf{T} = \{(\mathbf{x}_k, \mathbf{y}_k\}_{k=1}^N$, generative models attempt to attain a model $P_\lambda(\mathbf{x}, \mathbf{y})$ that maximizes the likelihood of the joint probability distribution

$$\max_{P_\lambda(\mathbf{x}, \mathbf{y})} \Gamma(P_\lambda(\mathbf{x}, \mathbf{y})) = \prod_{k=1}^N P_\lambda(\mathbf{x}_k, \mathbf{y}_k) \,, \qquad (9.23)$$

while discriminative models strive to find a model $P_\alpha(\mathbf{y}\,|\,\mathbf{x})$ that maximizes the likelihood of the conditional probability distribution

$$\max_{P_\alpha(\mathbf{y}\,|\,\mathbf{x})} \Gamma(P_\alpha(\mathbf{y}\,|\,\mathbf{x})) = \prod_{k=1}^N P_\alpha(\mathbf{y}_k\,|\,\mathbf{x}_k) \,. \qquad (9.24)$$

For generative and discriminative models using the exponential parametric family, such as the Gibbs distribution and the maximum entropy models, it is more convenient to use log-likelihood as the loss function. In such case, problems (9.23), (9.24) can be re-written as follows:

$$\max_{\mathcal{D}_\lambda(\mathbf{x},\mathbf{y})} \Gamma_{log}(\mathcal{D}_\lambda(\mathbf{x},\mathbf{y})) = \sum_{k=1}^{N} \log \frac{e^{\mathcal{D}_\lambda(\mathbf{x}_k,\mathbf{y}_k)}}{\sum_{\mathbf{x}_k,\mathbf{y}_k} e^{\mathcal{D}_\lambda(\mathbf{x}_k,\mathbf{y}_k)}}$$

$$= \sum_{k=1}^{N} \log \frac{e^{\mathcal{D}_\lambda(\mathbf{x}_k,\mathbf{y}_k)}}{e^{\mathcal{D}_\lambda(\mathbf{x}_k,\mathbf{y}_k)} + \sum_{\substack{\mathbf{x}\neq\mathbf{x}_k, \\ \mathbf{y}\neq\mathbf{y}_k}} e^{\mathcal{D}_\lambda(\mathbf{x},\mathbf{y})}} \quad (9.25)$$

$$\max_{\mathcal{D}_\alpha(\mathbf{y}|\mathbf{x})} \Gamma_{log}(\mathcal{D}_\alpha(\mathbf{y}|\mathbf{x})) = \sum_{k=1}^{N} \log \frac{e^{\mathcal{D}_\alpha(\mathbf{y}_k|\mathbf{x}_k)}}{\sum_{\mathbf{y}_k} e^{\mathcal{D}_\alpha(\mathbf{y}_k|\mathbf{x}_k)}}$$

$$= \sum_{k=1}^{N} \log \frac{e^{\mathcal{D}_\alpha(\mathbf{y}_k|\mathbf{x}_k)}}{e^{\mathcal{D}_\alpha(\mathbf{y}_k|\mathbf{x}_k)} + \sum_{\mathbf{y}\neq\mathbf{y}_k} e^{\mathcal{D}_\alpha(\mathbf{y}|\mathbf{x}_k)}} \quad (9.26)$$

where $\mathcal{D}_\lambda(\mathbf{x},\mathbf{y})$, $\mathcal{D}_\alpha(\mathbf{y}\,|\,\mathbf{x})$ are certain energy functions defined by respective models. It is obvious that maximizing the above two log-likelihood functions is equivalent to maximizing the terms $e^{\mathcal{D}_\lambda(\mathbf{x}_k,\mathbf{y}_k)}$ and $e^{\mathcal{D}_\alpha(\mathbf{y}_k|\mathbf{x}_k)}$ while minimizing the terms $\sum_{\substack{\mathbf{x}\neq\mathbf{x}_k, \\ \mathbf{y}\neq\mathbf{y}_k}} e^{\mathcal{D}_\lambda(\mathbf{x},\mathbf{y})}$ and $\sum_{\mathbf{y}\neq\mathbf{y}_k} e^{\mathcal{D}_\alpha(\mathbf{y}|\mathbf{x}_k)}$ at the same time. In other words, (9.25) and (9.26) are essentially equivalent to the following two maximization problems:

$$\max_{\mathcal{D}_\lambda(\mathbf{x},\mathbf{y})} \Gamma_{log}(\mathcal{D}_\lambda(\mathbf{x},\mathbf{y})) \;\Rightarrow\; \max_{\mathcal{D}_\lambda(\mathbf{x},\mathbf{y})} \sum_{k=1}^{N} \left(e^{\mathcal{D}_\lambda(\mathbf{x}_k,\mathbf{y}_k)} - \sum_{\substack{\mathbf{x}\neq\mathbf{x}_k, \\ \mathbf{y}\neq\mathbf{y}_k}} e^{\mathcal{D}_\lambda(\mathbf{x},\mathbf{y})} \right),$$

$$\quad (9.27)$$

$$\max_{\mathcal{D}_\alpha(\mathbf{y}|\mathbf{x})} \Gamma_{log}(\mathcal{D}_\alpha(\mathbf{y}|\mathbf{x})) \;\Rightarrow\; \max_{\mathcal{D}_\alpha(\mathbf{y}|\mathbf{x})} \sum_{k=1}^{N} \left(e^{\mathcal{D}_\alpha(\mathbf{y}_k|\mathbf{x}_k)} - \sum_{\mathbf{y}\neq\mathbf{y}_k} e^{\mathcal{D}_\alpha(\mathbf{y}|\mathbf{x}_k)} \right).$$

$$\quad (9.28)$$

From (9.27) and (9.28) we can see a clearer picture of the difference between the generative and the discriminative approaches. Discriminative models aim to find a model $\mathcal{D}_\alpha(\mathbf{y}\,|\,\mathbf{x})$ that gives a high score to the true label $\mathbf{y}_k$ of example $\mathbf{x}_k$, and low scores to all other wrong labels $\mathbf{y}$ (it is not guaranteed that the true label $\mathbf{y}_k$ will get the highest score because $e^{\mathcal{D}_\alpha(\mathbf{y}_k|\mathbf{x}_k)} - \sum_{\mathbf{y}\neq\mathbf{y}_k} e^{\mathcal{D}_\alpha(\mathbf{y}|\mathbf{x}_k)}$ is not necessarily larger than zero). In contrast, generative models strive to construct a model that compares the true label $\mathbf{y}_k$ of example $\mathbf{x}_k$ not only with all its wrong labels, but also with all labels of all other examples $\mathbf{x} \neq \mathbf{x}_k$. For the task of data classifications, the loss function used by discriminative models makes more sense because what we really need to compare is the scores of the true and wrong labels for the same example $\mathbf{x}_k$, we want the score for the true label as large as possible, and scores for wrong labels as small as possible at the same time. The loss function used by discriminative models partially reflects this principle while the one used by generative models does not. This difference gives another reason why discriminative models generally outperform generative models for classification tasks.

In Chap. 10, we will present one of the latest graphical models: the maximum margin Markov network, that explicitly uses the above principle as its loss function. We will further illustrate why such a loss function will lead to an improvement on data classification accuracies.

The modeling philosophy underpinning discriminative models agrees completely with the modeling imperative advocated by Vapnik (see Sect. 1.2.4):

Vapnik's Imperative: While solving a problem of interest, do not solve a more general problem as an intermediate step. Try to get the answer that you need, but not a more general one. It is quite possible that you have enough information to solve a particular problem of interest well, but not enough information to solve a general problem.

As evidenced by the examples given in this section, by trying to solve the exact problem we have, not a more general one, we gain the model simplicity, as well as the freedom of making fewer assumptions on data and features. These gains bring to us the ability to incorporate correlations/contexts among features comprising the observed variable. Such ability will undoubtedly produce more accurate performances for modeling complex data entities, such as a beach scene, a home run event, etc, where feature correlations and contexts play important roles in describing the problems.

9.4 Relation to Conditional Random Field

The conditional random field (CRF) is a discriminative probabilistic model proposed by John Lafferty, *et al* [72, 73] to overcome problems associated with generative models (see Sect. 9.3). CRF was originally designed to label and segment sequences of observations, but can be used more generally.

Let X, Y be random variables over observed data sequences and corresponding label sequences, respectively. For simplicity of descriptions, we assume that the random variable sequences X and Y have the same length, and use $\mathbf{x} = [x_1, x_2, \ldots, x_m]$ and $\mathbf{y} = [y_1, y_2, \ldots, y_m]$ to represent instances of

X and Y, respectively. CRF defines the conditional probability distribution $P(Y|X)$ of label sequences given observation sequences as follows

$$P_\lambda(Y|X) = \frac{1}{Z_\lambda(X)} \exp\left(\sum_{i=1}^{n} \lambda_i f_i(X, Y)\right),$$ (9.29)

where $Z_\lambda(X)$ is the normalizing factor that ensures $\sum_\mathbf{y} P_\lambda(\mathbf{y}|\mathbf{x}) = 1$, λ_i is a model parameter, and $f_i(X, Y)$ is a feature function (often binary-valued) that becomes positive (one for binary-valued feature function) when X contains a certain feature in a certain position and Y takes a certain label, and becomes zero otherwise.

Given a set of training data $\mathbf{T} = \{(\mathbf{x}_k, \mathbf{y}_k)\}_{k=1}^{N}$ with an empirical distribution $\tilde{P}(X, Y)$, CRF determines the model parameters $\boldsymbol{\lambda} = \{\lambda_i\}$ by maximizing the log-likelihood of the training set

$$\Gamma(P_\lambda) = \sum_{k=1}^{N} \log P_\lambda(\mathbf{y}_k|\mathbf{x}_k)$$

$$\propto \sum_{\mathbf{x}, \mathbf{y}} \tilde{P}(\mathbf{x}, \mathbf{y}) \log P_\lambda(\mathbf{y}|\mathbf{x}).$$ (9.30)

Interestingly, it can be shown by simple calculus that the log-likelihood defined in (9.30) is the same as the negative dual function $L(P_\lambda, \boldsymbol{\lambda})$ defined in (9.14) (see Problem 9.10 at the end of the chapter). In other words, the conditional random field discussed above is exactly the same as the maximum entropy model described in Sect. 9.2. Apparently, the two models are quite different: The maximum entropy model aims to be consistent with all the facts, but otherwise be as uniform as possible; that is $P_{me} = \arg\max_{P \in \mathcal{P}} H(P)$. On the other hand, the conditional random field model starts with an exponential model, and strives to maximize the log-likelihood of the model with respect to the empirical distribution; that is $P_{CRF} = \arg\max_{P_\lambda} \Gamma(P_\lambda)$. Nonetheless, we have shown that the two models are completely equivalent.

The above discussions directly lead to the following theorem. A complete proof of the theorem can be found in [69].

Theorem 9.1 (Equivalence of ME and CRF Models). *Assume that we are given an empirical distribution $\tilde{P}(X, Y)$, and a set of features $\mathbf{f} = (f_1, \ldots, f_n)$. Let $\mathcal{P}$ be the set of conditional probability distributions that agree with $\tilde{P}(X, Y)$ in terms of the expected values of the feature functions $\mathbf{f}$*

$$\mathcal{P} = \{P(Y|X) \mid P(f_i) = \tilde{P}(f_i), \ i = 1, 2, \ldots, n\},$$

and let $\mathcal{Q}$ be the set of conditional probability distributions that are based on an exponential model with the feature functions $\mathbf{f}$

$$\mathcal{Q} = \{P(Y|X) \,|\, P(Y|X) = \frac{1}{Z_\lambda(X)} \exp(\boldsymbol{\lambda} \cdot \mathbf{f}), \, \boldsymbol{\lambda} \in \mathbf{R}^n\}.$$

The maximum entropy model $P_{me} \in \mathcal{P}$ is equivalent with the maximum likelihood model $P_{CRL} \in \mathcal{Q}$, and this model is uniquely determined:

$$P^* = P_{me} = P_{CRL}.$$

9.5 Feature Selection

The maximum entropy method provides a mechanism for automatic feature selection in its model construction process [68]. This ability is very useful for problems for which we do not have sufficient knowledge about which features are actually relevant or useful. Using this ability, we can begin by specifying a large collection $\mathcal{F}$ of candidate features, let the model to discover the set of features that best characterize the problem, and employ only this best set of feature in the final model.

The feature selection ability is accomplished based on an incremental model growth process. Every stage of the process is characterized by a set of active features $\mathcal{S}$ which determine a space of models expressed by (9.31).

$$\mathcal{P}(\mathcal{S}) = \{P \,|\, P(f) = \widetilde{P}(f), \; f \in \mathcal{S}\}. \tag{9.31}$$

The optimal model $P_\mathcal{S}$ in this space is the one defined by

$$P_\mathcal{S} = \arg \max_{P \in \mathcal{P}(\mathcal{S})} H(P). \tag{9.32}$$

By adding a new feature $\hat{f}$ to $\mathcal{S}$, we obtain a new set of active features $\mathcal{S} \cup \hat{f}$ which determine a set of models

$$\mathcal{P}(\mathcal{S} \cup \hat{f}) = \{P \,|\, P(f) = \widetilde{P}(f), \; f \in \mathcal{S} \cup \hat{f}\}. \tag{9.33}$$

Again, the optimal model in this space is

$$P_{\mathcal{S} \cup \hat{f}} = \arg \max_{P \in \mathcal{P}(\mathcal{S} \cup \hat{f})} H(P). \tag{9.34}$$

Adding the feature $\hat{f}$ allows the model $P_{\mathcal{S} \cup \hat{f}}$ to better account for the training data. This results in a gain $\Delta\Gamma(\mathcal{S}, \hat{f})$ in the log-likelihood of the training data

$$\Delta\Gamma(\mathcal{S}, \hat{f}) = \Gamma(P_{\mathcal{S}\cup\hat{f}}) - \Gamma(P_{\mathcal{S}}). \tag{9.35}$$

Obviously, the more important the feature is for modeling the target problem, the more log-likelihood gain we will get by adding it to the active feature set. Therefore, at each stage of the model construction process, the goal of feature selection can be realized by selecting the candidate feature $\hat{f}$ which maximizes the log-likelihood gain $\Delta\Gamma(\mathcal{S}, \hat{f})$. This feature selection and model construction process can be terminated either when the specified number of features have been selected, or when the log-likelihood gain $\Delta\Gamma(\mathcal{S}, \hat{f})$ has fallen below the predefined threshold.

In summary, the feature selection algorithm is composed of the following operations:

1. Start with $\mathcal{S} = \emptyset$, thus $P_{\mathcal{S}}$ is uniform.
2. For each candidate feature $f \in \mathcal{F}$:
   (a) Compute the maximum entropy model $P_{\mathcal{S}\cup f}$ using either the gradient ascent or the iterative scaling algorithms described in Sect. 9.2.3.
   (b) Compute the log-likelihood gain $\Delta\Gamma(\mathcal{S}, f)$ using (9.35).
3. Select the feature $\hat{f}$ with the maximal gain $\Delta\Gamma(\mathcal{S}, \hat{f})$, and add $\hat{f}$ to $\mathcal{S}$.
4. Compute $P_{\mathcal{S}}$ using either the gradient ascent or the iterative scaling algorithms described in Sect. 9.2.3.
5. If the number of selected features reaches the specified threshold, or the gain $\Delta\Gamma(\mathcal{S}, \hat{f})$ falls below the predefined threshold, terminate the process; otherwise go to Step 2.

The above feature selection algorithm is computationally costly because for each candidate feature $f \in \mathcal{F}$, we have to compute the maximum entropy model $P_{\mathcal{S}\cup f}$ using a numerical method. The algorithm becomes impractical when the pool of candidate features is large. In the remaining part of this section, we introduce an approximate algorithm that will yield a great saving in computational complexity, but will generate only an approximate solution of the maximum entropy model [68].

Recall that a model $P_{\mathcal{S}}$ has a set of parameters $\boldsymbol{\lambda}$, one for each feature in $\mathcal{S}$. The model $P_{\mathcal{S}\cup f}$ contains this set of parameters, plus a single new parameter α corresponding to new feature f. To make the feature selection computation tractable, we make the assumption that the optimal values for $\boldsymbol{\lambda}$ do not change as the new feature f is added to $\mathcal{S}$. If this assumption holds, incorporating a new feature to the model would require only optimizing the single parameter α to maximize the likelihood. Translating the above statement into math, we have

$$P_{\mathcal{S}\cup f}^{\alpha} = \frac{1}{Z_{\alpha}(X)} P_{\mathcal{S}}(Y|X) e^{\alpha f(X,Y)},$$ (9.36)

where $Z_{\alpha}(X) = \sum_y P_{\mathcal{S}}(y|x) e^{\alpha f(x,y)}$. Among these models, we are interested in the one that maximizes the likelihood gain

$$\begin{aligned} G_{\mathcal{S}\cup f}(\alpha) &= \Gamma(P_{\mathcal{S}\cup f}^{\alpha}) - \Gamma(P_{\mathcal{S}}) \\ &= -\sum_x \tilde{P}(x) \log Z_{\alpha}(x) + \alpha \tilde{P}(f). \end{aligned}$$ (9.37)

The optimal model is defined as

$$\hat{P}_{\mathcal{S}\cup f}^* = \arg \max_{P_{\mathcal{S}\cup f}^{\alpha}} G_{\mathcal{S}\cup f}(\alpha).$$ (9.38)

Unfortunately, the assumption we made above is fault: when a new feature f is added to $\mathcal{S}$, the optimal values of all parameters λ change. Therefore, the model $\hat{P}_{\mathcal{S}\cup f}^*$ obtained by (9.38) is an approximation to the genuine maximum entropy model. Nonetheless, this approximation has reduced the computation of the maximum entropy model for a new feature set $\mathcal{S} \cup f$ to a simple one-dimensional optimization problem over the single parameter α, which can be solved by any popular line-search techniques. The saving in computational complexity is enormous, which makes the approximate algorithm a preferred choice for real applications. The price to be paid for the computational saving is, there is a reasonable chance that a less important feature f has a higher approximate gain $G_{\mathcal{S}\cup f}(\alpha)$ than the feature $\hat{f}$ that maximizes the exact gain $\Delta\Gamma(\mathcal{S}, \hat{f})$, so that f instead of $\hat{f}$ is selected to be include in the final model. Therefore, the feature set selected by the approximate algorithm may not be the optimal set in terms of the maximal log-likelihood gain.

9.6 Case Study: Baseball Highlight Detection Using Maximum Entropy Model

In this case study, we apply the maximum entropy model to the task of baseball highlight detection from TV broadcasted baseball videos [74]. We first provide an overview of the baseball highlight detection system, and then describe how the maximum entropy model is used to seamlessly integrating image, audio, and speech features to detect and classify baseball highlights. At the end of the section, we present experimental evaluations to reveal the performance accuracies of the ME-based system, and to compare it with the HMM-based system described in Sect. 7.7.

9.6.1 System Overview

The goals we set for our baseball highlight detection/classification system are:
(1) the system should be able to detect and classify all major types of highlights such as *home run, outfield hit, outfield fly, infield hit, infield out, strike
out, walk*, etc, and (2) the user should be able to give his/her definition of the
highlights that are of interest. To achieve these goals, we extract image, audio, and text features from the input video, and fuse these multimedia features
along with their contextual information using the maximum entropy model
(see Fig. 9.1). More precisely, for the image stream of the video, we segment
it into individual camera shots, compute color distribution, edge distribution,
camera motion, and detect players as well as their positions for each shot. For
the audio stream, we partition it into audio segments each of which possesses
coherent acoustic profiles, and detect the segments that contain such special
sounds as music, cheers, applaud, etc. For closed captions, we detect informative words/phrases and record their time codes within the video sequence. If
the closed captions are not available, we apply speech recognition to the audio stream to get the speech transcript of the video sequence. Although these
multimedia features correlate to each other, their presence is often unsynchronized. Particularly, text words always lag behind their corresponding image
and audio features. To cope with the asynchronous nature of different features, we use a set of rules defined in Section 9.6.4 to construct a multimedia
feature vector for each shot.

It is obvious that the above multimedia features are simple and low-level
features that can be extracted quickly and reliably. Using such features is
important to ensure the feasibility and scalability of our system in handling
long video sequences. It is also obvious that any of the above features alone will
not be sufficient to achieve our goals. For example, a video segment containing
audience's cheers does not necessarily correspond to a good play, because the
audience often cheer when they see their favorite players, or when they want
to invigorate their home town team. On the other hand, having detected
the phrase "home run" from the closed captions does not guarantee that the
associated video segment contains a home run event, because the reporter
may have just mentioned the past home run record of a particular player.
Similarly, observing a player running toward a base in a shot is not sufficient
to determine that the shot corresponds to a hit, because the player may have
been forced out before reaching the base.

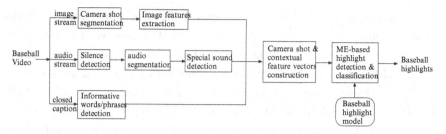

Fig. 9.1. The outline of the ME-based baseball highlight detection system

The above examples also demonstrate the problems of sports highlight detection using single medium features. The types of sports highlights/events that can be detected using single medium features are quite limited. However, highlight detection capabilities can be enhanced remarkably when a seamless integration of the above image, audio, and text features is realized, because these features are complementary, and bring a synergistic effect for capturing the semantics of the original video.

In addition to multimedia feature integration, incorporating contextual information of the multimedia features is also important. As described in Sect. 7.7.2, there are a few unique views, such as the pitcher's view, global infield view, global outfield view, global and closeup player running view, audience view, etc, that constitute most parts of baseball highlights. Each particular type of highlight generally has a similar transitional pattern of these unique views. For example, a typical home run highlight usually consists of four or more shots, which starts from a pitcher's view, followed by a panning outfield and audience view in which the video camera follows the flying ball, and ends with a global or closeup view of the player running to home base. To determine whether the current shot belongs to a home run highlight, the system has to examine not only the features of the current shot, but also the features of several following shots. In our proposed system, we assimilate the contextual information by extracting the multimedia features for n (=4 in our implementation) consecutive shots and combining them into one feature vector to form the input to the maximum entropy model.

We developed a unique Maximum Entropy Model (MEM)-based framework to perform the statistical modeling of highlight detection and classification. Traditionally, the Hidden Markov Model (HMM) described in Chap. 7 is the most common approach for modeling complex and context-sensitive data sequences. The HMM usually needs to first segment and classify the data sequence into a set of finite states, and then observe the state transitions during its data modeling process. Unlike the HMM-based approach, our MEM-based framework provides a simple platform to integrate the above multimedia features as well as their contextual information in a uniform fashion. Because this framework does not need to explicitly classify the data sequence into states, it remarkably simplifies the training data creation task and the highlight detection and classification process. In addition, the MEM is able to automatically select useful features from a given feature set during its learning process (see Sect. 9.5), which is particularly valuable for modeling complicated data with very high dimensions. Moreover, accomplishing baseball highlight detection/classification through a machine learning process is superior to rule-based approaches because machine learning methods are more powerful for discovering and expressing implicit, complex knowledge, and more flexible, adaptive for meeting specific needs. By providing to the learning process training data biased in certain directions, the user is able to give a definition of the highlights that reflects his/her preferences.

9.6.2 Highlight Detection Based on Maximum Entropy Model

For our baseball highlight detection and classification system, the task of the MEM is to build a statistical model which, given the feature vector $\mathbf{x}$ of a video segment, computes the probability $P(h|\mathbf{x})$ that the video segment contains the highlight h. To integrate the multimedia features as well as their contextual information in a uniform fashion, we use n (=4 in our implementation) consecutive shots to form a processing unit $\mathcal{X}$, and combine the image, audio, and text features extracted from these n consecutive shots to create the feature vector $\mathbf{x}$ of the processing unit $\mathcal{X}$. For each feature i in the feature vector $\mathbf{x}$ and each highlight type κ, we introduce a binary-valued feature function $f_{i\kappa}(\mathbf{x}, h)$ which is defined as follows:

$$f_{i\kappa}(\mathbf{x}, h) = \begin{cases} 1 : \text{if feature } i \text{ is present in } \mathbf{x} \text{ and } h = \kappa \\ 0 : \text{otherwise.} \end{cases} \tag{9.39}$$

Using the above feature functions, the MEM takes the following form to compute the probability $P(h|\mathbf{x})$ (see Sect. 9.2.2):

$$P(h|\mathbf{x}) = \frac{1}{Z(\mathbf{x})} \exp\left(\sum_{i,\kappa} \lambda_{i\kappa} f_{i\kappa}(\mathbf{x}, h) \right), \tag{9.40}$$

where $Z(\mathbf{x})$ is the normalizing constant, and $\lambda_{i\kappa}$ is the weight assigned to the feature function $f_{i\kappa}(\mathbf{x}, h)$.

Each feature function $f_{i\kappa}(\mathbf{x}, h)$ serves to connect a particular feature with a particular highlight category, and to provide a means for us to incorporate *a priori* domain knowledge. If we know for sure that certain features j in the feature vector $\mathbf{x}$ are independent of the highlight category h, we can set the corresponding feature functions $f_{jh}(\mathbf{x}, h)$ to zero. By initializing the feature functions to the appropriate binary values using domain knowledge, we can certainly reduce the number of parameters $\lambda_{i\kappa}$ to be estimated, and hence accelerate the learning process. On the other hand, if we don't have sufficient domain knowledge at hand, we can simply assume that every feature i is present in every highlight h (i.e. set all the feature functions $f_{i\kappa}(\mathbf{x}, \kappa) = 1$) and let the learning process automatically determine the appropriate weight for each feature function.

Our implementation of the MEM learning process is as follows: At the initialization stage, we set all the feature functions $f_{i\kappa}(\mathbf{x}, \kappa)$ to value one, and assume that they are all equally important (i.e. assign a uniform value to all the weights $\lambda_{i\kappa}$). During the training process, the weight $\lambda_{i\kappa}$ for each feature function $f_{i\kappa}(\mathbf{x}, \kappa)$ is iteratively adjusted by the learning algorithm. The training process terminates when all the $\lambda_{i\kappa}$'s have converged, and the final set of $\lambda_{i\kappa}$'s constitutes the estimated model of $P(h|\mathbf{x})$.

For each highlight h, the MEM models the multimedia features and their contextual information in the following fashion. If a particular feature j in the feature vector $\mathbf{x}$ plays a dominant role in identifying the highlight h, the weight λ_{jh} for the feature function $f_{jh}(\mathbf{x}, h)$ will obtain a large value through the learning process so that the probability $P(h|\mathbf{x})$ will become sufficiently large whenever feature j is present in $\mathbf{x}$. For those features that are either unimportant or unrelated to the highlight h, their associated weights will become either small or close to zero at the end of the learning process. On the other hand, if a feature subset $\{x_1, x_2, \ldots\} \in \mathbf{x}$ collectively identifies the highlight h, the corresponding weights λ_{1h}, λ_{2h}, ... will take moderate values and the probability $P(h|\mathbf{x})$ will become large only when the entire feature subset appears in $\mathbf{x}$. Because the input feature vector $\mathbf{x}$ embeds the time correlated multimedia features from n consecutive shots, we take the full advantage of the MEM-based framework to model both the correlations among the multimedia features and the contextual information embedded within patterns of view transitions. Furthermore, unlike the HMM and the

Bayes Network-based approaches, the proposed MEM-based framework takes low-level, compound multimedia features as its input, and does not need to explicitly classify each shot into states (i.e., perform view classification) in its operations, therefore, it remarkably simplifies the training data creation task and the highlight detection/classification process.

We use the iterative scaling algorithm described in Sect. 9.2.3 to compute the parameter set $\lambda_{i\kappa}$'s, and use the approximation algorithm described in Sect. 9.5 to conduct feature selection for building the maximum entropy model.

9.6.3 Multimedia Feature Extraction

As discussed in the preceding section, there are several important views that serve as the main components of baseball highlights. Each particular type of highlight typically has a similar pattern of view transitions. Therefore, to detect/classify baseball highlights, we need to extract features that capture and distinguish these view patterns. This task can be achieved to a certain extent by examining such image features as color and edge distributions, camera motions, players and their positions. Features from audio and closed captions often provide complementary, higher level clues to the detection/classification process. The multimedia features and their extractions are described as follows.

Image Features

Given an input video, we first segment the image stream of the video into individual shots and then conduct the following feature extractions for each shot.

- **Color distribution:** A standard baseball field mainly consists of grass areas and base areas. By computing the distribution of green and soil colors in keyframes of a shot, we can roughly figure out which part of the field the shot is displaying. Within our framework, each shot is represented by three keyframes: the first, the middle, and the last frames of the shot. Each keyframe is divided into 3 × 3 blocks, and the color distribution of a keyframe is composed of nine data pairs (g_i, s_i) where g_i and s_i represent the percentages of green and soil colors in block i, respectively. The color distribution of the entire shot is then derived by averaging the color distributions of the three keyframes.

- **Edge distribution:** This feature is useful for distinguishing field views from audience views. An audience view is usually a long shot of a large number of spectators who collectively form texture-like areas in video frames. Edge density in such views is higher on average than in other views. The edge distribution of a shot is computed in a manner similar to the color distribution. First, edge detection is conducted for each keyframe to obtain edge pixels (the pixels belonging to an edge). Next, the frame is divided into 3×3 blocks, and the percentages of edge pixels in the nine blocks are computed. These nine percentage values are then used to form the edge distribution of the frame. Finally, the edge distribution of the entire shot is derived by averaging the edge distributions of the three keyframes of the shot.

- **Camera motion:** Camera motion becomes conspicuous and intense in highlight scenes because cameras track either the ball or the players' motions to capture the entire play. We apply a simplified camera motion model [75] to estimate camera pan, tilt and zoom, which are the most commonly used camera operations in TV broadcasting. This model defines the relationship between two images by a six-parameter linear transformation:

$$\mathbf{x}' = P\mathbf{x}, \tag{9.41}$$

where

$$\mathbf{x}' = \begin{bmatrix} u' \\ v' \end{bmatrix} \quad P = \begin{bmatrix} s_f & 0 & -k_y \\ 0 & s_f & k_x \end{bmatrix} \quad \mathbf{x} = \begin{bmatrix} u \\ v \\ 1 \end{bmatrix} \tag{9.42}$$

and $\mathbf{x}$ and $\mathbf{x}'$ are the two image coordinates of a 3-D point in the real-world scene. The transformation P has three unknown parameters:

$$s_f = \frac{f'}{f} \qquad k_x = f'\theta_x \qquad k_y = f'\theta_y, \tag{9.43}$$

where s_f is the scale between the two focal lengths f and f', and θ_x, θ_y represent the pan and tilt angles, respectively. The above three unknown parameters are estimated using the algorithm developed by Szeliski and Shum [76]. This algorithm obtains the best estimate of the three parameters by minimizing the following error function E:

$$E(D) = \sum_i \left[I_0(\mathbf{x}_i) - \hat{I}_1(\mathbf{x}'_i) \right]^2, \tag{9.44}$$

where I_0, I_1 are the two consecutive frames, $\hat{I}_1$ is the warped image of I_1 obtained using the current transformation P. Initially, P is set to $s_f = 1$,

$\theta_x = 0$, $\theta_y = 0$. D is the incremental update for P,

$$(I + D)P \Longrightarrow P \qquad (9.45)$$

and each $\mathbf{x}'_i$ is calculated as,

$$\mathbf{x}'_i = (I + D)\mathbf{x}_i. \qquad (9.46)$$

In the above estimation process, the error function $E(D)$ is minimized using the Cholesky decomposition algorithm.

Since the acquisition of camera motion is computation-intensive, and is prone to error, we apply the random sample consensus scheme (RANSAC) [77] to make the computation faster and more robust. The RANSAC scheme randomly picks up a small number of pixels in video frames to obtain an initial camera motion estimation, and then repeats the process enough times on different set of pixels to get the best estimation which maximizes the number of pixels satisfying the estimation.

- **Player detection:** Players are the central actors in a baseball game, and their movements have strong correlations to each class of highlights. Although general human detections in cluttered environments are very challenging, player detection in baseball game videos is much easier due to the fact that players in the baseball field are sparsely positioned and are mostly surrounded by green or soil background colors. By examining the distribution of green and soil colors in a keyframe, we are able to figure out the location and the range of the baseball field within the frame. Then, within the range of the baseball field, we discover the areas that have non-background colors and higher edge densities. These areas are good candidates for baseball players. Among all the candidates, false candidates and outliers can be further discovered by tracking each candidate within the shot because genuine candidates possess stable image features (e.g. size and color) and consistent trajectories while false candidates do not.

Special Sound Detection

Certain sounds in a baseball game, such as cheers, applause, music, speech, and mixtures of music and speech, provide important clues for highlight detection. Figure 9.2 shows the process of our special sound detection module which consists of two stages. In the training stage, we construct a model for each type of sound listed above using annotated training data. The mel-cepstral coefficients from raw wave signals are used as the input feature vectors of the sound models, and the Gaussian mixture model (GMM) is used to model the distributions of the input vectors. With the GMM, the likelihood of feature vector $\mathbf{x}$ given sound model c is defined as:

$$P(\mathbf{x}|c) = \sum_{i}^{K^c} \eta_i^c N(\mathbf{x}; \mu_i^c, v_i^c) \qquad (9.47)$$

Where K^c is the number of mixtures in model c, η_i^c is the mixing coefficient, μ_i^c and v_i^c are the mean and the variance of each mixing Gaussian. Given the number of mixtures K^c, the well-known EM (Expectation-Maximization) algorithm [78] is used to estimate the parameters of each model. To account for the difference in the complexity and the training data size for different sound models, the number of mixtures K^c for each sound model is chosen differently based on the Bayesian Information Criterion (BIC) [79].

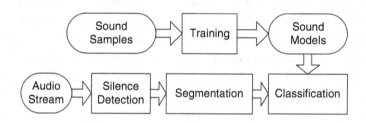

Fig. 9.2. Process of special sound detection

In the detection stage, we first detect and eliminate silent regions from the audio stream, and then partition those non-silent regions into audio segments each of which possesses similar acoustical profiles. Each audio segment then becomes the input to all the five sound models constructed in the training stage, which each outputs a probability showing the likelihood of the audio segment being a particular sound. These five likelihoods are then used as part of the multimedia features in forming the feature vector of a camera shot.

Closed Captions

Informative words from closed captions often provide the most direct and abstracted clues to the detection/classification process. We extract informative words based on the mutual information metric between a word w and a highlight h:

$$MI(w, h) = p(w, h) \log \frac{p(w, h)}{p(w)p(h)}$$

$$+p(\overline{w}, h) \log \frac{p(\overline{w}, h)}{p(\overline{w})p(h)}$$

$$+p(w, \overline{h}) \log \frac{p(w, \overline{h})}{p(w)p(\overline{h})}$$

$$+p(\overline{w}, \overline{h}) \log \frac{p(\overline{w}, \overline{h})}{p(\overline{w})p(\overline{h})} \tag{9.48}$$

where $p(w, h)$ denotes the probability that both the word w and the highlight h are present, $p(\overline{w}, h)$ the probability that w is absent but h is present, $p(w, \overline{h})$ the probability that w is present but h is absent, and $p(\overline{w}, \overline{h})$ the probability that both w and h are absent, in the context under consideration. Metric $MI(w, h)$ has the property that its value becomes large if the presence of the word w positively indicates the presence of the highlight h, whereas its value becomes small in the opposite situation. Therefore for our task, informative words for a particular highlight are those which have large mutual information measures with the highlight. From the training data, we have identified a list of 72 informative words for the major highlights, which include: *field, center, strike out, base, double out, score, home run*, etc. In forming the multimedia feature vector of a camera shot, we use 72 dimensions to indicate the presence/absence of the 72 informative words. For each dimension, value one indicates the presence of a particular word while value zero indicates otherwise.

9.6.4 Multimedia Feature Vector Construction

As described in the proceeding subsections, the image, audio, and text features are extracted separately from their respective streams of the input video program. Although these features correlate to each other, their presence is often unsynchronized. Particularly, text words always lag behind their corresponding image and audio features because the announcer will not start the descriptions until he/she has observed the entire event. To cope with the asynchronous nature of different features, we use the following rules for constructing the multimedia feature vector of a shot S_i.

1. All the image features extracted from S_i are used to form part of the multimedia feature vector of S_i.

2. Assuming that the shot S_i starts at time t_{i1} and ends at time t_{i2}, any special sounds whose occurrence period overlaps the time interval $[t_{i1}, t_{i2}]$ are included in the multimedia feature vector of S_i.

3. Assuming that the time window starts at time t_{i2} and lasts for T_w seconds ($T_w = 5$ in our implementation), any informative words which are present in the time interval $[t_{i2}, t_{i2} + T_w]$ are included in the multimedia feature vector of S_i.

Once the feature vector for each shot has been created using the above rules, we combine the feature vectors of n consecutive shots to form an input vector to the MEM engine. Because this input vector integrates the time correlated multimedia features from n consecutive shots, we take the full advantage of the MEM to model both the correlations among the multimedia features and the contextual information embedded within the view transitional patterns.

9.6.5 Experiments

We collected 10 baseball videos totalling 32 hours for training and testing purposes. These games were obtained from five major TV stations in the U.S. and consist of 16 teams playing in 9 stadiums.

All the games were manually labeled by three human operators who were not familiar with our baseball highlight detection/classification system. The labeling process is straightforward: when the operator observes a highlight from a video program, he/she labels the highlight by indicating the starting and ending points, and the category of the highlight. Using our MEM-based framework, there is no need to further decompose a highlight sequence into individual views, and to label the category of each of the constituent views. Currently, the highlight labels consist of seven categories: *home run, outfield hit, outfield out, infield hit, infield out, strike out, walk*. These categories have been chosen because they cover the major events in a typical baseball game. We used seven games as the training data and the remaining three games as the testing data. The labeled highlights in the testing data were used as the ground truth to evaluate the highlight detection/classification accuracy of our system.

Performance Evaluations

The proposed highlight detection and classification system starts with the extraction of the image, audio, and text features, and the creation of a feature vector for each processing unit of the input video. From each shot, we extract four image features (color, edge, camera motion and player), five audio features (speech, music, cheers, applause, mixtures of speech and music), detect the presence/absence of 72 informative words/phrases, and encode these image, audio, and text features into 109, 5, and 72 dimensions, respectively. As described in the preceding subsections, to incorporate contextual information into the MEM-based framework, we combine the features of n consecutive shots together to form a 744-dimensional feature vector for each processing unit.

The above feature vectors and the manually assigned labels in the training data are the input to the MEM-based framework during the learning process. The output contains a list of selected features and the set of λ_{ik}'s that maximize the log-likelihood of the training data. The learning process has selected the top 30 features which are most useful for detecting and classifying the above seven types of highlights.

Table 9.1. Recalls and precisions of baseball highlight classifications

Highlights	Multimedia Features		Image Features Only	
	Recall	Precision	Recall	Precision
home run	50.0%	50.0%	25.0%	25.0%
outfield hit	84.9%	75.7%	70.5%	61.2%
outfield out	83.4%	93.7%	78.9%	68.0%
infield hit	49.3%	47.9%	32.1%	32.3%
infield out	78.5%	56.3%	52.4%	56.8%
strike out	79.0%	63.4%	35.1%	47.2%
walk	65.2%	51.2%	11.7%	16.2%

On average, the recall and precision for highlight classification are 70.0% and 62.60%, respectively. Table 9.1 details the performance results for each type of highlight. The precisions for *infield hit* and *infield out* are relatively low because these two types of highlights usually have quite similar view transitional patterns which often lead to misclassifications (i.e., infield hit classified to infield out, and vice versa). We missed some *home runs* due to the fact that there were not enough training samples.

To understand how the multimedia features contribute to the highlight classification performances, we also conducted highlight classification using the image features only. The recall and precision for each type of highlight are shown in the right two columns of Table 9.1. As expected, the average recall and precision have dropped to 43.7% and 43.8%, respectively. The classification accuracies for *strike out* and *walk* are particularly low because these two categories usually start and end at pitching views, and present less contextual information compared to other types of highlights. These poor results demonstrate that image features alone are not sufficient for modeling major baseball game highlights.

To get a better insight of the system performance, we take a closer look at the performance statistics for one of the baseball games. The entire game consisted of 12 innings and 70 outs. There are 94 highlights that belong to one of the seven categories labeled by the operators. Our system detected 91 of those highlights, and classified 71 correctly. Table 9.2 lists the performance statistics for this game.

Table 9.2. Performance statistics on game five of the world series 2001

highlight	total	correct	misclassified	missed	false alarm	recall	precision
home run	3	2	0	1	0	66.6%	100%
outfield hit	13	11	2	0	2	84.62%	73.33%
outfield out	17	14	1	2	0	82.35%	93.33%
infield hit	6	3	1	2	3	50.00%	42.86%
infield out	30	26	2	2	5	86.67%	78.79%
strike out	16	11	0	5	2	68.75%	84.62%
walk	9	5	0	4	1	55.56%	83.33%

Performance Comparisons

We conducted performance comparisons between the MEM-based system and the HMM-based system described in Sect. 7.7. The HMM-based system uses the same set of image, audio, and text features as described in Section 9.6.3, and is evaluated using the same training and testing data sets as the MEM-based system. However, for training the HMM-based system, the training data set needed to be relabeled so that for each highlight sequence, in addition to the information labeled for the MEM-based system, the starting point, ending point and view category of each constituent view must be labeled as well. This training data labeling task is much more arduous and time consuming.

The HMM-based system consists of seven unique HMM's, each of which models a particular type of highlight. For each HMM, we define the following items:

1. State V: one of the seven types of views described in Section 7.7.2.
2. Observation M: the 186-dimensional multimedia feature vector created for a given shot (see the beginning of this section for a detailed description).
3. Observation probability $p(M|V)$: the probability of observing the feature vector M given the state V. We use the Bayes rule to compute $p(M|V)$ from the training data.
4. Transition probability $p(V_{t+1}|V_t)$: the probability that state V_t transits to state V_{t+1} at the next time instant. Given the class of highlights, the state (view) transition probability can be learned from the training data.
5. Initial state distribution π: which also can be learned from the training data.

Given the state V, the observation M, the observation probability $p(M|V)$, the transition probability $P(V_{t+1}|V_t)$, and the initial state distribution π, the HMM is uniquely defined. With the HMM H_k, the probability of observing the sequence $\mathbf{M} = M_{t_1} M_{t_2} \cdots M_T$ can be obtained as:

$$P(\mathbf{M}|H_k) = \sum_{\text{all } \mathbf{v}} \pi(V_{t_1})p(M_{t_1}|V_{t_1})p(V_{t_2}|V_{t_1})p(M_{t_2}|V_{t_2})$$
$$\times \cdots p(V_T|V_{T-1})p(M_T|V_T), \tag{9.49}$$

where $\mathbf{V}$ denotes a fixed state sequence $\mathbf{V} = V_{t_1} V_{t_2} \cdots V_T$.

The HMM-based system performs baseball highlight detection /classification as follows:

1. Segment the input video into individual shots.
2. For each shot S_i, compute the observation M_i.
3. Compute the observation probability $P(M_i|V_j)$ for each shot S_i and each view type V_j.
4. For each processing unit $\mathbf{M}_x$ (which consists of 3 to 5 shots, depending on the HMM model), compute the probability $P(\mathbf{M}_x|H_k)$ of the observation sequence $\mathbf{M}_x = M_{x1} M_{x2} \cdots M_{xT}$ using each HMM H_k. If $P = \max_{H_k} P(\mathbf{M}_x|H_k)$ exceeds the predefined threshold, then the highlight class represented by HMM $h = \text{argmax}_{H_k} P(\mathbf{M}_x|H_k)$ is assigned to $\mathbf{M}_x$.

Table 9.3 shows the evaluation results of the HMM-based system. For ease of comparisons, we have included the highlight classification accuracies of the MEM-based system in the left columns of the table as well. It is observed that the MEM-based system produced better performance than the HMM-based system on all highlight categories, and this advantage becomes very remarkable for the categories of *strike out* and *walk*. This phenomenon can be explained by the fact that the HMM-based system uses the naive Bayes to calculate the observation probability $P(M|V)$, which assumes that all the features extracted from each shot are independent of each other. Obviously this assumption reduces the system's ability to model the correlations among the multimedia features, leading to higher error rates in the computation of probabilities $P(M|V)$. For the highlight categories that have relatively short view transitional patterns, such as *strike out* and *walk*, the HMM might not be able to compensate for errors in the observation probabilities because less contextual information is contained within the sequence.

Table 9.3. Performance comparisons between the two systems.

Highlights	MEM-based System		HMM-based System	
	Recall	Precision	Recall	Precision
home run	50.0%	50.0%	50.0%	50.0%
outfield hit	84.9%	75.7%	83.4%	68.2%
outfield out	83.4%	93.7%	75.9%	88.0%
infield hit	49.3%	47.9%	44.1%	47.3%
infield out	78.5%	56.3%	67.5%	40.8%
strike out	79.0%	63.4%	55.1%	47.2%
walk	65.2%	51.2%	57.7%	46.2%

The above experimental evaluations demonstrate the superiority of the MEM-based system in its ability to detect more major baseball highlights and in its overall accuracy of detecting these major highlights. Because MEM and HMM are the representative discriminative and generative models, and we have tested the two models under exactly the same conditions, the above performance comparisons are a good demonstration of how much advantage a discriminative model can have over a generative model. Moreover, because the MEM-based framework does not need to explicitly segment and classify the input video into states during its data modeling process, it remarkably simplifies the training data creation and the highlight detection/classification tasks.

Problems

9.1. Suppose that the average number of rolling an uneven dice is 4, calculate the maximum entropy distribution of each number.

9.2. Find the maximum entropy distribution for positive real numbers with expectation μ.

9.3. Find the maximum entropy distribution for real numbers with expectation μ and variance σ^2

9.4. Show that entropy $H(P)$ is a concave function over probability distributions, i.e., for $\omega > 0$,

$$\omega H(P) + (1 - \omega)H(Q) < H(\omega P + (1 - \omega)Q)$$

9.5. Assume $P_\lambda(y|\mathbf{x})$ has the form in (9.12), show that $-\log P_\lambda(y|\mathbf{x})$ is a convex function over λ.

9.6. This chapter uses entropy as the measure of uniformity. A different measure of uniformity is the norm $\|p\|^2$ of the distribution function:

$$\|p\|^2 = \int_x (p(x))^2 dx$$

where a smaller value of $\|p\|^2$ means more uniform. Suppose that we are given a set of expectations:

$$E(f_i) = c_i, \ i = 1, 2 \cdots, n$$

show that the distribution that satisfies the expectation constraints while having the minimal norm has the following form:

$$p(x) = \lambda_0 + \sum_{i=1}^{n} \lambda_i f_i(x) .$$

9.7. Maximum entropy model with soft constraints:

$$P_{me} = \arg \max_{P \in \mathcal{P}} H(P) - \frac{\gamma}{2} \sum_{i=1}^{n} (E_P(f_i) - \hat{E}(f_i))^2 .$$

Show that the dual problem is

$$\lambda = \arg\min_{\lambda} - \sum_{x} \tilde{P}(\mathbf{x}) \log P_{\lambda}(y|\mathbf{x}) + \frac{1}{2\gamma}\|\lambda\|^2 ,$$

where

$$P_{\lambda}(y|\mathbf{x}) = \frac{1}{Z_{\lambda}(\mathbf{x})} \exp\left(\sum_{i=1}^{n} \lambda_i f_i(\mathbf{x}, y)\right) .$$

9.8. Let X be a d-dimensional random vector. Suppose that the marginal distribution of X_i and X_j, $1 \le i < j \le d$ is $p_{ij}(x_i, x_j)$. Show that the maximum entropy distribution of X has the form:

$$P(X) = \prod_{i<j} f_{ij}(x_i, x_j)$$

where f_{ij} are some nonnegative functions.

9.9. Show that

$$\frac{\partial L(P_{\lambda}, \lambda)}{\partial \lambda_i} = P_{\lambda}(f_i) - \tilde{P}(f_i) ,$$

where $L(P_{\lambda}, \lambda)$ is the dual function defined by (9.14).

9.10. Prove that the log-likelihood $\Gamma(P_{\lambda})$ defined in (9.30) is the same as the negative dual function $L(P_{\lambda}, \lambda)$ defined in (9.14): $\Gamma(P_{\lambda}) = L(P_{\lambda}, \lambda)$.

10

Max-Margin Classifications

So far we have described a variety of graphical models, either generative or discriminative. Graphical models are powerful statistical tools for modeling correlations and dependencies among different instances, often resulting in significant improvements in accuracy over approaches that classify instances independently. Because of this, graphical models are preferred choices for a broad range of multimedia content analysis applications.

In training a graphical model using a set of training samples, model parameters are usually determined by maximizing the likelihood between the model and the training samples. However, graphical models obtained this way are often plagued with the overfitting problem, and there is no guarantee that such graphical models have sufficient generalization powers to model unseen data as accurately as the training samples.

In recent years, Support Vector Machines (SVMs) proposed by Cortes and Vapnik [80, 7] have become the state-of-the-art classifier for supervised classification problems, and have demonstrated great successes in a broad range of tasks, including document categorization, character recognition, image classification, and many more. SVMs are famous for their strong generalization guarantees derived from the max-margin property, and for their ability to use very high dimensional feature spaces using the kernel trick. These are the characteristics that other classifiers do not have.

Despite many impressive successes, SVMs also have some significant limitations: They can assign only one label at a time, and their running time is polynomial in the number of classes. This means that SVMs can not jointly classify correlated instances in a systematic way, and can not take advantage of some precious information for problems with rich structures.

Clearly, we have two approaches that offer complementary strengths and weaknesses. The SVM approach can exploit very high dimensional feature spaces with strong generalization guarantees, but can only perform simple classifications of instances independently, whereas the graphical model approach can model correlations and dependencies among different instances in principled and efficient ways, but does not provide the same level of generalization ability as SVMs. So one natural question to ask is whether or not there is a way to unify both approaches and to get the best of them. The answer is yes. The new framework proposed by Tasker, Guestrin and Koller is called *Max-Margin Markov Networks* (M^3-nets in short) [81]. It is a major breakthrough in the machine learning field in recent years because it has enabled us to apply the SVM principles to a whole new set of problems.

In this chapter, we first provide an overview of SVMs, where the concepts of margin, kernel, generalization bound, etc. are introduced, and a SVM training algorithm, namely Sequential Minimal Optimization (SMO), is presented. In the second half of the chapter, we present the max-margin Markov network framework, which unifies all the ideas of the SVM and the graphical model approaches. We also compare the M^3-net with other graphical models, and provide some intuitive insights into why the M^3-net is superior to others.

10.1 Support Vector Machines (SVMs)

The development of SVMs is a significant product of the generalization bound analysis that aims to discover the relationship between the capacity of a learning machine and its performance accuracy. For a given learning task, with a given finite amount of training data, the best generalization performance will be achieved when the right balance is struck between the accuracy attained on that particular training set, and the "capacity" of the machine, that is, the ability of the machine to learn any training set without error [82]. A machine with too much capacity is like a person with a photographic memory who perceives every vehicle he/she has seen as a different type of vehicle, and would like to classify each individual vehicle into a different category, while a machine with too little capacity is like a person who can only observe the most prominent differences among different instances, and would like to declare all the objects with wheels as vehicles. Obviously, neither machines can generalize well. In this section, we will briefly introduce the concept of generalization

bound and its relationship with SVMs. We will focus our efforts mainly on
SVMs themselves, as well as their computing algorithms.

10.1.1 Loss Function and Risk

Given a set of labeled instances $S = \{(\mathbf{x}^{(i)}, y^{(i)})\}_{i=1}^n$, where $\mathbf{x}^{(i)}$ is the feature
vector of the i'th instance, and $y^{(i)}$ is a label assigned to the instance by a
trusted source, the goal of supervised classifications is to learn a mapping
function (a classifier) $f : \mathbf{x} \mapsto y$ from the training set S. In learning such a
mapping function $y = f(\mathbf{x})$, we need some ways to evaluate the classification
performance of $f(\mathbf{x})$. A popular tool for this purpose is the *loss function*
$L(\mathbf{x}, y, f(\mathbf{x}))$ that gives the cost of assigning label $f(\mathbf{x})$ to observation $\mathbf{x}$, given
that the correct label is y. $L(\mathbf{x}, y, f(\mathbf{x}))$ is usually defined over the domain
$[0, \infty]$, and the minimum value 0 is reached when $f(\mathbf{x})$ assigns the correct
label to $\mathbf{x}$: $L(\mathbf{x}, y, y) = 0$.

A rational goal for learning a classifier $y = f(\mathbf{x})$ would be to minimize
the total loss on the labels to be predicted. In the case where one does not
know what objects will have to be classified in the future, it makes sense
to minimize the expected loss on future data, called the *expected risk* $R(f)$,
which is a function of the classifier f:

$$R(f) = \int_{\mathbf{x}, y} L(\mathbf{x}, y, f(\mathbf{x})) dP(\mathbf{x}, y), \tag{10.1}$$

where $P(\mathbf{x}, y)$ is the joint probability distribution over $\mathbf{x}$ and y. In real applications, since $P(\mathbf{x}, y)$ can not be obtained for all but very simple problems, it
is impossible in general to compute the expected risk $R(f)$. A more practical
approach is to compute the *empirical risk* $R_{emp}(f)$ evaluated on the training
set S:

$$R_{emp}(f) = \frac{1}{n} \sum_{i=1}^n L(\mathbf{x}^{(i)}, y^{(i)}, f(\mathbf{x}^{(i)})), \tag{10.2}$$

where n is the number of training samples in S.

10.1.2 Structural Risk Minimization

For a given classification task, a classifier $y = f(\mathbf{x})$ is generally chosen from
some appropriately selected parametric family $\mathcal{F} = \{f(\mathbf{x}, \boldsymbol{\alpha}), \boldsymbol{\alpha} \in \mathcal{H}\}$, where
$\mathcal{H}$ is some parameter space. Thus the goal for learning a classifier can be
rephrased as determination of the parameter set $\boldsymbol{\alpha}$ such that the empirical
risk $R_{emp}(f)$ is minimized.

The choice of the parametric family $\mathcal{F}$ is very important. If $\mathcal{F}$ is too expressive, we will have a classifier with a photographic memory which is prone to overfitting. If it is not expressive enough, then the learned classifier may not be able to approximate the real function. This qualitative statement is made explicit with the following *risk bound*: For any sample $\mathcal{S}$ of size n, threshold $\delta > 0$, and $f \in \mathcal{F}$, we have

$$R(f) \leq R_{emp}(f) + \Omega(\mathcal{F}, n, \delta^{-1}), \tag{10.3}$$

where $\Omega(\mathcal{F}, n, \delta^{-1})$ is a measure of the *capacity* of the parameter class $\mathcal{F}$, which is related to its expressiveness.

There are several important characteristics and implications about this bound. First, it is independent of $P(\mathbf{x}, y)$. It only assumes that both the training and testing data are drawn independently according to some $P(\mathbf{x}, y)$. Second, it generalizes the large number law in function space and tells us when the empirical risk $R_{emp}(f)$ will be a good approximation to the expected risk $R(f)$. From (10.3) it is clear that, the more expressive the parameter class $\mathcal{F}$, the larger the capacity measure $\Omega(\mathcal{F}, n, \delta^{-1})$, and hence the less approximate the empirical risk $R_{emp}(f)$ to $R(f)$. This is nothing but the characterization of overfitting, and explains why classifiers with large capacities do not generalize well. On the other hand, if we use a parameter class $\mathcal{F}$ that is not expressive enough, although the capacity measure $\Omega(\mathcal{F}, n, \delta^{-1})$ becomes smaller, the empirical risk $R_{emp}(f)$, which represents the training error, will become larger. Therefore, compromise has to be made to find a parameter class $\mathcal{F}$ that has the smallest capacity measure $\Omega(\mathcal{F}, n, \delta^{-1})$, but at the same time, can yield small enough training error $R_{emp}(f)$, where $f \in \mathcal{F}$.

The risk bound defined by (10.3) gives a principled method for choosing a classifier, which is called *structural risk minimization* [7]. Let $\mathcal{F}_k = \{f(\mathbf{x}, \boldsymbol{\alpha}), \boldsymbol{\alpha} \in \mathcal{H}_k\}$ be a subset of the parametric family: $\mathcal{F}_k \subset \mathcal{F}$. The essence of the structural risk minimization is that we define a structure of nested subsets

$$\mathcal{F}_1 \subset \mathcal{F}_2 \subset \cdots \subset \mathcal{F}_k \subset \cdots \tag{10.4}$$

such that the corresponding capacity measure $h_k = \Omega(\mathcal{F}_k, n, \delta^{-1})$ of each subset $\mathcal{F}_k$ satisfies

$$h_1 \leq h_2 \leq \cdots \leq h_k \leq \cdots \tag{10.5}$$

For a given set of training data $\mathcal{S} = \{(\mathbf{x}^{(i)}, y^{(i)})\}_{i=1}^n$, we iterate through the subsets $\mathcal{F}_k$ in the order of increased capacity. At each iteration step, we find the function $f_k^* \in \mathcal{F}_k$ that produces the minimal training error. Once we get all the functions f_k^*, the optimal classifier is the one that minimizes the right hand side of (10.3) (the risk bound). The bound is not necessarily tight, and thus it does not guarantee that a classifier with a higher bound will have worse generalization performance than the one with a lower bound. But it does give a theoretical bound on the generalization error for a given classifier which is independent of the distribution $P(\mathbf{x}, y)$, and hence provide a more principled heuristic for choosing classifiers. We will see in Sect. 10.1.4 how this has motivated a powerful learning algorithm with nice generalization guanrantees, the support vector machines.

10.1.3 Support Vector Machines

A support vector machine is a linear classifier that attempts to maximize the confidence margin for classifying the given training data. We first consider the simplest case of linear SVMs trained on separable data, and will later cover the general case of nonlinear SVMs trained on non-separable data.

Separable Case

Consider the set of training data that consist of two classes $\mathcal{S} = \{\mathbf{x}^{(i)}, y^{(i)}\}_{i=1}^n$, $y^{(i)} \in \{-1, 1\}$, $\mathbf{x}^{(i)} \in \mathbb{R}^d$. A linear classifier able to separate the positive from the negative examples will be a hyperplane in $\mathbb{R}^d$ characterized by a normal $\mathbf{w}$ and an offset b:

$$h(\mathbf{x}) = \mathbf{w}^T \mathbf{x} + b. \tag{10.6}$$

For a linearly separable data set $\mathcal{S}$, there exists a hyperplane that satisfies all the points in $\mathcal{S}$:

$$\mathbf{w}^T \mathbf{x}^{(i)} + b \geq 0 \quad \text{for } y^{(i)} = +1, \tag{10.7}$$

$$\mathbf{w}^T \mathbf{x}^{(i)} + b < 0 \quad \text{for } y^{(i)} = -1. \tag{10.8}$$

The above two equations can be written more succinctly as

$$y^{(i)}(\mathbf{w}^T \mathbf{x}^{(i)} + b) \geq 0 \quad \forall i. \tag{10.9}$$

There are an infinite number of $(\mathbf{w}, b)$ pairs satisfying the inequality (10.9), since for any $(\mathbf{w}, b)$ satisfying (10.9), $(a\mathbf{w}, ab)$, $\forall a > 0$, also satisfies it. To make the solution unique, we can rescale $(\mathbf{w}, b)$ so that the closest points to the hyperplane satisfy $|(\mathbf{w}^T \mathbf{x}^{(i)} + b)| = 1$. This normalization leads to the following canonical form for SVM

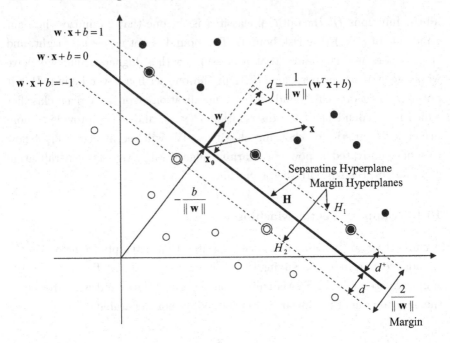

Fig. 10.1. Linear SVM for the separable case. The circled points are the support vectors

$$y^{(i)}(\mathbf{w}^T\mathbf{x}^{(i)} + b) \geq 1 \quad \forall i. \tag{10.10}$$

Figure 10.1 shows the geometry of the canonical SVM setting. From (10.10) and the figure one can easily verify that the hyperplane has the following properties:

1. For any two points $\mathbf{x}_1$ and $\mathbf{x}_2$ lying on the hyperplane, $\mathbf{w}^T(\mathbf{x}_1 - \mathbf{x}_2) = 0$. Therefore, $\mathbf{w}$ is the vector normal to the surface of the hyperplane.
2. For any point $\mathbf{x}_h$ on the hyperplane, $\mathbf{w}^T\mathbf{x}_h = -b$.
3. The signed distance from a point $\mathbf{x}$ to the hyperplane is given by

$$d = \frac{\mathbf{w}}{||\mathbf{w}||}(\mathbf{x} - \mathbf{x}_0)$$

$$= \frac{1}{||\mathbf{w}||}(\mathbf{w}^T\mathbf{x} - \mathbf{w}^T\mathbf{x}_0)$$

$$= \frac{1}{||\mathbf{w}||}(\mathbf{w}^T\mathbf{x} + b) \tag{10.11}$$

where $\mathbf{x}_0$ is the intersection point between the normal vector $\mathbf{w}$ and the hyperplane. Since $\mathbf{x}_0$ lies on the hyperplane, it satisfies the equality

$\mathbf{w}^T\mathbf{x}_0 = -b$ in item 2, which leads to the last equality in the above derivation.

4. The perpendicular distance from the hyperplane to the origin equals $|b|/||\mathbf{w}||$ (see Problem 10.2 at the end of the chapter).

5. The points for which the equality in (10.10) holds are those points that lie on the hyperplanes $\mathbf{w}^T\mathbf{x} + b = \pm 1$ (denoted as H_1, H_2, respectively), and have the perpendicular distance $1/||\mathbf{w}||$ to the separating hyperplane $\mathbf{w}^T\mathbf{x} + b = 0$.

Let d^+, d^{-1} be the distances from the separating hyperplane to the closest positive, negative examples, respectively. The *margin* of the separating hyperplane is defined as $d^+ + d^{-1}$. It is obvious from Fig. 10.1 that, the closest positive, negative examples to the separating hyperplane are those points lying on the hyperplanes H_1, H_2, respectively, and hence the margin size equals

$$d^+ + d^{-1} = \frac{1}{||\mathbf{w}||} + \frac{1}{||\mathbf{w}||} = \frac{2}{||\mathbf{w}||}. \qquad (10.12)$$

The goal of SVM is to find the pair of hyperplanes H_1, H_2 that maximize the margin, subject to the constraints (10.10). This can be formulated as the following constrained optimization problem:

$$\min_{\mathbf{w},b} \; \frac{1}{2}\mathbf{w}^T\mathbf{w}, \qquad (10.13)$$
$$\text{subject to} \quad y^{(i)}(\mathbf{w}^T\mathbf{x}^{(i)} + b) \geq 1 \quad \forall i.$$

This is a convex optimization problem for which we are guaranteed to obtain its global optimal solution.

Non-Separable Case

In the real world, there are many data sets that are not linearly separable. When the SVM derived above is applied to non-separable data sets, some data points $\mathbf{x}^{(i)}$ could be at a distance $\xi_i/||\mathbf{w}||$ on the wrong side of the margin hyperplane (see Fig. 10.2). To extend the SVM to handle non-separable data, we can relax the constraint (10.10), and add a further cost for doing so. More precisely, we introduce positive slack variables ξ_i, one for each data point $\mathbf{x}^{(i)}$, and transform the constraint (10.10) to

$$y^{(i)}(\mathbf{w}^T\mathbf{x}^{(i)} + b) \geq 1 - \xi_i, \quad \xi_i \geq 0 \quad \forall i. \qquad (10.14)$$

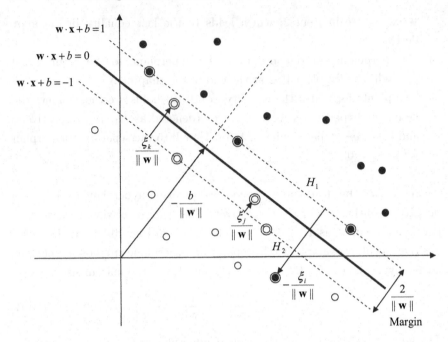

Fig. 10.2. Linear SVM for the non-separable case

For a misclassification error to occur, the corresponding ξ_i must exceed unity, hence $\frac{1}{n}\sum_{i=1}^{n}\xi_i$ is an upper bound of the average loss on the training data. Therefore, a natural way to assign an extra cost for errors is to add a new term $\frac{C}{n}\sum_{i=1}^{n}\xi_i$ to the cost function, where C is a parameter to be chosen by the user. A larger C corresponds to a higher penalty to errors, with $C = \infty$ meaning that no error can be tolerated at all (its cost is infinite).

With the above preparations, now the SVM for non-separable case can be casted as the following optimization problem:

$$\min_{\mathbf{w},b,\xi_i}\ \frac{1}{2}\mathbf{w}^T\mathbf{w} + \frac{C}{n}\sum_{i=1}^{n}\xi_i\,, \tag{10.15}$$

$$\text{subject to}\quad y^{(i)}(\mathbf{w}^T\mathbf{x}^{(i)} + b) \geq 1 - \xi_i\,,\quad \xi_i \geq 0\ \ \forall i\,.$$

Again, this is a convex optimization problem, and the Lagrange multiplier method can be applied to obtain the globally optimal solution.

10.1.4 Theoretical Justification

Before describing the algorithm for solving the optimization problem (10.15), let's see why choosing a classifier by maximizing the margin is a rational thing to do. One informal reason is that, if we believe that the Euclidean distance is a good measure of the dissimilarity between instances, then the bigger the margin, the more confidence we have on the classification. This is because the more room we have between the two different classes, the less chance we have to misclassify data in future classification.

A more formal argument is that, by choosing only the hyperplanes that have the maximal margin, we restrict the size of the parameter class for candidate classifiers, and hence minimize the capacity measure $\Omega(\mathcal{F}, n, \delta^{-1})$ in the right hand side of (10.3). In fact, for the $0-1$ loss which assigns 1 for misclassification and 0 otherwise, it has been shown by Vapnik that the capacity measure can be written as follows [7]

$$\Omega(\mathcal{F}, n, \delta^{-1}) = \left(\frac{V(\log(2n/V) + 1) + \log(4/\delta)}{n} \right)^{\frac{1}{2}}, \qquad (10.16)$$

where V is the VC-dimension of the class of classifiers $\mathcal{F}$, and n is the size of the training sample. This bound is called the *VC confidence*, and shows the dependence on V and n of the capacity measure. Furthermore, for the class of linear classifiers with a specific margin, Vapnik derived an expression indicating that bigger margins yield smaller capacity measures, giving considerable justification for maximizing the margin.

In fact, the cost function (10.15) for SVMs can be easily justified from the structural risk minimization point of view. The term $\frac{1}{n} \sum_{i=1}^{n} \xi_i$ in the cost function is an upper bound of the average loss on the training data. Minimizing this term is equivalent to minimizing the empirical risk $R_{emp}(f)$. On the other hand, the term $\frac{1}{2} \mathbf{w}^T \mathbf{w}$ is a reciprocal of the margin of the separating hyperplane. Minimizing this term is equivalent to maximizing the margin of the linear classifier, which, according to Vapnik, is equivalent to reducing the capacity $\Omega(\mathcal{F}, n, \delta^{-1})$. Therefore, the cost function for SVMs is related to the risk bound defined in (10.3). Classifiers that minimize the risk bound are guaranteed to have good performance accuracies for classifying future unseen data. The strong theoretical justification and generalization guarantee for SVMs are the unique properties that differentiate SVMs from other classifiers in the literature.

10.1.5 SVM Dual

In this subsection, we apply the Lagrange multiplier method to compute the solution to the constrained optimization problem (10.15). The Lagrange multiplier method first defines a Lagrange function using a set of non-negative lagrangian multipliers $\boldsymbol{\alpha} = \{\alpha_i\}$ and $\boldsymbol{\beta} = \{\beta_i\}$

$$L_P = \frac{1}{2}\mathbf{w}^T\mathbf{w} + \frac{C}{n}\sum_{i=1}^{n}\xi_i - \sum_{i=1}^{n}\alpha_i(y^{(i)}(\mathbf{w}^T\mathbf{x}^{(i)}+b) - 1 + \xi_i) - \sum_{i=1}^{n}\beta_i\xi_i. \quad (10.17)$$

Next, the unconstrained minimum of the Lagrangian function L_P is computed with respect to $\mathbf{w}$, b, and ξ_i. Setting the respective derivatives to zero, we have

$$\frac{\partial L_P}{\partial \mathbf{w}} = \mathbf{w} - \sum_{i=1}^{n}\alpha_i y^{(i)}\mathbf{x}^{(i)} = 0 \quad \Rightarrow \quad \mathbf{w} = \sum_{i=1}^{n}\alpha_i y^{(i)}\mathbf{x}^{(i)}, \quad (10.18)$$

$$\frac{\partial L_P}{\partial b} = -\sum_{i=1}^{n}\alpha_i y^{(i)} = 0 \quad \Rightarrow \quad 0 = \sum_{i=1}^{n}\alpha_i y^{(i)}, \quad (10.19)$$

$$\frac{\partial L_P}{\partial \xi_i} = \frac{C}{n} - \alpha_i - \beta_i = 0 \quad \Rightarrow \quad \alpha_i = \frac{C}{n} - \beta_i. \quad (10.20)$$

Substituting these solutions to (10.17), we obtain the dual objective function

$$L_D = \sum_{i=1}^{n}\alpha_i - \frac{1}{2}\sum_{i=1}^{n}\sum_{j=1}^{n}\alpha_i\alpha_j y^{(i)}y^{(j)}\mathbf{x}^{(i)} \cdot \mathbf{x}^{(j)}. \quad (10.21)$$

Since the primal problem is convex and strictly feasible, its minimum solution can be obtained by equivalently maximizing the dual objective function

$$\max_{\boldsymbol{\alpha}} L_D(\boldsymbol{\alpha}) = \sum_{i=1}^{n}\alpha_i - \frac{1}{2}\sum_{i=1}^{n}\sum_{j=1}^{n}\alpha_i\alpha_j y^{(i)}y^{(j)}\mathbf{x}^{(i)} \cdot \mathbf{x}^{(j)} \quad (10.22)$$

$$\text{subject to} \quad \sum_{i=1}^{n}\alpha_i y^{(i)} = 0, \quad 0 \leq \alpha_i \leq \frac{C}{n} \ \forall i.$$

Once the optimal $\boldsymbol{\alpha}$ set is obtained, the optimal classifier is then given by

$$f_{\boldsymbol{\alpha}}(\mathbf{x}) = \text{sign}\left(\sum_{i=1}^{n}\alpha_i y^{(i)}(\mathbf{x}^{(i)} \cdot \mathbf{x}) + b\right). \quad (10.23)$$

In addition to (10.18), (10.19), and (10.20), the KKT conditions for the dual problem (10.22) also include the constraints

$$\alpha_i(y^{(i)}(\mathbf{w}^T\mathbf{x}^{(i)} + b) - 1 + \xi_i) = 0, \quad (10.24)$$

$$\beta_i\xi_i = 0, \quad (10.25)$$

$$y^{(i)}(\mathbf{w}^T\mathbf{x}^{(i)} + b) - 1 + \xi_i \geq 0, \quad (10.26)$$

for all i. Together these equations (10.18)–(10.26) uniquely characterize the solution to the primal and the dual problems.

From (10.18) we see that the maximal margin hyperplane $\mathbf{w}$ can be written as a linear combination of the training samples

$$\mathbf{w} = \sum_{i=1}^{n} \alpha_i y^{(i)} \mathbf{x}^{(i)}.$$

The data points $\mathbf{x}^{(i)}$ for which $\alpha_i \neq 0$ are called the *support vectors*, since $\mathbf{w}$ is defined by these points. By the KKT condition (10.24), support vectors are those points that satisfy $y^{(i)}(\mathbf{w}^T\mathbf{x}^{(i)} + b) - 1 + \xi_i = 0$, that is, they lie at a distance $\xi_i/\|\mathbf{w}\|$ on the wrong side of the margin hyperplane. Among these support vectors, points with $\xi_i = 0$ lie on the margin hyperplanes. From (10.25) and (10.20), points on the margin hyperplanes have $0 < \alpha_i < C/n$, while other support points have $\alpha_i = C/n$. From (10.24), we see that any support points lying on the margin hyperplane ($\alpha_i > 0$, $\xi_i = 0$) can be used to compute the offset b. In real implementations, we typically use an average of all the solutions for numerical stability.

10.1.6 Kernel Trick

The support vector machine described so far finds a linear boundary in the input feature space which divides data into two classes. In this subsection, we extend the ideas of linear SVM to enable the generation of a nonlinear classification boundary using the *kernel trick* technique. Kernel trick is a technique that attempts to implicitly map the original feature space into an enlarged feature space using a kernel function, and to use a linear classifier to conduct data classifications in this enlarged space. Generally speaking, linear boundaries in the enlarged feature space translate to nonlinear boundaries in the original feature space, which results in better separations of data sets that are non-separable by linear boundaries.

Figure 10.3 demonstrates a data set that can not be separated by a linear SVM without using the kernel trick. Figure 10.3(a) shows a 1-D data set that consists of two classes. Obviously, this data set is not separable by any linear boundary. However, if we project the data set into a 3-D space using the mapping function $\Phi(x) = [1, \sqrt{2}x, x^2]$, we obtain the data distribution shown in Fig. 10.3(b), where the horizontal and vertical axes correspond to $\sqrt{2}x$ and x^2, respectively. In this 3-D space, the projected data set becomes separable by a linear boundary that is shown by the dot line. The dot line in the 3-D

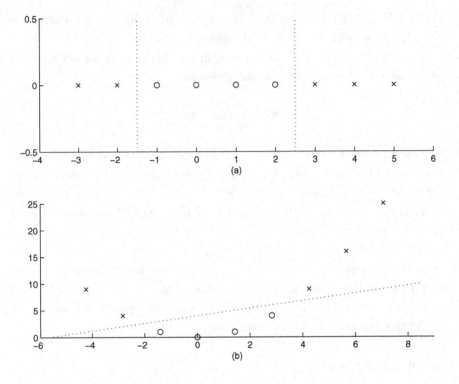

Fig. 10.3. A two-class data set that can not be separated by a linear SVM without using the kernel trick. The two classes of data are depicted by 'o' and 'x', respectively

space is equivalent to the two threshold (two dot lines) shown in Fig. 10.3(a), which is obviously a nonlinear boundary in the 1-D space.

The idea of kernel trick is simple. The Lagrange dual function (10.21) has the form

$$L_D = \sum_{i=1}^{n} \alpha_i - \frac{1}{2} \sum_{i=1}^{n} \sum_{j=1}^{n} \alpha_i \alpha_j y^{(i)} y^{(j)} \mathbf{x}^{(i)} \cdot \mathbf{x}^{(j)},$$

and the SVM classifier is given by

$$f_{\boldsymbol{\alpha}}(\mathbf{x}) = \text{sign} \left(\sum_{i=1}^{n} \alpha_i y^{(i)} (\mathbf{x}^{(i)} \cdot \mathbf{x}) + b \right).$$

Note that in these equations, the input feature vectors appear only in the form of dot products $(\mathbf{x}^{(i)} \cdot \mathbf{x}^{(j)})$. This is a remarkable property because it means that we do not need to care about individual components of the input vectors, and that all we need to know is dot products between the input vectors. Assume that we want to enlarge the original feature space by mapping the data into some high dimensional (possibly infinite dimensional) Euclidean space $\mathcal{N}$ using a mapping function $\Phi : \mathbb{R}^d \mapsto \mathcal{N}$. In the enlarged feature space $\mathcal{N}$, because the SVM depends on the data only through dot products $\Phi(\mathbf{x}^{(i)}) \cdot \Phi(\mathbf{x}^{(j)})$, if there is a "kernel function" K such that $K(\mathbf{x}^{(i)}, \mathbf{x}^{(j)}) = \Phi(\mathbf{x}^{(i)}) \cdot \Phi(\mathbf{x}^{(j)})$, then we will only need to use K in the computation, and will never need to explicitly know what Φ is. Using this kernel trick, we obtain the nonlinear SVM as follows:

$$f_{\boldsymbol{\alpha}}(\mathbf{x}) = \text{sign}\left(\sum_{i=1}^{n} \alpha_i y^{(i)} \Phi(\mathbf{x}^{(i)}) \cdot \Phi(\mathbf{x}) + b\right)$$

$$= \text{sign}\left(\sum_{i=1}^{n} \alpha_i y^{(i)} K(\mathbf{x}^{(i)}, \mathbf{x}) + b\right). \tag{10.27}$$

The concept of kernel trick can be illustrated by a simple example. Consider a feature space with two inputs $\mathbf{x} = [x_1, x_2]$. Applying the degree-2 polynomial kernel $K(\mathbf{x}, \mathbf{x}') = (1 + \mathbf{x} \cdot \mathbf{x}')^2$ to this feature space yields [83]

$$K(\mathbf{x}, \mathbf{x}') = (1 + \mathbf{x} \cdot \mathbf{x}')^2$$
$$= (1 + x_1 x_1' + x_2 x_2')^2$$
$$= 1 + 2x_1 x_1' + 2x_2 x_2' + (x_1 x_1')^2 + (x_2 x_2')^2 + 2x_1 x_1' x_2 x_2'.$$

If we choose the mapping function $\Phi(\mathbf{x})$ as

$$\Phi(\mathbf{x}) = [1, \sqrt{2}x_1, \sqrt{2}x_2, x_1^2, x_2^2, \sqrt{2}x_1 x_2]^T, \tag{10.28}$$

which is the function that maps the two dimensional feature space into a six dimensional one, then

$$K(\mathbf{x}, \mathbf{x}') = \Phi(\mathbf{x}) \cdot \Phi(\mathbf{x}'). \tag{10.29}$$

What this example reveals is that the degree-2 polynomial kernel function serves to map the original two dimensional feature space into a six dimensional one, and to conduct dot products in the six dimensional feature space without the need to explicitly compute $\Phi(\mathbf{x})$ for each input data. As the SVM depends on the data only through dot products, for the purpose of space enlargement, all we need to know is a kernel function $K(\mathbf{x}, \mathbf{x}') = \Phi(\mathbf{x}) \cdot \Phi(\mathbf{x}')$. Once we attain the kernel function, we no longer need to explicitly map the original feature space into a high dimensional one, and in fact, we do not even need to know what the mapping function $\Phi(\mathbf{x})$ is. Therefore, using kernel trick, we can generalize the linear SVM to a nonlinear one with a minimal change in the framework and a minimal computational cost.

Here, we list three popular kernel functions that have been widely used in the SVM literature:

Degree-d polynomial: $K(\mathbf{x}, \mathbf{x}') = (1 + \mathbf{x} \cdot \mathbf{x}')^d$.
Radial basis: $K(\mathbf{x}, \mathbf{x}') = \exp\left(-\frac{\|\mathbf{x} - \mathbf{x}'\|^2}{c}\right)$.
Neural network: $K(\mathbf{x}, \mathbf{x}') = \tanh(\kappa_1 \mathbf{x} \cdot \mathbf{x}' + \kappa_2)$.

10.1.7 SVM Training

The goal of SVM training is to obtain an optimal set of Lagrangian multipliers $\boldsymbol{\alpha}$ that maximize the dual objective function $L_D(\boldsymbol{\alpha})$ in (10.22). This is a typical quadratic optimization problem that can be solved using quadratic programming (QP) algorithms. However, the quadratic form for SVMs involves a matrix that consists of as many elements as the square of the number of training examples, and this immense size makes many standard QP techniques unapplicable.

To solve the scalability problem of standard QP techniques, there have been research studies that strive to break a large QP problem into a series of smaller QP subproblems, and to solve each QP subproblem using some standard QP techniques [84, 85]. In this subsection, we describe the Sequential Minimal Optimization (SMO) method that attempts to decompose the SVM QP problem into the smallest possible QP subproblem, and to solve the smallest subproblem analytically at every step [86]. For the SVM problem setting, the smallest possible QP subproblem involves two Lagrange multipliers because the Lagrange multipliers must obey a linear equality constraint $\sum_i \alpha_i y^{(i)} = 0$. At each step, SMO picks two Lagrange multipliers according to some heuristical rules, optimizes the two multipliers jointly, and updates the SVM to reflect the the optimal values.

Compared to other SVM training algorithms in the literature, SMO has much better scaling properties because it completely avoids matrix computation and storage by decomposing the SVM QP problem into the smallest possible QP subproblems. SMO is also faster and easier to implement because it solves the smallest QP subproblems analytically, rather than invoking an entire iterative QP numerical routine at each step. With the SMO approach, even though more optimization subproblems need to be solved during the course of the optimization, each subproblem is so fast that the overall QP problem can be solved quickly without any scalability problems.

There are three components of SMO: an analytic method to jointly optimize two Lagrange multipliers, heuristics for choosing pairs of multipliers to optimize, and a method for computing the offset b. In the remaining part of this subsection, we describe each of these components in details.

Jointly Optimizing Two Lagrange Multipliers

This is the smallest possible QP subproblem for solving the overall SVM QP problem. The KKT conditions which are the necessary and sufficient conditions for a point $\boldsymbol{\alpha}$ to be the solution to (10.22) are

$$\alpha_i = 0 \quad \Rightarrow \quad \xi_i = 0,\ y^{(i)}(\mathbf{w}^T\mathbf{x}^{(i)} + b) \geq 1, \qquad (10.30)$$

$$0 < \alpha_i < \frac{C}{n} \quad \Rightarrow \quad \xi_i = 0,\ y^{(i)}(\mathbf{w}^T\mathbf{x}^{(i)} + b) = 1, \qquad (10.31)$$

$$\alpha_i = \frac{C}{n} \quad \Rightarrow \quad \xi_i \neq 0,\ y^{(i)}(\mathbf{w}^T\mathbf{x}^{(i)} + b) \leq 1, \qquad (10.32)$$

$$\sum_{i=1}^{n} \alpha_i y^{(i)} = 0. \qquad (10.33)$$

The KKT conditions (10.30), (10.31), and (10.32) correspond to the points that are correctly classified, on the margin hyperplanes, and on the wrong side of the margin hyperplanes, respectively. These KKT conditions can be evaluated one example at a time, and the dual objective function (10.22) reaches its maximum when every α_i obeys these KKT conditions. For convenience, we denote the first, second Lagrange multipliers by α_1, α_2, respectively.

Given two Lagrange multipliers α_1 and α_2, the strategy used by SMO to jointly optimize α_1 and α_2 consists of the following steps:

1. Compute the unconstrained optimal values for α_1, α_2 first.
2. Compute the bounds that make the two multipliers obey all the KKT conditions.
3. Compute the constrained optimal values for α_1, α_2 by clipping the unconstrained optimal values with the bounds.

To compute the unconstrained optimal values for α_1, α_2, we need to first express the dual objective function $L_D(\boldsymbol{\alpha})$ as a function of α_1, α_2. Let $k_{ij} = K(\mathbf{x}^{(i)}, \mathbf{x}^{(j)})$, $v_i = \sum_{j=3}^{n} y^{(j)}\alpha_j k_{ij}$, and $s = y^{(1)}y^{(2)}$. Then $L_D(\boldsymbol{\alpha})$ can be re-written as follows

$$L_D(\alpha_1, \alpha_2) = \sum_{i=1}^{n} \alpha_i - \frac{1}{2}\sum_{i=1}^{n}\sum_{j=1}^{n} \alpha_i\alpha_j y^{(i)}y^{(j)} k_{ij}$$

$$= \alpha_1 + \alpha_2 - \frac{1}{2}k_{11}\alpha_1^2 - \frac{1}{2}k_{22}\alpha_2^2 - sk_{12}\alpha_1\alpha_2$$

$$-y^{(1)}v_1\alpha_1 - y^{(2)}v_2\alpha_2 + L_{const}, \qquad (10.34)$$

where $L_{const} = \sum_{i=3}^{n} \alpha_i - \frac{1}{2} \sum_{i=3}^{n} \sum_{j=3}^{n} \alpha_i \alpha_j y^{(i)} y^{(j)} k_{ij}$.

Since $\alpha_1 = \gamma - s\alpha_2$ (see the derivations of (10.39) and (10.40) below), we can rewrite $L_D(\boldsymbol{\alpha})$ as a function of α_2 as follows

$$
\begin{aligned}
L_D(\alpha_2) &= \gamma - s\alpha_2 + \alpha_2 - \frac{1}{2}k_{11}(\gamma - s\alpha_2)^2 - \frac{1}{2}k_{22}\alpha_2 - sk_{12}(\gamma - s\alpha_2)\alpha_2 \\
&\quad - y^{(1)}v_1(\gamma - s\alpha_2) - y^{(2)}v_2\alpha_2 + L_{const} \\
&= \gamma - s\alpha_2 + \alpha_2 - \frac{1}{2}k_{11}\gamma^2 + k_{11}s\gamma\alpha_2 - \frac{1}{2}k_{11}\alpha_2^2 - \frac{1}{2}k_{22}\alpha_2^2 \\
&\quad - sk_{12}\gamma\alpha_2 + k_{12}\alpha_2^2 - y^{(1)}v_1\gamma + y^{(1)}v_1s\alpha_2 - y^{(2)}v_2\alpha_2 + L_{const}
\end{aligned}
$$

$$(10.35)$$

The first derivative of L_D with respect to α_2 is

$$
\frac{\partial L_D}{\partial \alpha_2} = -s + 1 + sk_{11}(\gamma - s\alpha_2) - k_{22}\alpha_2 + k_{12}\alpha_2 - sk_{12}(\gamma - s\alpha_2) + y^{(2)}(v_1 - v_2),
$$

$$(10.36)$$

and the second derivative of L_D with respect to α_2 is

$$
\frac{\partial^2 L_D}{\partial \alpha_2^2} = 2k_{12} - k_{11} - k_{22} = \eta.
$$

$$(10.37)$$

Let E_i be the error on the i'th training example: $E_i = (\mathbf{w}^{old} \cdot \mathbf{x}^{(i)} + b) - y^{(i)}$. One can verify that the following equality holds (see Problem 10.3 at the end of this chapter)

$$
\alpha_2^{new} = \alpha_2^{old} - \frac{y^{(2)}(E_1 - E_2)}{\eta}.
$$

$$(10.38)$$

This is the equation that gives the unconstrained optimal value for the Lagrange multiplier α_2.

Next, we need to find the bound for α_2 to obey all the KKT conditions. The bound constraint (10.31) requires that the Lagrange multipliers lie within a box, and the linear equality constraint (10.33) requires that they lie one a diagonal line (see Fig. 10.4). Let $\gamma = -\sum_{i=3}^{n} \alpha_i y^{(i)}$, then

$$
\alpha_1 y^{(1)} + \alpha_2 y^{(2)} + \sum_{i=3}^{n} \alpha_i y^{(i)} = 0 \quad \Rightarrow \quad \alpha_1 y^{(1)} + \alpha_2 y^{(2)} = \gamma. \quad (10.39)
$$

Since $y^{(i)} \in \{1, -1\}$, and we have set $s = y^{(1)}y^{(2)}$, (10.39) can be rewritten as

$$
\alpha_1 + s\alpha_2 = \gamma. \quad (10.40)
$$

Note that γ does not change before and after optimization, and hence

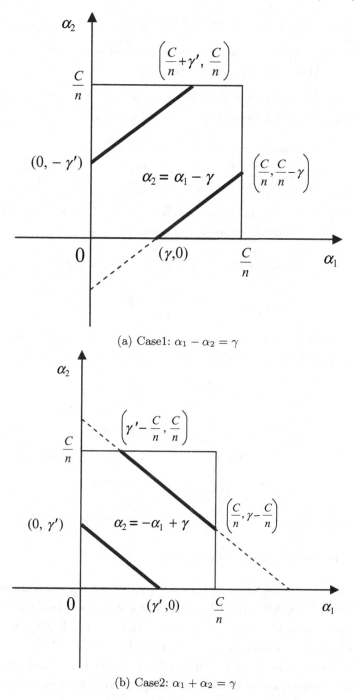

(a) Case1: $\alpha_1 - \alpha_2 = \gamma$

(b) Case2: $\alpha_1 + \alpha_2 = \gamma$

Fig. 10.4. Two cases of joint optimization of α_1 and α_2

$$\alpha_1^{old} + s\alpha_2^{old} = \gamma. \tag{10.41}$$

The end points of the diagonal line segment can be expressed quite simply in terms of α_2. There are two cases to consider:

1. $y^{(1)} \neq y^{(2)}$ (see Fig. 10.4(a)). Then $\alpha_1 - \alpha_2 = \alpha_1^{old} - \alpha_2^{old} = \gamma$. The lower and higher end points expressed in terms of α_2 are

$$L = \max(0, -\gamma) = \max(0, \alpha_2^{old} - \alpha_1^{old}), \tag{10.42}$$

$$H = \min\left(\frac{C}{n}, \frac{C}{n} - \gamma\right) = \min\left(\frac{C}{n}, \frac{C}{n} + \alpha_2^{old} - \alpha_1^{old}\right). \tag{10.43}$$

2. $y^{(1)} = y^{(2)}$ (see Fig. 10.4(b)). Then $\alpha_1 + \alpha_2 = \alpha_1^{old} + \alpha_2^{old} = \gamma$. The lower and higher end points expressed in terms of α_2 are

$$L = \max\left(0, \gamma - \frac{C}{n}\right) = \max\left(0, \alpha_1^{old} + \alpha_2^{old} - \frac{C}{n}\right), \tag{10.44}$$

$$H = \min\left(\frac{C}{n}, \gamma\right) = \min\left(\frac{C}{n}, \alpha_1^{old} + \alpha_2^{old}\right). \tag{10.45}$$

Using the bounds derived for the above two cases, we attain the constrained optimal value for α_2 as follows:

$$\alpha_2^{new,clipped} = \begin{cases} H, & \text{if } \alpha_2^{new} \geq H, \\ \alpha_2^{new}, & \text{if } L < \alpha_2^{new} < H, \\ L, & \text{if } \alpha_2^{new} \leq L. \end{cases} \tag{10.46}$$

Using $\alpha_2^{new,clipped}$, the constrained optimal value for α_1 is computed as

$$\alpha_1^{new} = \alpha_1^{old} + s(\alpha_2^{old} - \alpha_2^{new,clipped}), \tag{10.47}$$

where $s = y^{(1)}y^{(2)}$.

Heuristics for Choosing Multipliers

The SMO algorithm is based on the evaluation of the KKT conditions. When every multiplier satisfies the KKT conditions of the problem, the algorithm terminates. To speed up the convergence, SMO uses two heuristics to choose pairs of Lagrange multipliers to jointly optimize. The first heuristic provides the outer loop of the SMO algorithm. The outer loop of the algorithm first iterates over the entire set of training examples to decide whether an example violates the KKT conditions. If it does, then that example is chosen for immediate optimization. A second example is chosen using the second heuristic, and the two multipliers are jointly optimized. The SVM is then updated using these two new multiplier values, and the outer loop resumes looking for KKT violators.

After one pass through the entire training set, the outer loop switches to the second mode in which it only iterates over those examples that reside on the margin hyperplanes, i.e. the non-bound examples whose Lagrange multipliers are within the open interval $(0, \frac{C}{n})$. Again, each non-bound example is checked against the KKT conditions, and violating examples are chosen for immediate optimization and update. The outer loop makes repeated passes over the non-bound examples until they all obey the KKT conditions within ϵ. After that, the outer loop switches back to the first mode in which it goes over the entire training set again. The outer loop keeps alternating between the entire training set and the non-bound set until all the multipliers obey the KKT conditions within ϵ. At that point, the algorithm terminates.

Once a first Lagrange multiplier is chosen, SMO uses the second heuristic to choose the second multiplier. The second heuristic attempts to maximizing the step size that can be taken during the joint optimization. Equation (10.38) is used at this step. The goal is to choose the maximum possible step size by having the largest value of $||E_1 - E_2||$ in (10.38). SMO keeps a cached error value E for every non-bound example in the training set. If E_1 is positive, then the example with the minimum error E_2 is chosen. If E_1 is negative, then the example with the largest error E_2 is chosen.

There are cases where SMO can not make positive progress using the second heuristic described above. For example, positive progress can not be made if the first and second training examples share the same input vector $\mathbf{x}$. To avoid this problem, SMO uses a hierarchy of choices in choosing the second multiplier. If there is no positive progress, then SMO iterates through the non-bound example starting at a random position, searching for a second example that can make positive progress. If none of the non-bound example makes positive progress, then the algorithm starts at a random position and iterates through the entire training set until an example is found that makes positive progress. The randomness in choosing the starting position is to avoid bias towards examples stored at the beginning of the training set. In very extreme degenerative cases where none of the examples will make an adequate second example, SMO will skip the first multiplier and start with another multiplier.

Updating Offset b

After each optimization step, we need to re-evaluate the offset b so that the KKT conditions are fulfilled for both optimized examples.

Let u_1 be the SVM output for the training sample $\mathbf{x}^{(1)}$ with the old α_1 and α_2:

$$u_1 = \mathbf{w}^{old} \cdot \mathbf{x}^{(1)} + b^{old}$$

$$= \alpha_1^{old} y^{(i)} k_{11} + \alpha_2^{old} y^{(2)} k_{12} + \sum_{j=3}^{n} \alpha_j y^{(j)} k_{1j} + b^{old} . \qquad (10.48)$$

Since

$$E_1 = (\mathbf{w}^{old} \cdot \mathbf{x}^{(1)} + b^{old}) - y^{(1)} ,$$

we have

$$u_1 - E_1 = y^{(1)} . \qquad (10.49)$$

If $0 < \alpha_1^{new} < \frac{C}{n}$, then $\mathbf{x}^{(1)}$ will lie on a margin hyperplane, and hence the SVM output for $\mathbf{x}^{(1)}$ will be $y^{(1)}$. Therefore,

$$y^{(1)} = \alpha_1^{new} y^{(1)} k_{11} + \alpha_2^{new} y^{(2)} k_{12} + \sum_{j=3}^{n} \alpha_j y^{(j)} k_{1j} + b_1 . \qquad (10.50)$$

Substituting (10.48) and (10.50) into (10.49), we get

$$b_1 = E_1 + b^{old} + y^{(1)} (\alpha_1^{new} - \alpha_1^{old}) k_{11} + y^{(2)} (\alpha_2^{new} - \alpha_2^{old}) k_{12} . \qquad (10.51)$$

Similarly, we can obtain the equation for b_2 when $0 < \alpha_2^{new} < \frac{C}{n}$

$$b_2 = E_2 + b^{old} + y^{(1)} (\alpha_1^{new} - \alpha_1^{old}) k_{11} + y^{(2)} (\alpha_2^{new} - \alpha_2^{old}) k_{12} . \qquad (10.52)$$

When both b_1 and b_2 are valid, they are equal. When both new Lagrange multipliers are at bound (i.e. $\alpha_1^{new} = \alpha_2^{new} = \frac{C}{n}$, $\xi_1 > 0$, $\xi_2 > 0$), and $L \neq H$, then any value in the closed interval $[b_1, b_2]$ is consistent with the KKT conditions. In this case, SMO chooses $b^{new} = \frac{b_1 + b_2}{2}$ to be the new offset. If one multiplier is at bound and the other is not, then b^{new} is set to the offset value computed using the non-bound multiplier.

A cached error value E is kept for every example whose Lagrange multiplier is neither zero nor $\frac{C}{n}$. When a Lagrange multiplier is non-bound and is involved in a joint optimization, its cached error becomes zero. The stored errors of other non-bound multipliers not involved in joint optimization are updated as follows:

$$E_j^{new} - E_j^{old} = u_j^{new} - u_j^{old}, \tag{10.53}$$

where u_j^{new} and u_j^{old} are the new and old SVM output values for the j'th training example, and this change is due to the change in α_1, α_2, and b. Therefore, we can compute $u_j^{new} - u_j^{old}$ as follows:

$$u_j^{new} - u_j^{old} = y^{(1)} \alpha_1^{new} k_{1j} + y^{(2)} \alpha_2^{new} k_{2j} + b^{new} - y^{(1)} \alpha_1^{old} k_{1j} - y^{(2)} \alpha_2^{old} k_{2j} - b^{old}. \tag{10.54}$$

Substituting (10.54) into (10.53), we have

$$E_j^{new} = E_j^{old} + y^{(1)}(\alpha_1^{new} - \alpha_1^{old})k_{1j} + y^{(2)}(\alpha_2^{new} - \alpha_2^{old})k_{2j} + b^{new} - b^{old}. \tag{10.55}$$

10.1.8 Further Discussions

As described in Sect. 10.1.3, the SVM for non-separable case can be casted as the following optimization problem:

$$\min_{\mathbf{w}, b, \xi_i} \frac{1}{2} \mathbf{w}^T \mathbf{w} + \frac{C}{n} \sum_{i=1}^{n} \xi_i, \tag{10.56}$$

$$\text{subject to} \quad y^{(i)}(\mathbf{w}^T \mathbf{x}^{(i)} + b) \geq 1 - \xi_i, \quad \xi_i \geq 0 \quad \forall i.$$

It can be easily verified that the above optimization problem is equivalent to minimizing the following function $L(\mathbf{w})$ (see Problem 10.4 at the end of the chapter):

$$\min_{\mathbf{w}} L(\mathbf{w}) = \sum_i |1 - y^{(i)} f(\mathbf{x}^{(i)})|_+ + \frac{1}{2} \mathbf{w}^T \mathbf{w}, \tag{10.57}$$

where $f(\mathbf{x}^{(i)}) = \mathbf{w}^T \mathbf{x}^{(i)} + b$, $|x|_+$ equals x if $x > 0$, and equals 0 otherwise. The first and second terms in $L(\mathbf{w})$ can be considered as a loss function and a regularization term, respectively, which is a familiar paradigm in function estimations. The loss function $|1 - y^{(i)} f(\mathbf{x}^{(i)})|_+$ is called *hinge loss*, and takes the form shown in Fig. 10.5. This loss function has the characteristics of giving zero penalty to data points that are correctly classified (i.e. reside at the right side of the margin hyperplanes), and assigning penalties to data points if they reside at the wrong side of the margin hyperplanes. The penalties are proportional to the distance on the wrong side of the margin hyperplanes. On the other hand, the regularization term makes explicit the size constraint on the model parameters. When there are many correlated variables in constructing a classification model, their coefficients can become poorly determined, and exhibit high variances. A wildly large positive coefficient on one variable can

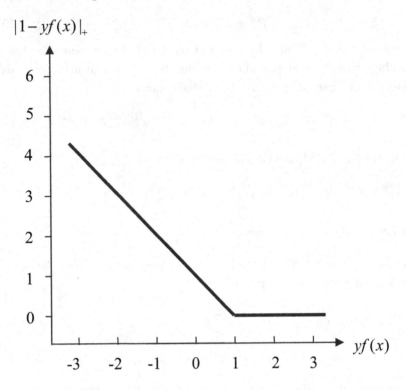

Fig. 10.5. The hinge loss function used by SVMs

be canceled by a large negative coefficient on its correlated cousin. By impos-
ing a size constraint on the coefficients, this phenomenon is prevented from
occurring.

Because $L(\mathbf{w})$ contains the non-smooth term $|1 - y^{(i)}f(\mathbf{x}^{(i)})|_+$, its mini-
mization is a non-trivial problem. A common solution is to convert it into a
constrained optimization problem, such as the one same as (10.56), and use
the SMO algorithm described in this section to compute its solution. It is
noteworthy that there are research efforts that strive to approximate the non-
smooth hinge loss function with a smooth function, so that $L(\mathbf{w})$ becomes
differentiable, and standard unconstrained optimization methods such as the
gradient descent algorithm can be used to compute its solution (see Problem
10.5 at the end of the chapter).

10.2 Maximum Margin Markov Networks

For single-label binary classification problems, SVMs provide an effective method of learning a maximum-margin decision boundary. For multi-label, multi-class classification problems, graphical models offer the most powerful tool for learning a joint probabilistic model over the set of variables (see Chap. 4 for detailed descriptions). Max-Margin Markov Networks (M^3-nets) strives to get the best of the two approaches by incorporating the max-margin concept into the framework of conditional random fields [81].

10.2.1 Primal and Dual Problems

Let $\mathbf{x} = [x_1, x_2, \ldots, x_m]$ be the feature vector of a sequence of m instances, and $\mathbf{y} = [y_1, y_2, \ldots, y_m]$ be the vector of labels of the m instances, where $y_i \in \{l_1, l_2, \ldots, l_k\}$. For simplicity of descriptions, we assume that the sequences $\mathbf{x}$ and $\mathbf{y}$ have the same length. From Sect. 9.4, conditional random fields generally define the conditional probability $P(\mathbf{y}|\mathbf{x})$ of a label sequence $\mathbf{y}$ given an observation sequence $\mathbf{x}$ using the following exponential form:

$$P_{\boldsymbol{\lambda}}(\mathbf{y}|\mathbf{x}) = \frac{1}{Z_{\boldsymbol{\lambda}}(\mathbf{x})} \exp\left(\sum_{i=1}^{l} \lambda_i f_i(\mathbf{x}, \mathbf{y})\right), \tag{10.58}$$

where $Z_{\boldsymbol{\lambda}}(X)$ is the normalizing factor that ensures $\sum_{\mathbf{y}} P_{\boldsymbol{\lambda}}(\mathbf{y}|\mathbf{x}) = 1$, λ_i is a model parameter, and $f_i(\mathbf{x}, \mathbf{y})$ is a feature function (often binary-valued) that connects certain important features with a certain class label. Now define the feature vector $\mathbf{F}(\mathbf{x}, \mathbf{y})$ as

$$\mathbf{F}(\mathbf{x}, \mathbf{y}) = [f_1(\mathbf{x}, \mathbf{y}), f_2(\mathbf{x}, \mathbf{y}), \ldots, f_l(\mathbf{x}, \mathbf{y})], \tag{10.59}$$

we can re-write (10.58) as

$$P_{\boldsymbol{\lambda}}(\mathbf{y}|\mathbf{x}) \propto \exp\left(\mathbf{w}^T \mathbf{F}(\mathbf{x}, \mathbf{y})\right), \tag{10.60}$$

where $\mathbf{w} = [\lambda_1, \lambda_2, \ldots, \lambda_l]$. With conditional random fields, the parameter set $\mathbf{w}$ is estimated by maximizing the log-likelihood of the model during the training stage. Here, instead of using the maximum likelihood estimate, we want to exploit a loss function that embodies the max-margin concept. In general, we are not interested in the exact form of $P(\mathbf{y}|\mathbf{x})$. We are rather interested in the classifier

$$\mathbf{f}_{\mathbf{w}}(\mathbf{x}) = \arg\max_{\mathbf{y}} \mathbf{w}^T \mathbf{F}(\mathbf{x}, \mathbf{y}), \tag{10.61}$$

and with what confidence the classification is done.

A suitable notion of margin in this case is the difference between the value $\mathbf{w}^T\mathbf{F}(\mathbf{x}, \mathbf{t}(\mathbf{x}))$ for the true label $\mathbf{t}(\mathbf{x})$ of $\mathbf{x}$ and the value $\mathbf{w}^T\mathbf{F}(\mathbf{x}, \mathbf{y})$ for a wrong label $\mathbf{y} \neq \mathbf{t}(\mathbf{x})$. If the data is linearly separable, in analogy to the canonical form (10.10) for SVMs, we can rescale $\mathbf{w}$ so that the minimal distance between the above two values is 1:

$$\mathbf{w}^T\mathbf{F}(\mathbf{x}, \mathbf{t}(\mathbf{x})) - \mathbf{w}^T\mathbf{F}(\mathbf{x}, \mathbf{y}) \geq 1, \quad \forall \mathbf{y} \neq \mathbf{t}(\mathbf{x}), \quad \mathbf{x} \in \mathcal{S}. \tag{10.62}$$

Again, for non-separable data, we introduce non-negative slack variables $\xi_\mathbf{x}$, one for each training sample. We also define

$$\Delta \mathbf{F}_\mathbf{x}(\mathbf{y}) = \mathbf{F}(\mathbf{x}, \mathbf{t}(\mathbf{x})) - \mathbf{F}(\mathbf{x}, \mathbf{y})$$

for brevity of notation. The inequality (10.62) then becomes:

$$\mathbf{w}^T \Delta \mathbf{F}_\mathbf{x}(\mathbf{y}) \geq 1 - \xi_\mathbf{x}, \quad \forall \mathbf{y} \neq \mathbf{t}(\mathbf{x}), \quad \mathbf{x} \in \mathcal{S}. \tag{10.63}$$

The constraint (10.63) stipulates that the margin between the value for the true label and the value for a wrong label must be more than 1. For multi-label, multi-class classification problems, however, the loss function is usually not the simple $0 - 1$ loss $I(\arg\max_\mathbf{y} \mathbf{w}^T\mathbf{F}(\mathbf{x}, \mathbf{y}) = \mathbf{t}(\mathbf{x}))$, but rather the per-label loss, which is the proportion of incorrect individual labels in $\mathbf{y}$. Therefore, it makes more sense to use a margin that is proportional to the number of wrong labels in $\mathbf{y}$

$$\Delta \mathbf{t}_\mathbf{x}(\mathbf{y}) = \sum_{i=1}^{m} I(y_i \neq \mathbf{t}(\mathbf{x})_i), \tag{10.64}$$

where $\mathbf{t}(\mathbf{x})_i$ denotes the i'th element of the label vector $\mathbf{t}(\mathbf{x})$. Similar to SVMs, using the margin (10.64), the term $\frac{C}{n}\sum_{\mathbf{x}\in\mathcal{S}} \xi_\mathbf{x}$ will then correspond to an upper bound of the empirical risk.

With all the above preparations, the maximum margin Markov network becomes the following quadratic optimization problem:

$$\min_{\mathbf{w}, \xi} \frac{1}{2}\mathbf{w}^T\mathbf{w} + \frac{C}{n}\sum_{\mathbf{x}\in\mathcal{S}} \xi_\mathbf{x}, \tag{10.65}$$

$$\text{subject to} \quad \mathbf{w}^T \Delta \mathbf{F}_\mathbf{x}(\mathbf{y}) \geq \Delta \mathbf{t}_\mathbf{x}(\mathbf{y}) - \xi_\mathbf{x}, \quad \mathbf{x} \in \mathcal{S}, \quad \forall \mathbf{y}.$$

Note that the constraints in (10.65) include the case $\mathbf{y} = \mathbf{t}(\mathbf{y})$. Again, similar to the derivation of the SVM dual problem (see Sect. 10.1.5), we can derive

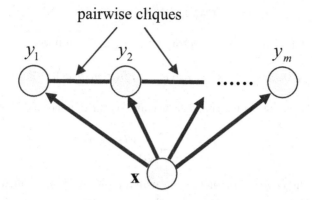

Fig. 10.6. Chain graph that contains only the pairwise cliques

the dual objective function of this problem by introducing the Lagrangian multipliers, constructing the Lagrangian function, minimizing the Lagrangian function with respect to $\mathbf{w}$ and $\xi_{\mathbf{x}}$, and then substituting the solution back to the Lagrangian function. Because there is one constraint for each pair of $\mathbf{x} \in \mathcal{S}$ and $\mathbf{y}$, we need to introduce a $|\mathcal{S}| \times |\mathbf{y}|$ number of Lagrangian multipliers $\alpha_{\mathbf{x}}(\mathbf{y})$. The dual problem of M^3-nets is very similar to that of SVMs, which is shown as follows:

$$\max_{\alpha_{\mathbf{x}}(\mathbf{y})} \sum_{\mathbf{x},\mathbf{y}} \alpha_{\mathbf{x}}(\mathbf{y}) \Delta t_{\mathbf{x}}(\mathbf{y}) - \frac{1}{2} \sum_{\mathbf{x},\mathbf{y}} \sum_{\mathbf{x}',\mathbf{y}'} \alpha_{\mathbf{x}}(\mathbf{y}) \alpha_{\mathbf{x}'}(\mathbf{y}') (\Delta \mathbf{F}_{\mathbf{x}}(\mathbf{y}) \cdot \Delta \mathbf{F}_{\mathbf{x}'}(\mathbf{y}'))$$

$$\text{subject to} \quad \sum_{\mathbf{y}} \alpha_{\mathbf{x}}(\mathbf{y}) = \frac{C}{n}, \forall \mathbf{x} \in \mathcal{S}, \quad \alpha_{\mathbf{x}}(\mathbf{y}) \geq 0, \forall \mathbf{x} \in \mathcal{S}, \forall \mathbf{y}. \quad (10.66)$$

Unfortunately, the number of constraints in (10.65) and (10.66) are exponential in the number of labels l, and both the primal and the dual problems are untractable in their original forms.

10.2.2 Factorizing Dual Problem

We can explore the sparsity of interactions within the network to factorize the original problem. The factorized problem can generally reduce the number of parameters to be estimated from an exponential order to a polynomial one, making the untractable problem tractable.

For simplicity of presentations, we focus on the chain graph that contains only the pairwise cliques (see Fig. 10.6). With such a graph, feature functions $f_i(\mathbf{x}, \mathbf{y})$ in (10.58) becomes

$$f_i(\mathbf{x}, \mathbf{y}) = f_i(\mathbf{x}, y_i, y_{i+1}). \tag{10.67}$$

We further define the feature vector $\mathbf{F}(\mathbf{x}, y_i, y_{i+1})$ as follows:

$$\mathbf{F}(\mathbf{x}, y_i, y_{i+1}) = [f_1(\mathbf{x}, y_i, y_{i+1}), \dots, f_l(\mathbf{x}, y_i, y_{i+1})] \in \mathbb{R}^l. \tag{10.68}$$

Using the above notations, the joint feature vector defined in (10.59) becomes

$$\mathbf{F}(\mathbf{x}, \mathbf{y}) = \sum_{(y_i, y_{i+1}) \in E} \mathbf{F}(\mathbf{x}, y_i, y_{i+1}), \tag{10.69}$$

where E is the edge set of the graph, which consists of only pairwise edges.

The key insight to the M^3-net is that the variables (Lagrangian multipliers) $\alpha_{\mathbf{x}}(\mathbf{y})$ in the dual problem 10.66 can be interpreted as a density function over $\mathbf{y}$ conditioned on $\mathbf{x}$, because they satisfy the constraints $\sum_{\mathbf{y}} \alpha_{\mathbf{x}}(\mathbf{y}) = \frac{C}{n}$ and $\alpha_{\mathbf{x}}(\mathbf{y}) \geq 0$. The dual objective function is a function of expectations of $\Delta t_{\mathbf{x}}(\mathbf{y})$ and $\Delta \mathbf{F}_{\mathbf{x}}(\mathbf{y})$ with respect to $\alpha_{\mathbf{x}}(\mathbf{y})$. Since both $\Delta t_{\mathbf{x}}(\mathbf{y}) = \sum_i \Delta t_{\mathbf{x}}(y_i)$ and $\Delta \mathbf{F}_{\mathbf{x}}(\mathbf{y}) = \sum_{(i,j)} \Delta \mathbf{F}_{\mathbf{x}}(y_i, y_j)$ are sums of functions over nodes and edges, we can factorize the dual variables $\alpha_{\mathbf{x}}(\mathbf{y})$ in exactly the same way as $\Delta t_{\mathbf{x}}(\mathbf{y})$ and $\Delta \mathbf{F}_{\mathbf{x}}(\mathbf{y})$. We define the marginal dual variables as follows:

$$\mu_{\mathbf{x}}(y_i, y_j) = \sum_{\mathbf{y} \sim [y_i, y_j]} \alpha_{\mathbf{x}}(\mathbf{y}), \quad \forall (i,j) \in E, \ \forall y_i, y_j, \ \forall \mathbf{x}, \tag{10.70}$$

$$\mu_{\mathbf{x}}(y_i) = \sum_{\mathbf{y} \sim [y_i]} \alpha_{\mathbf{x}}(\mathbf{y}), \quad \forall i, \ \forall y_i, \ \forall \mathbf{x}, \tag{10.71}$$

where E is the edge set of the graph, and $\mathbf{y} \sim [y_i, y_j]$ denotes a full assignment $\mathbf{y}$ consistent with partial assignment y_i, y_j.

Using the above marginal dual variables, we can re-write the first and second terms of the dual objective function as follows:

$$\sum_{\mathbf{x}, \mathbf{y}} \alpha_{\mathbf{x}}(\mathbf{y}) \Delta t_{\mathbf{x}}(\mathbf{y}) = \sum_{\mathbf{x}} \sum_{\mathbf{y}} \sum_{i=1}^{l} \alpha_{\mathbf{x}}(\mathbf{y}) \Delta t_{\mathbf{x}}(y_i)$$

$$= \sum_{\mathbf{x}} \sum_{y_i} \Delta t_{\mathbf{x}}(y_i) \sum_{\mathbf{y} \sim [y_i]} \alpha_{\mathbf{x}}(\mathbf{y})$$

$$= \sum_{\mathbf{x}} \sum_{y_i} \mu_{\mathbf{x}}(y_i) \Delta t_{\mathbf{x}}(y_i). \tag{10.72}$$

$$\sum_{\mathbf{x}, \mathbf{y}} \sum_{\mathbf{x}', \mathbf{y}'} \alpha_{\mathbf{x}}(\mathbf{y}) \alpha_{\mathbf{x}'}(\mathbf{y}') (\Delta \mathbf{F}_{\mathbf{x}}(\mathbf{y}) \cdot \Delta \mathbf{F}_{\mathbf{x}'}(\mathbf{y}'))$$

$$= \sum_{\mathbf{x},\mathbf{x}'} \sum_{\mathbf{y},\mathbf{y}'} \alpha_{\mathbf{x}}(\mathbf{y}) \alpha_{\mathbf{x}'}(\mathbf{y}') \sum_{(y_i,y_{i+1}) \in E} \sum_{(y'_i,y'_{i+1}) \in E} (\Delta \mathbf{F}(\mathbf{x}, y_i, y_{i+1}) \cdot \Delta \mathbf{F}(\mathbf{x}', y_{i'}, y_{i'+1}))$$

$$= \sum_{\mathbf{x},\mathbf{x}'} \sum_{(y_i,y_{i+1}) \in E} \sum_{(y'_i,y'_{i+1}) \in E} (\Delta \mathbf{F}(\mathbf{x}, y_i, y_{i+1}) \cdot \Delta \mathbf{F}(\mathbf{x}', y_{i'}, y_{i'+1}))$$

$$\cdot \left(\sum_{\mathbf{y} \sim [y_i, y_{i+1}]} \alpha_{\mathbf{x}}(\mathbf{y}) \right) \left(\sum_{\mathbf{y}' \sim [y_{i'}, y_{i'+1}]} \alpha_{\mathbf{x}'}(\mathbf{y}') \right)$$

$$= \sum_{\mathbf{x},\mathbf{x}'} \sum_{(y_i,y_{i+1}) \in E} \sum_{(y'_i,y'_{i+1}) \in E} \mu_{\mathbf{x}}(y_i, y_{i+1}) \mu_{\mathbf{x}'}(y_{i'}, y_{i'+1})$$

$$\cdot (\Delta \mathbf{F}(\mathbf{x}, y_i, y_{i+1}) \cdot \Delta \mathbf{F}(\mathbf{x}', y_{i'}, y_{i'+1})) . \tag{10.73}$$

Obviously, (10.72) and (10.73) contain only a polynomial number of dual variables (Lagrangian multipliers) $\mu_{\mathbf{x}}(y_i)$ and $\mu_{\mathbf{x}}(y_i, y_{i+1})$. Therefore, the above two factorizations have transformed the exponential summation into a polynomial one, and have turned the untractable problem into a tractable one.

To produce an equivalent quadratic optimization problem, we must also ensure that the dual variables $\mu_{\mathbf{x}}(y_i)$, $\mu_{\mathbf{x}}(y_i, y_{i+1})$ are the marginals resulting from a legal density $\alpha(\mathbf{y})$. In particular, we must enforce consistency between the pairwise and singleton marginals:

$$\sum_{y_i} \mu_{\mathbf{x}}(y_i, y_j) = \mu_{\mathbf{x}}(y_j), \quad \forall y_j, \ \forall (i,j) \in E, \ \forall \mathbf{x}. \tag{10.74}$$

Using the above definitions and notations, we obtain the following factored dual problem that is equivalent to the original dual problem:

$$\max_{\substack{\mu_{\mathbf{x}}(y_i), \\ \mu_{\mathbf{x}}(y_i,y_{i+1})}} \sum_{\mathbf{x}} \sum_{y_i} \mu_{\mathbf{x}}(y_i) \Delta \mathbf{t}_{\mathbf{x}}(y_i)$$

$$- \frac{1}{2} \sum_{\mathbf{x},\mathbf{x}'} \sum_{\substack{(y_i,y_{i+1}) \in E \\ (y'_i,y'_{i+1}) \in E}} \mu_{\mathbf{x}}(y_i, y_{i+1}) \mu_{\mathbf{x}'}(y_{i'}, y_{i'+1})(\Delta \mathbf{F}(\mathbf{x}, y_i, y_{i+1}) \cdot \Delta \mathbf{F}(\mathbf{x}', y_{i'}, y_{i'+1})),$$

$$\text{subject to} \sum_{y_i} \mu_{\mathbf{x}}(y_i, y_j) = \mu_{\mathbf{x}}(y_j), \ \sum_{y_i} \mu_{\mathbf{x}}(y_i) = \frac{C}{n}, \ \mu_{\mathbf{x}}(y_i, y_j) \geq 0. \tag{10.75}$$

Similar to SVMs, the solution to the factorized dual problem takes the form of

$$\mathbf{w} = \sum_{\mathbf{x}} \sum_{(y_i,y_{i+1}) \in E} \mu_{\mathbf{x}}(y_i, y_{i+1}) \Delta \mathbf{F}(\mathbf{x}, y_i, y_{i+1}), \tag{10.76}$$

and this formulation can also make use of the kernel trick as everything is expressed in terms of dot products.

10.2.3 General Graphs and Learning Algorithm

In the proceeding subsections, we have derived the framework of the Maximum Margin Markov Networks using the chain graph and pairwise cliques. It is noteworthy that the derived framework applies to arbitrary graph structures. More specifically, if the graph is triangulated, then we can easily create the factorized dual problem by defining the clique marginals with the consistency conditions. If the graph is non-triangulated, then we have to first triangulate it and then obtain an equivalent optimization problem. In this case, we need to add to the problem a number of new constraints that is exponential in the size of cliques.

In [81], Taskar, *et al.* presented an extended version of SMO as the learning algorithm for M^3-nets (see Sect. 10.1.7 for detailed descriptions). They also derived a generalization bound on the expected risk for their max-margin approach.

10.2.4 Max-Margin Networks vs. Other Graphical Models

In Sect. 9.3, we discussed pros and cons of generative and discriminative graphical models. We pointed out that, for the task of data classifications, what we really need to compare is the scores of the true and wrong labels for the same training example $\mathbf{x}_k$, and we want the score for the true label as large as possible, and scores for wrong labels as small as possible. The loss function used by discriminative models partially reflects this principle while the one used by generative models does not.

In fact, the M^3-nets presented in this section is one of the few graphical models that explicitly use the above principle as its loss function. The loss function defined in (10.62) mandates that the minimal distance between the score assigned to the true label $\mathbf{t}(\mathbf{x})$ of $\mathbf{x}$ and the score assigned to a wrong label $\forall \mathbf{y} \neq \mathbf{t}(\mathbf{x})$ must be 1.

The advantage of using the loss function (10.62) can be illustrated using Fig. 10.7. In this figure, the horizontal axis represents all possible labels for a specific training example $\mathbf{x}_k$, while the vertical axis represents the score given to each label by a learning model under discussion. Assume that at the initial stage of the training process, the model gives randomized, relatively uniform scores to all possible labels of the training example $\mathbf{x}_k$ (see Fig. 10.7(a)). The ideal model we want to construct is the one that assigns the highest score to the true label $\mathbf{t}(\mathbf{x}_k)$ of $\mathbf{x}_k$, and penalizes wrong labels $\forall \mathbf{y} \neq \mathbf{t}(\mathbf{x}_k)$ by assigning

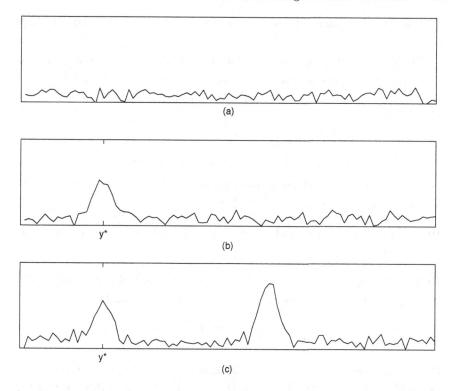

Fig. 10.7. An intuitive illustration of the differences between max-margin networks and other graphical models. In each of the figures, the horizontal axis represents all possible labels for a specific training example $\mathbf{x}_k$, and the vertical axis represents the score given to each label by a learning model under discussion. y^* is the true label of the training example $\mathbf{x}_k$

low scores to them (see Fig. 10.7(b)). There is another possible scenario where the training process produces a model that assigns a high score to the true label $\mathbf{t}(\mathbf{x}_k)$ of $\mathbf{x}_k$, but assigns even a higher score to some labels $\mathbf{y}_j \neq \mathbf{t}(\mathbf{x}_k)$ (see Fig. 10.7(c)).

Obviously, M^3-nets have the lowest probability of generating a model shown in Fig. 10.7(c), because the loss function adopted by M^3-nets penalizes such a model. Discriminative graphical models are inferior to M^3-nets because their loss functions do not completely reflect the principle discussed above. Among the three types of approaches, generative models have the highest probability of getting trapped into the scenario shown in Fig. 10.7(c) because their loss functions only intend to increase the score of the true label $\mathbf{t}(\mathbf{x}_k)$ of

$\mathbf{x}_k$, but do not compare it with scores of wrong labels for the same example $\mathbf{x}_k$.

The above illustration provides us with an intuitive insight into the reasons why M^3-nets are superior to other graphical models, and why discriminative models are more likely to attain a better model than generative models.

Problems

10.1. Let $\mathbf{x}, \mathbf{y} \in R^d$. What is the dimension of the space implied by the polynomial kernel $k(\mathbf{x}, \mathbf{y}) = (\mathbf{x}^T \mathbf{y} + 1)^n$?

10.2. Show that the distance between the origin and the hyperplane $\mathbf{w}^T \mathbf{x} + b = 0$ is $|b|/\|\mathbf{w}\|$.

10.3. SMO algorithm. Let E_i be the error on the i'th training example: $E_i = (\mathbf{w}^{old} \cdot \mathbf{x}^{(i)} + b) - y^{(i)}$. Prove that the following equality holds

$$\alpha_2^{new} = \alpha_2^{old} - \frac{y^{(2)}(E_1 - E_2)}{\eta}.$$

10.4. Hinge loss. Given the set of training data that consists of two classes $\mathcal{S} = \{\mathbf{x}_i, y_i\}_{i=1}^n$, $y_i \in \{-1, 1\}$, show that the following two optimization problems are equivalent:

(a)

$$\min_{\mathbf{w}} \sum_i \xi_i + \frac{1}{2} \|\mathbf{w}\|^2,$$

$$\text{subject to} \quad y_i \mathbf{w}^T \mathbf{x}_i \geq 1 - \xi_i, \quad \xi_i \geq 0 \quad \forall i.$$

(b)

$$\min_{\mathbf{w}} \sum_i |1 - y_i \mathbf{w}^T \mathbf{x}_i|_+ + \frac{1}{2} \|\mathbf{w}\|^2,$$

where $|x|_+$ equals x if $x > 0$, and equals 0 otherwise. The loss function $|1 - y_i f(x_i)|_+$ is called *hinge loss*.

10.5. Smoothed hinge loss. The hinge loss (Problem 10.4) used by SVM is not a smooth function, which introduces difficulty for optimization. A smoothed approximation to hinge loss is often used so that unconstrained optimization methods can be used to solve the problem. Show that the following loss function with $\gamma > 0$ is an upper bound of hinge loss and converges to hinge loss when $\gamma \to 0$

$$L(y, f(x)) = \gamma \log \left(1 + \exp \left(\frac{1}{\gamma} (1 - y f(x)) \right) \right).$$

10.6. Let $L(y, x)$ be a convex cost function over x. The conjugate function $\hat{L}$ of L is defined as

$$\hat{L}(y, \theta) = \max_x \theta x - L(y, x),$$

where θ is the parameter of $\hat{L}$. Given the set of training data that consists of two classes $\mathcal{S} = \{\mathbf{x}_i, y_i\}_{i=1}^n$, $y_i \in \{-1, 1\}$, show that the following two optimization problems are equivalent:

(a)

$$\min_{\mathbf{w}} \sum_{i=1}^n L(y_i, \mathbf{w}^T \mathbf{x}_i) + \frac{1}{2} \|\mathbf{w}\|^2$$

(b)

$$\min_{\alpha} \sum_{i=1}^n \hat{L}(y_i, -\alpha_i) + \frac{1}{2} \alpha^T \mathbf{K} \alpha$$

where $\mathbf{K} = [K_{ij}]$ is a kernel matrix, and $K_{ij} = \mathbf{x}_i^T \mathbf{x}_j$. Furthermore, the solutions of (a) and (b) are related by

$$\mathbf{w} = \sum_{i=1}^n \alpha_i \mathbf{x}_i.$$

[Hint: Use $\xi_i = \mathbf{w}^T \mathbf{x}_i$ as constraints and apply the Lagrange multiplier method to (a)]

10.7. Kernel CRF. In problem 9.7, we can define a feature mapping function $\Phi(x, y) = [f_1(x, y), \cdots, f_n(x, y)]^T$. Show that the inner products $\langle \Phi(x_i, y_i), \Phi(x_j, y_j) \rangle$ among data points are sufficient to uniquely specify the problem (i.e., the actual value of $\Phi(x, y)$ is not necessary). Compare this with the M^3 network.

10.8. Given the set of training data $\mathcal{S} = \{\mathbf{x}_i, \mathbf{y}_i\}_{i=1}^n$, $\mathbf{y}_i = [y_{i1}, y_{i2}, \ldots, y_{im}]$, $y_{ij} \in \{l_1, l_2, \ldots, l_k\}$, show that the optimization problem of M^3 network is equivalent to

$$\min_{\mathbf{w}} \sum_{i=1}^n \max_{\mathbf{y}} (\Delta \mathbf{t}_{\mathbf{x}_i}(\mathbf{y}) + \mathbf{w}^T \Phi(\mathbf{x}_i, \mathbf{y}) - \mathbf{w}^T \Phi(\mathbf{x}_i, \mathbf{y}_i)) + \frac{\lambda}{2} \|\mathbf{w}\|^2.$$

10.9. Download a hand written digit data set from http://www.ics.uci.edu/mlearn/databases/optdigits/readme.txt. Use LIBSVM (http://www.csie.ntu.edu.tw/cjlin/libsvm/) to train a SVM classifier for digit classification. Use 80% of the data for training and 20% for evaluation. Try linear kernel $\mathbf{x} \cdot \mathbf{x}'$ and radial basis function (RBF) kernel. Select proper C in (10.15) and radius of RBF using 5-fold cross validation on the training data.

10.10. For M^3 network, show that the consistency constraints in (10.74) are sufficient to guarantee that the marginal dual variables μ are from valid dual variable α if the graph is tree-structured, i.e., valid α can uniquely determined by the marginal dual variables.

10.11. Consider a M^3 network of 3 nodes with pairwise cliques, each node is binary valued. Consider following hypothetical assignment of marginal dual variables:

$$\mu_1(1) = \mu_2(1) = \mu_3(1) = 0.5$$

$$\mu_{12}(0,1) = \mu_{12}(1,0) = 0.5$$

$$\mu_{23}(0,1) = \mu_{23}(1,0) = 0.5$$

$$\mu_{31}(0,1) = \mu_{31}(1,0) = 0.5$$

Verify that this assignment satisfies the consistency constraints in (10.74). Prove that this assignment of marginal dual variables cannot come from any valid dual variable α.

A

Appendix

In this appendix, we give the solution to the weighted BiNMF. Assume that each data point has the weight γ_i, the weighted sum of squared errors is:

$$
\begin{aligned}
J &= \frac{1}{2} \sum_i \gamma_i (X_i - \mathbf{X}\mathbf{W}V_i^T)^T (X_i - \mathbf{X}\mathbf{W}V_i^T) \\
&= \frac{1}{2} \text{trace}((\mathbf{X} - \mathbf{X}\mathbf{W}\mathbf{V}^T)\mathbf{\Gamma}(\mathbf{X} - \mathbf{X}\mathbf{W}\mathbf{V}^T))^T \\
&= \frac{1}{2} \text{trace}((\mathbf{X}\mathbf{\Gamma}^{1/2} - \mathbf{X}\mathbf{\Gamma}^{1/2}\mathbf{W}'\mathbf{V}'^T)(\mathbf{X}\mathbf{\Gamma}^{1/2} - \mathbf{X}\mathbf{\Gamma}^{1/2}\mathbf{W}'\mathbf{V}'^T)^T) \\
&= \frac{1}{2} \text{trace}((\mathbf{X}\mathbf{\Gamma}^{1/2} - \mathbf{X}\mathbf{\Gamma}^{1/2}\mathbf{W}'\mathbf{V}'^T)^T(\mathbf{X}\mathbf{\Gamma}^{1/2} - \mathbf{X}\mathbf{\Gamma}^{1/2}\mathbf{W}'\mathbf{V}'^T)) \\
&= \frac{1}{2} \text{trace}((\mathbf{I} - \mathbf{W}'\mathbf{V}'^T)^T\mathbf{\Gamma}^{1/2}\mathbf{K}\mathbf{\Gamma}^{1/2}(\mathbf{I} - \mathbf{W}'\mathbf{V}'^T)) \\
&= \frac{1}{2} \text{trace}((\mathbf{I} - \mathbf{W}'\mathbf{V}'^T)^T\mathbf{K}'(\mathbf{I} - \mathbf{W}'\mathbf{V}'^T)),
\end{aligned}
\tag{A.1}
$$

where $\mathbf{\Gamma}$ is the diagonal matrix with γ_i as its diagonal elements, $\mathbf{W}' = \mathbf{\Gamma}^{-1/2}\mathbf{W}$, $\mathbf{V}' = \mathbf{\Gamma}^{1/2}\mathbf{V}$ and $\mathbf{K}' = \mathbf{\Gamma}^{1/2}\mathbf{K}\mathbf{\Gamma}^{1/2}$.

Notice that the above equation has the same form as (3.40) in Section 3.3.2, so the same algorithm can be used to find the solution.

References

1. T. M. Mitchell, *Machine Learning*. McGraw Hill, 1997.
2. L. Wasserman, *All of Statistics – A Concise Course in Statistical Inference*. Springer, 1997.
3. F. Jelinek, *Statistical Methods for Speech Recognition*. The MIT Press, 1997.
4. L. R. Rabiner, "A tuorial on hidden markov models and selected applications in speech recognition," *Proceedings of IEEE*, vol. 77, no. 2, pp. 257–286, 1989.
5. C. R. Rao, "R. A. Fisher: The founder of modern statistics," *Statistical Science*, vol. 7, Feb. 1992.
6. V. Vapnik, *Estimation of Dependences Based on Empirical Data*. Berlin: Springer Verlag, 1982.
7. V. Vapnik, *The Nature of Statistical Learning Theory*. New York: Springer Verlag, 1995.
8. Y. Gong, *Intelligent Image Databases – Towards Advanced Image Retrieval*. Boston: Kluwer Academic Publishers, 1997.
9. A. del Bimbo, *Visual Information Retrieval*. San Francisco: Morgan Kaufmann, 1999.
10. O. Margues and B. Furth, *Content-Based Image and Video Retrieval*. New York: Springer, 2002.
11. G. Golub and C. Loan, *Matrix Computations*. Baltimore: Johns-Hopkins, 2 ed., 1989.
12. A. Hyvarinen and E. Oja, "Independent component analysis: Algorithms and applications," *Neural Networks*, vol. 13, pp. 411–430, 2000.
13. A. Hyvarinen, "New approximations of differential entropy for independent component analysis and projection pursuit," *Advances in Neural Information Processing Systems*, vol. 10, pp. 273–279, 1998.
14. S. Roweis and L. Saul, "Nonlinear dimensionality reduction by locally linear embedding," *Science*, vol. 290, no. 5500, pp. 2323–2326, 2000.
15. "Mnist database website." http://yann.lecun.com/exdb/mnist.

16. P. Willett, "Document clustering using an inverted file approach," *Journal of Information Science*, vol. 2, pp. 223–231, 1990.

17. W. Croft, "Clustering large files of documents using the single-link method," *Journal of the American Society of Information Science*, vol. 28, pp. 341–344, 1977.

18. P. Willett, "Recent trend in hierarchical document clustering: a critical review," *Information Processing and Management*, vol. 24, no. 5, pp. 577–597, 1988.

19. J. Y. Zien, M. D. F. Schlag, and P. K. Chan, "Multilevel spectral hypergraph partitioning with artibary vertex sizes," *IEEE Transactions on Computer-Aided Design*, vol. 18, pp. 1389–1399, sep 1999.

20. J. Shi and J. Malik, "Normalized cuts and image segmentation," *IEEE Transactions on Pattern Analysis and Machine Intelligence*, vol. 22, no. 8, pp. 888–905, 2000.

21. C. Ding, X. He, H. Zha, M. Gu, and H. D. Simon, "A min-max cut algorithm for graph partitioning and data clustering," in *Proceedings of IEEE ICDM 2001*, pp. 107–114, 2001.

22. H. Zha, C. Ding, M. Gu, X. He, and H. Simon, "Spectral relaxation for k-means clustering," in *Advances in Neural Information Processing Systems*, vol. 14, 2002.

23. A. Y. Ng, M. I. Jordan, and Y. Weiss, "On spectral clustering: Analysis and an algorithm," in *Advances in Neural Information Processing Systems*, vol. 14, 2002.

24. W. Xu and Y. Gong, "Document clustering based on non-negative matrix factorization," in *Proceedings of ACM SIGIR 2003*, (Toronto, Canada), July 2003.

25. W. Xu and Y. Gong, "Document clustering by concept factorization," in *Proceedings of ACM SIGIR 2004*, (Sheffield, United Kingdom), July 2004.

26. D. P. Bertsekas, *Nonlinear Programming*. Belmont, Massachusetts: Athena Scientific, second ed., 1999.

27. D. D. Lee and H. S. Seung, "Algorithms for non-negative matrix factorization," in *Advances in Neural Information Processing Systems*, vol. 13, pp. 556–562, 2001.

28. K.-R. Muller, S. Mika, G. Ratsch, K. Tsuda, and B. Scholkopf, "An introduction to kernel-based learning algorithms," *IEEE Transactions on Neural Networks*, vol. 12, no. 3, pp. 181–202, 2001.

29. F. Sha, L. K. Saul, and D. D. Lee, "Multiplicative updates for nonnegative quadratic programming in support vector machines," in *Advances in Neural Information Processing Systems*, vol. 14, 2002.

30. G. Salton and M. McGill, *Introduction to Modern Information Retrieval*. McGraw-Hill, 1983.

31. P. Bremaud, *Markov Chains, Gibbs Fields, Monte Carlo Simulation, and Queues*. Springer, 2001.

32. T. Lindvall, *lectures on the Coupling Method.* New York: Wiley, 1992.

33. F. R. Gantmacher, *Applications of the Theory of Matrices.* New York: Dover Publications, 2005.

34. R. A. Horn and C. R. Johnson, *Matrix Analysis.* Cambridge University Press, 1985.

35. N. Metropolis, M. Rosenbluth, A.W.Rosenbluth, A. Teller, and E. Teller, "Equations of state calculations by fast computing machines," *Journal of Chemistry and Physics*, vol. 21, pp. 1087–1091, 1953.

36. A. Barker, "Monte carlo calculations of the radial distribution functions for proton-electron plasma," *Australia Journal of Physics*, vol. 18, pp. 119–133, 1965.

37. G. Grimmett, "A theorem on random fields," *Bulletin of the London Mathematical Society*, pp. 81–84, 1973.

38. S. Kirkpatrick, C. Gelatt, and M. Vechhi, "Optimization by simulated annealing," *Science*, vol. 220, no. 4598, pp. 671–680, 1983.

39. V. Cerny, "A thermodynamical approach to the travelling salesman problem: An efficient simulation algorithm," *Journal of Optimization Theory and Applications*, vol. 45, pp. 41–51, 1985.

40. M. Han, W. Xu, and Y. Gong, "Video object segmentation by motion-based sequential feature clustering," in *Proceedings of ACM Multimedia Conference*, (Santa Barbara, CA), pp. 773–781, Oct. 2006.

41. A. D. Jepson and M. Black, "Mixture models for optical flow computation," in *Proceedings of IEEE CVPR*, (New York, NY), June 1993.

42. S. Ayer and H. S. Sawhney, "Layered representation of motion video using robust maximum-likelihood estimation of mixture models and MDL encoding," in *Proceedings of ICCV*, (Washington, DC), June 1995.

43. T. Darrell and A. Pentland, "Cooperative robust estimation using layers of support," *IEEE Transactions on Pattern Analysis and Machine Intelligence*, vol. 17, no. 5, pp. 474–487, 1995.

44. P. H. Torr, R. Szeliski, and P. Anandan, "An integrated bayesian approach to layer extraction from image sequences," *IEEE Transactions on Pattern Analysis and Machine Intelligence*, vol. 23, no. 3, pp. 297–303, 2001.

45. A. D. Jepson, D. J. Fleet, and M. J. Black, "A layered motion representation with occlusion and compact spatial support," in *Proceedings of ECCV*, (London, UK), pp. 692–706, May 2002.

46. E. Adelson and J. Wang, "Representing moving images with layers," in *IEEE Transactions on Image Processing*, vol. 3, pp. 625–638, Sept. 1994.

47. J. Shi and J. Malik, "Motion segmentation and tracking using normalized cuts," in *Proceedings of ICCV*, pp. 1154–1160, Jan. 1998.

48. N. Jojic and B. Frey, "Learning flexible sprites in video layers," in *Proceedings of IEEE CVPR*, (Maui, Hawaii), Dec. 2001.

49. J. Xiao and M. Shah, "Motion layer extraction in the presence of occlusion using graph cut," *IEEE Transactions on PAMI*, vol. 27, pp. 1644–1659, Oct. 2005.

50. S. Khan and M. Shah, "Object based segmentation of video using color motion and spatial information," in *Proceedings of IEEE CVPR*, (Maui, Hawaii), pp. 746–751, Dec. 2001.

51. Q. Ke and T. Kanade, "A subspace approach to layer extraction," in *Proceedings of IEEE CVPR*, (Maui, Hawaii), pp. 255–262, Dec. 2001.

52. Y. Wang and Q. Ji, "A dynamic conditional random field model for object segmentation in image sequences," in *Proceedings of IEEE CVPR*, (San Diego, CA), pp. 264–270, June 2005.

53. J. Wang and M. F. Cohen, "An iterative optimization approach for unified image segmentation and matting," in *Proceedings of ICCV*, (Beijing, China), pp. 936–943, 2005.

54. Y. Li, J. Sun, and H.-Y. Shum, "Video object cut and paste," *ACM Transactions on Graphics*, vol. 24, pp. 595–600, July 2005.

55. J. Sun, J. Jia, C.-K. Tang, and H.-Y. Sham, "Poisson matting," in *Proceedings of ACM SIGGRAPH*, (Los Angeles, CA), pp. 315–321, Aug. 2004.

56. N. Apostoloff and A. Fitzgibbon, "Bayesian video matting using learnt image priors," in *Proceedings of IEEE CVPR*, (Washington, DC), pp. 407–414, June 2004.

57. Y. Chuang, A. Agarwala, B. Curless, D. Salesin, and R. Szeliski, "Video matting of complex scenes," in *Proceedings of ACM SIGGRAPH*, (San Antonio, Texas), pp. 243–248, July 2002.

58. Y. Chuang, B. Curless, D. Salesin, and R. Szeliski, "A bayesian approach to digital matting," in *Proceedings of IEEE CVPR*, (Maui, Hawaii), pp. 264–271, Dec. 2001.

59. M. Ruzon and C. Tomasi, "Alpha estimation in natural images," in *Proceedings of IEEE CVPR*, (Hilton Head Island, South Carolina), pp. 18–25, June 2000.

60. H.-Y. Shum, J. Sun, S. Yamazaki, Y. Li, and C. keung Tang, "Pop-up light field: An interactive image-based modeling and rendering system," *ACM Transactions on Graphics*, vol. 23, pp. 143–162, Apr. 2004.

61. J. Canny, "A computational approach to edge detection," *IEEE Transacions on PAMI*, vol. 8, pp. 679–714, 1986.

62. B. Lucas and T. Kanade, "An iterative image registration technique with an application to stereo vision," in *IJCAI81*, pp. 674–679, Apr. 1981.

63. P. Chang, M. Han, and Y. Gong, "Extract highlights from baseball game videos with hidden markov models," in *IEEE International Conference on Image processing (ICIP)*, (Rochester, NY), Sept. 2002.

64. F. R. Kschischang, B. J. Frey, and H.-A. Loeliger, "Factor graphs and the sum-product algorithm," *IEEE Transactions on Information Theory*, vol. 47, no. 2, 2002.

65. S. L. Lauritzen, *Graphical Models*. Oxford University Press, 1996.

66. M. I. J. (ed), *Learning in Graphical Models*. Kluwer Academic Publishers, 1998.

67. J. Yedidia, "An idiosyncratic journey beyond mean field theory," in *Advanced Mean Field Methods, Theory and Practice*, (MIT Press), pp. 21–36, 2001.

68. A. Berger, S. D. Pietra, and V. D. Pietra, "A maximum entropy approach to natural language processing," *Journal of Computational Linguistics*, vol. 22, 1996.

69. S. D. Pietra, V. D. Pietra, and J. Lafferty, "Inducing features of random fields," *IEEE Transactions on Pattern Analysis and Machine Intelligence*, vol. 19, Apr. 1997.

70. D. Brown, "A note on approximations to discrete probability distributions," *Journal of Information and Control*, vol. 2, pp. 386–392, 1959.

71. J. N. Darroch and D. Ratcliff, "Generalized iterative scaling for log-linear models," *Annals of Mathematical Statistics*, vol. 43, pp. 1470–1480, 1972.

72. J. Lafferty, A. McCallum, and F. Pereira, "Conditional random fields: Probabilistic models for segmenting and labeling sequence data," in *Proceedings of International Conference on Machine Learning*, (Williams College, MA), June 2001.

73. C. Sutton, K. Rohanimanesh, and A. McCallum, "Dynamic conditional random fields: Factorized probabilistic models for labeling and segmenting sequence data," in *Proceedings of International Conference on Machine Learning*, (Banff, Canada), July 2004.

74. Y. Gong, M. Han, W. Hua, and W. Xu, "Maximum entropy model-based baseball highlight detection and classification," *International Journal on Computer Vision and Image Understanding*, vol. 96, pp. 181–199, 2004.

75. Y. T. Tse and R. L. Baker, "Camera zoom/pan estimation and compensation for video compression," *Image Processing Algorithms and Techniques*, vol. 1452, pp. 468–479, 1991.

76. R. Szeliski and H. Shum, "Creating full view panoramic image mosaics and texture-mapped models," in *SIGGRAPH97*, pp. 251–258, 1997.

77. M. Fischler and R. Bolles, "Random sample consensus: A paradigm for model fitting with applications to image analysis and automated cartography," *CACM*, vol. 24, pp. 381–395, June 1981.

78. A. Dempster, N. Laird, and D. Rubin, "Maximum-likelihood from incomplete data via em algorithm," *Royal Statistics Society Series B*, vol. 39, 1977.

79. G. Schwarts, "Estimating the dimension of a model," *Annals of Statistics*, vol. 6, pp. 461–464, 1990.

80. C. Cortes and V. Vapnik, "Support-vector networks," *Machine Learning Journal*, vol. 20, no. 3, pp. 273–297, 1999.

81. B. Taskar, C. Guestrin, and D. Koller, "Max-margin markov networks," in *Neural Information Processing Systems Conference (NIPS)*, (Vancouver, Canada), Dec. 2003.

82. C. J. C. Burges, "A tutorial on support vector machines for pattern recognition," *Data Mining and Knowledge Discovery Journal*, vol. 2, no. 2, pp. 121–167, 1998.

83. T. Hastie, R. Tibshirani, and J. Friedman, *The Elements of Statistical Learning*. Springer, 2001.

84. V. Vapnik, *Estimation of Dependences Based on Empirical data*. Springer-Verlag, 1982.

85. E. Osuna, R. Freund, and F. Girosi, "Improved training algorithm for support vector machines," in *Proceedings of IEEE NNSP*, (Amelia Island, FL), Sept. 1997.

86. J. C. Platt, "Sequential minimal optimization: A fast algorithm for training support vector machines," in *Technical Report 98-14, Microsoft Research*, (Redmond, WA), 1998.

Index